In These Great Times

CARCANET

a Karl Kraus reader

edited by

HARRY ZOHN

with translations by

JOSEPH FABRY

MAX KNIGHT

KARL F. ROSS

HARRY ZOHN

First published in Great Britain by
CARCANET PRESS LIMITED
208-212 Corn Exchange Buildings
Manchester M4 3BQ

Original publication by Engendra Press Ltd., Montreal

Werke by Karl Kraus are published in German
under the editorship of Heinrich Fischer,
Copyright © Kösel-Verlag GmbH & Co., Munich

English translations Copyright© 1976, 1984 by Joseph Fabry,
Max Knight, Karl F. Ross and Harry Zohn respectively

Introduction Copyright© 1976, 1984 by Harry Zohn

Frontispiece illustration property of Harry Zohn
Photograph of the death mask of Karl Kraus property of
Landesbildstelle Wien-Burgenland
All other photographs included in the text, reproduced
with the kind permission of Mr Friedrich Pfäfflin

British Library Cataloguing in Publication Data
Kraus, Karl
In these great times.
I. Title
838'.91209   PT2621.R27
ISBN 0 85635 516 X

Published with financial assistance from
the Arts Council of Great Britain

Printed by SRP Ltd., Exeter

To the memory of

Paul Hatvani (Hirsch)

Editor's Note

I should like to express my appreciation to my fellow translators, Max Knight, Joseph Fabry, and Karl F. Ross, without whose great ability and dedication this comprehensive sampler of Karl Kraus's creativity could not have been realized.

Friedrich Pfäfflin and Friedrich Jenaczek have put me in their debt by sharing their understanding of some knotty passages in the title essay, "In dieser grossen Zeit," which address sometimes made me think that it must have been delivered in an amphibolytheater. I am grateful also to Edward Timms for a critical reading of part of the manuscript.

A special word of gratitude is due the director of Engendra Press, Ronald Rosenthall, who has the distinction of being the first publisher in the English-speaking world to issue authorized book-length translations of Kraus's writings in the four decades since the author's death. His unerring stylistic taste, his imaginative approach, and — last but not least — his confidence in me have been a source of gratification.

This book, finally, is dedicated to the memory of Paul Hirsch (1892–1975), who came under Kraus's spell in his youth in Austria and perceptively wrote about him (under the nom de plume Paul Hatvani) in his old age in Australia.

Harry Zohn

BRANDEIS UNIVERSITY
WALTHAM, MASSACHUSETTS
January 1976

Contents

SELECTED POEMS
(translated by Max Knight and Karl F. Ross)

THE LAST DAYS OF MANKIND
(Selections arranged and translated by Max Knight and Joseph Fabry)   157

Illustrations

Introduction

by

Harry Zohn

1. A Karl Kraus Chronology

1874 Karl Kraus is born at Jičín (Bohemia) on 28 April
as the ninth child (and fifth son) of Jakob Kraus,
a well-to-do paper manufacturer, and Ernestine
Kantor Kraus.

1877 The Kraus family moves to Vienna where Karl Kraus
is to spend the rest of his life (". . . My hatred of
Vienna is not love gone astray. It's just that I've discovered a completely new way of finding it unbearable").

1884–92 Kraus attends secondary school, the Franz-Josephs-
Gymnasium, where he is a mediocre student.

1891 Kraus's mother dies on 24 October.

1892–98 Kraus studies law, philosophy, and German literature
at the University of Vienna, but attends few lectures
and does not take a degree.

1892–99 Kraus contributes book reviews, drama criticism, and
satirical sketches to such periodicals and newspapers
as *Die Gesellschaft* (Leipzig), *Magazin für Literatur*
(Berlin), *Neue literarische Blätter* (Bremen), *Wiener
Literatur-Zeitung*, *Wiener Rundschau*, *Liebelei*, *Die
Wage*, and *Neue Freie Presse* (all Vienna).

1893 In January Kraus makes an unsuccessful debut as an
actor at a theater in suburban Vienna.

1896 Kraus's first major work, *Die demolirte Literatur*
(A Literature Demolished), appears in the *Wiener
Rundschau* and as a pamphlet the following year. In
the form of a witty obituary of the Café Griensteidl, the
headquarters of Austria's men of letters, particularly
the "Young Vienna" circle, the work lampoons many
of Kraus's literary contemporaries.

3

1898	Kraus's pamphlet *Eine Krone für Zion* (A Crown for Zion) attacks political Zionism and its leader Theodor Herzl from the standpoint of an assimilated European Jew in sympathy with Socialism.
1899	Kraus turns down an editorial position offered him by the *Neue Freie Presse*, a newspaper he is to attack for the rest of his life ("There are two fine things in the world: to be part of the *Neue Freie Presse* or to despise it. I did not hesitate for one moment as to what my choice had to be"). Kraus founds his own aggressive periodical, *Die Fackel* (The Torch), the first issue of which appears on 1 April and soon becomes a Viennese institution. Initially it is published three times a month; after 1904 it appears at irregular intervals and with a fluctuating number of pages. Some fifty noted writers and artists contribute to the journal during its first decade. Setting out to "drain a swamp of clichés," Kraus announces as his motto not the usual "Was wir bringen" (What We Shall Do) but "Was wir umbringen" (What We Shall Undo). "May the *Fackel* provide light for a land in which — unlike the empire of Charles the Fifth — the sun never rises." On 12 October Kraus leaves the Jewish fold and becomes *konfessionslos* (religiously unaffiliated).
1900	Kraus's father dies on 5 April. Kraus detaches himself from his family, from which he continues to receive a subvention, and goes to live in a bachelor apartment.
1901	Kraus mourns the death, on 2 May, of Annie Kalmar, a young actress for whom he had great admiration and affection.
1902	Kraus's essay "Sittlichkeit und Kriminalität" (Morality and Criminal Justice) focuses on the glaring contrast between private and public morality and exposes the hypocrisy inherent in the administration of justice in Austria.

1903–07	Polemics with the German-Jewish essayist Maximilian Harden, Kraus's one-time mentor.
1908	The book edition of *Sittlichkeit und Kriminalität* appears with forty-one essays on the above theme drawn from the pages of the *Fackel*.
1909	Kraus's first collection of aphorisms appears under the title *Sprüche und Widersprüche* (Dicta and Contradictions).
1910	Kraus gives his first public reading from his writings and the works of others ("When I read, it is not acted literature; but what I write is written acting"). In his pamphlet *Heine und die Folgen* (Heine and the Consequences) Kraus attacks the German-Jewish writer for establishing the deleterious tradition of feuilletonistic journalism, a dangerous intermediary between art and life and a parasite on both ("To write a feuilleton is to curl locks on a bald head — but the public likes such curls better than a lion's mane of thought"; "Heinrich Heine so loosened the corsets of the German language that today every little salesman can fondle her breasts").
1911	Kraus carries on a polemic with the Berlin critic Alfred Kerr. On 8 April Kraus is baptized and joins the Catholic church. Starting with the *Fackel* no. 338 in December, Kraus writes the entire contents of the journal himself ("I no longer have collaborators. I used to be envious of them. They repel those readers whom I want to lose myself").
1912	With his address (and pamphlet) *Nestroy und die Nachwelt* (Nestroy and Posterity) Kraus revives interest in the nineteenth-century Viennese comic playwright and actor whom he presents in his full stature as a great German dramatist and social satirist who, like Kraus himself, achieves his critical and satirical effects through an inspired use of language. Kraus's second collection of aphorisms, *Pro domo et mundo*, appears.

5

1913	Kraus meets Baroness Sidonie Nádherný and unsuccessfully proposes marriage to her on several occasions. Despite her engagement to an Italian and her brief marriage to an Austrian fellow aristocrat in 1920, Kraus's affectionate relationship with her continues (with a few periods of estrangement) for the rest of his life ("To love, to be deceived, to be jealous — that's easy enough. The other way is less comfortable: To be jealous, to be deceived, and to love!"). For many years Kraus finds relaxation and inspiration at Sidonie's family estate at Janowitz (Janovice, south of Prague) and on trips taken with her.
1914	The outbreak of World War I inspires the outraged pacifist and humanitarian to produce his most powerful and characteristic work, beginning with the address "In dieser grossen Zeit" (In These Great Times), delivered in Vienna on 19 November.
1915	Kraus begins work on his mammoth drama *Die letzten Tage der Menschheit* (The Last Days of Mankind) and reads parts of it at numerous wartime recitals. The publisher Kurt Wolff founds the Verlag der Schriften von Karl Kraus for the dissemination of the satirist's work.
1916	The first collection of Kraus's poetry appears. By 1930 eight additional volumes are published under the collective title *Worte in Versen* (Words in Verse).
1918	Kraus publishes *Nachts* (At Night), his third and last collection of aphorisms.
1918–19	*Die letzten Tage der Menschheit* appears in special issues of the *Fackel*.
1919	A two-volume compilation of *Fackel* articles appears as *Weltgericht* (Last Judgment).
1921	Kraus publishes *Literatur oder Man wird doch da sehn* (Literature or We Shall See about That), a "magical operetta" satirizing literary Expressionism in general

and Franz Werfel, one of several apostles turned apostates, in particular ("A poem is good until one knows by whom it is"; "Something I cannot get over: that a whole line could be written by half a man. That a work could be built on the quicksand of a character"). Kraus breaks with Kurt Wolff, and his writings henceforth appear in the Verlag *Die Fackel*, Vienna.

1922 In the collection *Untergang der Welt durch schwarze Magie* (End of the World by Black Magic) Kraus concentrates on the pernicious press and its deleterious mixture of intellect and information. At Christmastime he writes his one-act verse play *Traumstück* (Dream Play), a surrealistic dramatic fantasy.

1923 On 7 March Kraus officially leaves the Catholic church in protest against the perceived collusion between the church and dubious artistic, journalistic, and commercial aspects of the Salzburg Festival. He publishes *Wolkenkuckucksheim* (Cloudcuckooland), a "fantastic verse play in three acts" after Aristophanes.

1924 Kraus publishes *Traumtheater* (Dream Theater), a one-act philosophical-dramatic vignette about the nature of theater, and dedicates it to the memory of Annie Kalmar.

1925 Kraus designates his recitals as "Theater der Dichtung" (Theater of Poetry, or Literary Theater) and regularly puts on one-man performances of plays by Nestroy, operettas by Offenbach, and Shakespeare dramas in his adaptation. He polemicizes against the "Buda pest," Imre Békessy, Vienna's corrupt press czar, and the following year manages to "kick the crook out of Vienna." A group of professors at the Sorbonne in Paris propose Kraus for the Nobel Prize in literature.

1927 Kraus concerns himself with the police riot touched off by the burning of the Ministry of Justice in response to the acquittal of killers in a clash of two Austrian paramilitary organizations.

7

1927–28	Kraus writes *Die Unüberwindlichen* (The Unconquer-able), a four-act documentary drama about Johannes Schober, Vienna's chief of police (and sometime Austrian prime minister), and his collusion with Békessy.
1927–30	Polemics and litigation with Alfred Kerr.
1929	Kraus's collection *Literatur und Lüge* (Literature and Lies) appears.
1930–32	Kraus's adaptations of Offenbach and Shakespeare are broadcast by the Berlin and Vienna radio.
1931	Publication of *Zeitstrophen*, a collection of topical stanzas which Kraus interpolated in Offenbach operettas and Nestroy plays.
1932	Kraus attends an international pacifist congress in Amsterdam.
1933	Kraus works on *Die Dritte Walpurgisnacht* (The Third Walpurgis Night). He delivers the funeral oration for his friend, the architect Adolf Loos.
1933–35	Kraus's versions of Shakespeare are published as *Sonette* and *Dramen*.
1936	The last *Fackel* (no. 922) appears in February. On 2 April Kraus gives his 700th (and last) public reading. He dies of heart failure on 12 June.

2. About This Reader

The centennial of Kraus's birth has come and gone, but the satirist's name still is anything but a household word in English-speaking countries, and most of his work is accessible only to those able to read it in the original German. Even though the bibliography at the end of this book lists some thirty studies on Kraus in English, only a small fraction of Kraus's vast output has been translated into any foreign language. The present volume is the first attempt to bring together representative selections from an uncommonly rich and multifaceted *oeuvre* and introduce a larger readership in the English-speaking world to a man and an artist whose life work constitutes an unsparing critique of his time — in the words of Egon Friedell, "a fanatically imaginative, superhumanly delineated work which will permanently preserve the traits of our age."[1]

Since a general introduction to Kraus is now readily available in a number of monographs, reference works, and journals (including *Half-Truths & One-and-a-Half Truths: Selected Aphorisms*, the first volume of the Engendra Kraus series), it was thought best to limit the prefatory matter in this Reader to a chronological table and to the following ancillary remarks on the contents of the book. An attempt will thus be made to distill some salient features of Kraus's mind and art from a variety of prose pieces and poems as well as an abridgment of his dramatic masterpiece, *The Last Days of Mankind*. The essential untranslatability of Karl Kraus has been axiomatic for so long that a breakthrough in this area seems overdue and highly desirable. It may, of course, be argued that any selection from a European writer's work that is predicated largely on its translatability or lack of it cannot be completely representative and satisfactory, and it must be admitted that many of Kraus's most powerful and characteristic writings are so wedded to the genius of the German language, so allusive in their style and so elusive in their arcane context, that no translation is possible. Still, one hopes that in some instances Kraus's aphorism according to which "a linguistic work translated into another language is like someone going across the border without his skin and donning the local garb on the other side" will be perceived as a half-truth rather than one and a half truths. The editor derives some comfort from the fact that many of the pieces that could be included in this Reader may also be found in a number of German-language volumes containing selections from the best of Kraus's writings.

A word is in order about the annotation of the prose pieces. The late Heinrich Fischer, Kraus's literary executor and the editor of the Kösel-Verlag's comprehensive edition of Kraus's works, was unalterably opposed to such annotation, feeling that background information and explanatory notes tended to impede rather than promote an understanding and appreciation of Kraus. There is indeed ample evidence that Kraus himself was more concerned with the symbolic force, the universality, and the timeless significance of his writings than with their particularity, with the persons, places, actions, conditions, and events that triggered his satires. "An

---

1. *A Cultural History of the Modern Age*, trans. Charles Francis Atkinson (New York: Knopf, 1930), vol. 1, p. 148.

understanding of my work is impeded by a knowledge of my material," Kraus once wrote. "People don't realize that what is there must first be invented, and that it is worth inventing. Nor do they see that a satirist for whom people exist as though he had invented them needs more strength than one who invents persons as though they existed." Elsewhere he asked: "Am I to blame if hallucinations and visions are alive and have names and permanent residences?" Another Kraus aphorism expresses a similar view of his artistry, the kind that makes riddles out of solutions: "My readers think that I write for the day because my writings are based on the day. So I shall have to wait until my writings are obsolete. Then they may acquire timeliness." And a verse epigram by Kraus is a dictum in the guise of a contradiction:

> Only those distant in time and space
> Can know my satire's true face.
> Neighbor Meyer sees my outlook worsen
> Because he knows Herr Mueller in person.

Some justification for the editor's approach, to be sure, may be found in Kraus's statement that his comments need a commentary, for "otherwise they are too easily understood"; and another line of defense would be to note that whereas allusions to Germanic literary creations (the stuff of many of the footnotes) are likely to ring a bell in the minds of literate Germans, they are less likely to be understood by English readers. For the rest, it may be argued that in the case of Kraus even the most careful translation and annotation is bound to leave enough obscurities and ambiguities to keep the author's intended depth and universality inviolate. Any editor of Kraus must be aware of the awesome responsibility involved in presenting the work of a man who once said that even thirty years after his death he would care more about a comma being in its proper place than about the dissemination of his complete writings. One is also reminded of Alfred Polgar's advice to his fellow writers not to hunt too assiduously for printer's errors, for "you never know what is going to make you profound."

The Prose

The selections in this Reader extend over three decades, and the prose ranges from torture in Austria to torture in Germany.

Our sole selection from the earliest years of the *Fackel* (which is untitled in the original) displays a dramatic concision not usually found in Kraus.[2] As the satirist exposes his native country's treatment of several composers of genius (to whose list might be added the names of Mozart, Schubert, and so many others), he is by implication concerned with his own fate as a *persona non grata* with the Establishment of his day. Kraus's self-chosen isolation as a satirical gadfly was motivated by his recognition that work within the literary "system" would have been hedged in with multifarious taboos and considerations of a personal, ideological, and commercial nature. Kraus realized that the vaunted Austrian *Gemütlichkeit* and disarming slackness might have absorbed a milder satirist and neutralized him as just another literary entertainer and culture clown. Thus he knew even in young years that the incomprehension, indifference, and philistine aggressiveness which bedeviled a Bruckner or a Wolf was likely to be his lot as well.[3]

The next five prose pieces first appeared in book form in *Die chinesische Mauer* (The Great Wall of China), the third volume drawn from material published in the *Fackel* and Kraus's most successful book in his lifetime, achieving five editions between 1910 and 1930. Like "The World of Posters" and "The Beaver Coat," "In Praise of a Topsy-Turvy Life-Style" first appeared in the humorous journal *Simplicissimus*, published in Munich. Kraus, like Balzac, was a night worker. Far from being accidental or merely eccentric, Kraus's working habits were one more aspect of his opposition to his time, of the satirist's self-imposed burden. In the late afternoon or evening Kraus would go to a café and read the newspapers, the primary source material of the man bent on pinning down his age between quotation marks and literally taking it at its word. After conversing with a few friends, Kraus would work all night, sifting the world through the sieve of the word (in his own phrase). Using a cheap wooden pen holder and a steel nib, Kraus would cover one blank proofsheet after another with his minuscule handwriting, which only a few typesetters in Vienna were able to decipher. Kraus's printer used to call in the morning for what had been written during the night, and on the next evening the galleys were already on his desk for his revision and emendation. Some of his writings had to be set in type up to a dozen times before he gave his

2. Indeed, there are doubts surrounding the authorship of "Torture in Austria": in its early years the *Fackel* had numerous contributors, much of whose work (like the piece under discussion) appeared anonymously. But several factors, including the closing slur of the Viennese operetta, indicate that the essay is in fact Kraus's.

3. In 1974, on the occasion of the 100th and 150th anniversaries of their respective births, the Austrian government honored Kraus and Bruckner with four-schilling stamps.

final approval ("No one who sees one of my works in print will recognize a seam. And yet everything has been torn open a hundred times").

"The Good Conduct Medal" harks back to the subject matter of the 1908 collection *Sittlichkeit und Kriminalität* (Morality and Criminal Justice) in which Kraus attacked the hypocrisy of a male-dominated society that condemned by day what it enjoyed by night. Here Kraus plays with the standards of morality and immorality in Austrian society and carries them *ad absurdum* by describing a case in which the *machismo* symbolized by a military medal caused a female's "guiltless guilt" during the perennial "open season on women." Since the physical prostitution of women seemed far less deleterious to Kraus than the intellectual prostitution of men, he repeatedly excoriated the self-righteous hypocrisy of Austrian society and its legal system in particular. "Squeeze human nature into the straitjacket of crimininal justice and crime will appear!" In those years he frequently concerned himself with various aspects of prostitution. The very word *Schandlohn* (wages of shame), he pointed out, was symptomatic of a state and a society that relegated sexual intercourse to the dark area of disreputable silence. Kraus once quoted a statement made at the Munich Congress to Combat White Slavery to the effect that the patrons of bordellos ought to pay the inmates badly so as to make the girls think twice before attaching themselves to such establishments. A Christian-Socialist paper having demanded that prostitution be stripped of its esthetic attractiveness and made plain and unappealing, the police promptly removed the piano from the salon of a brothel! Kraus made the point that for a prostitute to be licensed, her "total moral depravity" had to be demonstrated. To furnish such proof, a woman would have to be encouraged to practice a little illicit, clandestine prostitution first! Kraus concluded that it was made very difficult for a prostitute to mend her ways and return to a more respectable existence, for these women were duped and entrapped at every turn. The prostitute who thought of "nothing" while giving public display to her "wages of shame" is a case in point.

Plus ça change, plus c'est la même chose . . . The old-fashioned but timeless quality of Kraus's lament at the invasion of privacy and assault upon the senses perpetrated by an earlier form of advertising may arouse our sympathy and identification all the more as we realize that the television commercials which have long since relegated posters or billboards to a position of relative insignificance convey the same kind of "horror-content of life in extract form" and only produce a considerably heightened sort of phantasmagoria.

Similarly, now that mankind has taken the giant step to the moon and voyages there are no longer associated with an Offenbach operetta but threaten to become commonplace in the near future, the discovery of the North Pole is bound to seem "old hat." Yet the accuracy of Kraus's insight into human nature can be verified every day. He was not so much concerned with great events and exploits as with the petty popular reactions to them. In this instance Kraus was almost morbidly fascinated by what crawled out of the woodwork of the lower depths when an idealistic "summit of the world" was scaled. The great gulf between the heights of nature and the depths of human nature is revealed, and the basic (and still timely) question is implied whether a mankind that seems to be rushing headlong toward its last days is ready for, deserving of, or can be saved by, extraterrestrial excursions. Science was, generally speaking, one of Kraus's blind spots. It is true that he preferred traveling by car or by plane even at a time when those modes of transportation were not common. But he had little appreciation of modern technology and the benefits it might bestow on a humanity that was morally unprepared for them. The availability of radio, for example, only made Kraus comment that Viennese janitors would now be connected with the cosmos. The conquest of the North Pole was to him but another Pyrrhic victory over nature, and surely there is an awful prescience in his remark that progress tends to make purses out of human skin. In the early 1900s stupidity reached the North Pole; in the 1960s stupidity reached the moon. The ice fields of the intellect have grown in the interim and have still not stopped growing, and who can say that we are any closer to "transforming the world of human forces into a realm of reason" than were Kraus's contemporaries?

"The Beaver Coat" is one of Kraus's most light-hearted and funniest pieces. The theft of his coat turned Kraus into a public figure and willy-nilly exposed him to "the accursed popularity that a grinning Vienna bestows," as he put it in another context. Once again, the important thing is not the event itself but what follows in its train. These developments make Kraus yearn for a return to his accustomed splendid isolation. He prefers being obscure for the right reasons to being prominent for the wrong ones.

During his ongoing fight with the *Neue Freie Presse*, then Vienna's foremost daily and one of the most respected liberal newspapers of Europe, Kraus frequently had occasion to comment on a pandering, profiteering press which condemned immorality on its editorial pages while its advertising departments gratefully accepted money for dubious promotions. Themis, the personification of justice, seemed to play blind man's buff with Eros. Kraus once remarked that the same issue of the *Neue Freie Presse* in which sexual perverseness was editorially decried ran ads of "masseuses" named Hedwig Faust (Fist), Wanda Stock (Stick), Paula Ruthner (Rodner), Carola Prügler (Flogger), Wanda Schläger (Beater), and Minna Beinhacker (Legchopper). Contraceptive promotions and other sexually suggestive or explicit newspaper advertisements may seem tame and trivial in our age of "new morality," youth culture, "underground" newspapers and sexually oriented massage parlors, but it is well to remember that in exposing the elastic ethics of journalism and commerce Kraus was concerned with absolute standards of integrity.

That Swiss printer's gremlin of 1912 touched a raw nerve in Kraus: his antipathy to the Viennese operetta after Johann Strauss, which he regarded as journalistically deceptive and meretricious, unlike the operettas of Jacques Offenbach (a "genius of gaiety") which Kraus loved from his boyhood on and frequently performed in his one-man "Theater of Poetry," singing all the parts in German translation (and frequently with the addition of his own *Zeitstrophen*, or topical stanzas) to the accompaniment of a pianist.

In a more serious vein, the journalists who conducted an interview with a dying child grimly foreshadowed the war correspondents who a few years later were recorded by Kraus as racing with Death to reach mortally wounded soldiers in time to question them about their "sensations" and ask them to look "transfigured." The plague of the sensational interview has not abated, and in our own time it is difficult to open a newspaper or focus one's eyes on the television screen without encountering the latest victim of rape or kidnapping or attempted murder surrounded by reporters with ball-point or microphone at the ready, trampling human dignity in their effort to titillate the increasingly unfeeling buyers of their product with the last word in catastrophes.

If prewar Austria had seemed like a "proving ground for world destruction" to Kraus, the outbreak of World War I forced him to bear witness to what he regarded as the beginning of the end. The war not only confirmed the satirist's dire predictions but caused his visions of doom to assume apocalyptic dimensions. Like a vast funnel, the war and what was happening to the human spirit in wartime caught and intensified Kraus's satire, leading the satirist not only to vary, refine, and deepen the diverse themes of his prewar writings but to set himself up as the lonely, indomitable, inexorable, and incorruptible chronicler of "the last days of mankind" for the benefit of a posterity that might no longer inhabit this planet. As Walter Benjamin has pointed out, Kraus's writings are an inverted silence, with the storm of events sweeping into the black cloak of this silence and turning its loud lining inside out. Kraus's initial reaction to the new "great times" was silence. The torch was temporarily extinguished, and for several months the torch-bearer was too stunned to participate in the flood of words all around him; he refused to join the majority of his literary contemporaries in proclaiming their patriotism, rushing to the ramparts of rhyme, and boarding the bandwagon of banality. The fact that his physical condition precluded military service was reason enough for him to fear that any early or insufficiently considered reaction on his part would be widely misinterpreted. Yet he did feel constrained to speak out. "In dieser grossen Zeit," the speech he made in Vienna on 19 November 1914, and published in the *Fackel* the following month, is the germ cell of Kraus's extensive wartime output and is so characteristic of his work as a whole that it rightly serves as the title essay of the present Reader. Kraus believed that "an ear which hears the trumpets of the Last Judgment certainly is not closed to the trumpets of the day." It was, in fact, in the cacophonous blaring of the latter that Kraus heard the former. Considering the keen acoustic sense which informs his writings, it follows that Kraus's wartime work is, as it were, an enormous phonomontage based on these trumpets; they gave rise to it and are preserved in it.

Kraus was not only a master of the art of punning — a deep seriousness and symbolism underlay his verbal play — but a skillful practitioner of amphibology, the ambiguity of speech that stems from the uncertainty of grammatical construction rather than the meaning of words, with a phrase or a sentence capable of being constructed in more than one way. To a greater extent than is customary in German, one finite verb in Kraus can resolve several phrases; the links between nouns and pronouns are not always readily apparent; conjunctions are often dispensed with; and the style is generally elliptical. A good example of the intensity and tension in Kraus's prose — a quality which, unfortunately, cannot always be reproduced in translation — is the beginning of "In these great times." Kraus constructs this dialectical, periodic sentence around an "inspiring" platitude mouthed by every orator, militarist, politician and educator in wartime: we live in "great times." Deflating this cliché by depriving it of its aura and bathing it in irony, Kraus dismembers and varies the title of his speech while he withholds the rest of the main clause. His central assertion is the great rift between thought and action, events and the imagination, the sword and the word, language and experience, the press and truth. After usurping from the outward world one of its hateful, deceitful phrases, Kraus "places it before the court of his linguistic conscience and imagination, cross-examines the phrase by means of various antithetic devices, exploring a wealth of denotations, of literal, metaphorical and idiomatic meanings, and the record of the cross-examination turns out to be the portrait of an age."[4] The collusion of commerce with

4. J. P. Stern, "Karl Kraus's Vision of Language," *Modern Language Review* 61 (1966): 76–77.

militarism and the role of the press in wartime are themes on which Kraus supplies many variations in this address. "What mythological confusion is this?" he asked in a different context. "Since when has Mars been the god of commerce and Mercury the god of war?" And another of his aphorisms is pertinent here: "Someone said: 'This command will be carried out promptly.' What he meant to say was: 'This battle will be supplied promptly.' "

After the pathos of this address, two other wartime pieces, "A Minor Detail" and "Yolkwik Egg Substitute," may seem trivial indeed. Yet these seemingly minor matters are evidence of the same kind of spiritual malaise that gave mankind the "great times" it deserved. The sardonic realization that in some circles *Monogamie* (monogamy) was translated literally as, or equated with, *Einheirat* (marrying into a business) was one of many insights that Kraus owed to his language. "Yolkwik Egg Substitute" represents a further deflation of those whose "great" priorities diminish the quality of life. "What good are flame throwers to us," asked Kraus aphoristically, "when we are running out of matches?"

The story of Kraus's postwar writings and polemics is basically the history of his disillusionment as his "homeland's loyal hater." "The real end of the world," he wrote, "is the destruction of the spirit; the other kind depends on the insignificant attempt to see whether after such a destruction the world can go on." The best Kraus could say about the Austrian republic was that it had replaced the monarchy and freed him of that "burdensome companion," the other K.K. (*kaiserlich-königlich*, or imperial-royal, the designation of many institutions in the Austro-Hungarian empire). But after the great carnage the old ghosts still had not been exorcised, there was no end to "the parasites remaining from the imperial age as well as the blackheads of the revolution," and the tragic triad *Tinte, Technik, Tod* was still firmly entrenched. In "After Twenty Years," a poem written on the twentieth anniversary of the *Fackel* in 1919, Kraus enumerated his themes — past, present, and future: "Sex and untruth, stupidity, abuses, cadences and clichés, printer's ink, technology, death, war and society, usury, politics, the insolence of office and the spurns that patient merit of the unworthy takes, art and nature, love and dreams . . ."

More and more Kraus came to liken his situation in postwar Austria to Peer Gynt's futile struggle with the Great Boyg ("The Boyg does not fight — and does not lose"), with certain mentalities and conditions proving to be unconquerable. The ghoulishness of the survivors might have been foreseen. In a prose piece publicly read on 11 November 1917, Kraus quoted a report of the Lower Austrian Tourist Board regarding an expected increase in tourism on the Adriatic coast of Austria and in the

Alpine regions after the war, for these areas "with their outstanding war mementos will be a magnet for Central European tourists, and there will be a lively traffic as a consequence of reverent visits to heroes' graves and military cemeteries." In *Die Wiedergeburt in Kain* (The Rebirth in Cain, 1920), the Austrian writer Carl Julius Haidvogel attacks the notion of moonlight tours of the old battlefields, arguing that these might make the dead rise up in desperation and indignation.[5] Still, no one who has heard Kraus read "Promotional Trips to Hell" (it is one of the selections available on a commercially produced recording) will ever forget the *saeva indignatio* with which Kraus castigated the ghastly mentality displayed by a Basel newspaper which offered reasonably priced round trips for "rubber-necks" to places where thousands had died miserable deaths but a few years previously. Present-day parallels will readily suggest themselves to the reader; surely there is no dearth of either battlefields or of travel and advertising agencies not above pandering to morbid curiosity and organizing tours to Vietnam or elsewhere. Such tourism obviously deserves to be demoted rather than promoted.

Kraus's attitude toward psychoanalysis is best indicated by this widely quoted (or misquoted) aphorism: "Psychoanalysis is that mental illness for which it regards itself as therapy." There is some evidence to indicate that Kraus respected Sigmund Freud the man and the scientist, and Freud did have some early contact with Kraus, hoping to enlist him in the service of his movement. But by 1910 the lines were clearly drawn, and Kraus's rejection of psychoanalysis and the "psychoanals" was definitive. Early that year Fritz Wittels, a Kraus apostle turned apostate, presented a paper on "The *Fackel* Neurosis" at a meeting of the Vienna Psychoanalytic Society, and later he included uncomplimentary depictions of Kraus in several of his works of fiction. Kraus in turn took many satiric potshots at a movement and its practitioners which, in his estimation, only served to crush the human spirit.

"Mir fällt zu Hitler nichts ein" (I cannot think of anything to say about Hitler). This is the striking first sentence of Kraus's *Die Dritte Walpurgisnacht* (The Third Walpurgis Night — the title refers to both parts of Goethe's *Faust* as well as to the Third Reich), a prose work written in the late spring and summer of 1933 but not published in its entirety during Kraus's lifetime. That sentence, the embryo of the misunderstandings and

---

5 In 1931 another Austrian author Hans von Chlumberg wrote *Wunder um Verdun* (The Miracles of Verdun), a latter-day expressionistic play set in a war cemetery in northern France which is visited by tourists; the dead awaken to persuade the people to mend their ways.

conflicts that marked and marred Kraus's last years, may be indicative of resignation and impotence (though Kraus *could* think of many things to say about Hitler and Hitlerism and did indeed say them on hundreds of pages), but it is also a hyperbolic, heuristic device for depicting the witches' sabbath of the time. The *Dritte Walpurgisnacht* had been set in type to appear as *Fackel* nos. 888–907, but it was withheld to prevent hell from unleashing its furies on innocent people. There had been no *Fackel* for ten months when no. 888 appeared in October 1933. Its four pages contained only Kraus's funeral oration on his architect friend Adolf Loos and what was to be the satirist's last poem, with its poignant closing line, "The word expired when that world awoke." Kraus sadly realized the incommensurability of the human spirit with the brutal power structure across the German border, and on the second page of his work he asks this anguished question: "Is that which has been done to the spirit still a concern of the spirit?" The equally anguished answer he gives himself is this: "Force is no object of polemics, madness no object of satire."

Once again language was in mortal danger; Kraus's remarks on this subject anticipate and confirm the studies and dictionaries of the language of inhumanity (what Viktor Klemperer called the "LTI," *lingua tertii imperii*) and the murderers' lexica which were published after the end of Hitler's self-styled "Thousand-Year Reich" by men like Storz, Sternberger, Süskind, and Wulf. As Kraus attempts to deal, on the basis of newspaper and eyewitness reports, with the early excesses of the Nazi regime — which led him to foresee much of the full *furor Teutonicus* to come — he seems engaged in a desperate rear-guard action; his writing is like the rambling monologue of a worried man who talks incessantly in an effort to keep the demons at bay. The haunting rhetorical questions at the end of this excerpt from *Die Dritte Walpurgisnacht* (which has been titled by the editor) bear witness to Kraus's awful foreknowledge. In voicing genuine concern over Nazi Germany's pressure on his homeland, Kraus for once found himself in Austria's corner. Paradoxically, this led him to side with those who had suppressed the Social Democrats (to whom Kraus had been close at various times in his life), the clerico-fascist regime of Chancellor Engelbert Dollfuss, whose assassination in 1934 came as a severe blow to Kraus. Many of the satirist's erstwhile adherents, some of them now communists and/or emigrants, expected unequivocal support from Kraus in their struggle — as though he could have stopped Hitlerism with a special issue of the *Fackel* — and concluded from his vacillation that the essentially apolitical Kraus had been wrong from Dreyfus to Dollfuss.

The *Fackel* lost numerous readers, and Kraus, who said that "when the end of the world comes, I want to be living in retirement," was content to reduce his readership to those who not only heard the trumpets of the day but also were interested in Shakespeare, Nestroy, Offenbach, and German style, including Kraus's unique "comma problems." As he pathetically and futilely tried to pit the word against the sword, Kraus prepared to "live in the safe sentence structure." His death of heart failure in June of 1936, after a long period of physical and spiritual exhaustion, mercifully saved Kraus from witnessing the Nazi take-over of Austria to the cheers of most of its population, the destruction of his belongings, the deaths of close friends in concentration camps, and untold other horrors.

The Poetry

Karl Kraus has never been known primarily as a poet, but his lyric poetry has increasingly come to be regarded as an integral and important part of his *oeuvre*. Critics like Werner Kraft, Leopold Liegler, and Caroline Kohn have written perceptively about this aspect of Kraus's creativity. When one realizes that much of Kraus's prose is lyrical or poetic, it is easy to see his poetry as only a special coinage from the same mint.

Kraus began to write poetry comparatively late in life; his first poems did not appear in the *Fackel* until 1912 and 1913. But then nine volumes of poems and rhymed epigrams were published between 1916 and 1930 under the collective title *Worte in Versen* (Words in Verse — now available in one volume). In his verse Kraus admittedly is an epigone rather than an innovator; the poet is indebted to the Goethean and Shakespearean traditions. He was "unoriginal" in that he usually needed some occasion to trigger his art, the way an oyster needs the irritation of a grain of sand to produce a pearl. His poems are seldom "romantic" in the sense of being products of poetic rapture or intoxication; rather, they spring from the rapture of language and logic.

Kraus made little distinction between lyrical or pathetic prose satire and the poetic language of his verse. Some of his poems are versified glosses and polemics, lyrical versions of *Fackel* texts, or satiric ideas given purified form; others represent autobiographic excursions. Their abstractness and concision often presuppose familiarity with Kraus's other works, his life, and his personality. "I do not write poetry and then work with dross," Kraus once wrote; "I turn the dross into poetry and organize rallies in support of poetry." To a certain extent Kraus's poetry is *Gedankenlyrik* in Schiller's sense — poetry with a cargo of thought, reflecting a tradition coming to an end. Yet it also represents a sort of satirist's holiday in that Kraus is here free to reveal himself fully and unabashedly in his love of mankind, the human spirit, nature, and animals. Poetry, to him, was like a freer, purer world, one harking back to the German classical tradition, in which the poet, freed from the goads of the satiric occasion and an ever-wakeful moral conscience, was able to reflect on love, nature, dreams, fear, and wonderment.

In his poetry Kraus was guided by his conviction that the quality of a poem depended on the moral stature of the poet ("A poem is good until one knows by whom it is"). In his view, a satirist was only a deeply hurt lyricist, the artist wounded by the ugliness of the world. In *Worte in Versen*, rhyme and meaning are inseparably fused. Kraus's conception of rhyme is similar to that of Friedrich Schlegel, who described it as the surprising reunion of friendly ideas after a long separation. To give an idea from Kraus's poem "The Rhyme" macaronic form, "Rhyme is the landing shore / for two thoughts *en rapport*."

Caroline Kohn has classified Kraus's poetic output under these rubrics: Women, Desire, Love; Nature; Personal, Philosophical; Artist, Language; Dream; Society; Justice; Clichés, Ink, Press; Technology, War; Vienna, Austria; Berlin, Germany. The first two of the two dozen poems included in this Reader make reference to Kraus's working habits. "Nocturnal Hour" has been set to music by Eugen Auerbach (1929) and by Ernst Křenek; the latter's song cycle *Durch die Nacht* (Through the Night), composed in 1930–31, also contains settings of "Der Tag" ("The Day"), "Fernes Licht mit nahem Schein" ("Distant Light with Glow So Near"), and four other Kraus poems.

One of Kraus's most beautiful and most poignant poems, "Nocturnal Hour" is a profound expression of his situation, written with great visionary power and economy of symbolism and syntax. It is structurally notable for the recurring unrhymed first and last lines of each stanza (although these, in Karl F. Ross's English version, coincidentally do rhyme in the first verse) and the reiteration of the idea of transitoriness in the opening line of each. There is an increase in inwardness and depth until the final synthesis of night, winter, life, spring, and death. Kraus himself pointed out that three times the unrhymed last line belongs to "the bird's voice which accompanies the experience of work through the stages of night, winter, and life." What the poet considers, weighs and grades presumably is the possibility of changing this "language-forsaken" world through his efforts; a hero of creative work, he continues to do his duty even as death approaches.

The no less beautiful and poignant poem "The Day," which was also set by Kraus's longtime piano accompanist Franz Mittler, is based on the theme night-day-death as well. Kraus's first reading of it took place in Berlin in April of 1922. As the day breaks through the window, daring to disturb the claustrophobic intensity of Kraus's noctural labors, the bleary-

20

eyed writer expresses surprise at the fact that the impure, desecrated day can have the effrontery to dawn after an apocalyptic night of struggle with the affairs of an ungodly, corrupt world — matters which the *Zeitgeist* keeps bringing up in violation of an ideal, undefiled realm of pure humanity. The satirist has borne witness to the possibility of such humanity and has in mute, joyless labor erected an edifice of words in its support. The *memento mori* supplied by the hearse outside brings him an awareness of earthly vanity and evanescence and fills him with boundless sympathy with human suffering. Yet his self-effacing, fanatical work in the service of the word, of language, and his search for eternal truths as a bulwark against the encroachments of the age is a necessary humanizing function with distinct religious overtones. His prayer is for the poor soul outside as well as for himself, but especially for a mankind gone astray. Yet it is properly understood only in a larger context. Franz Kafka once described his obsessive writing as a form of prayer, and this was also Kraus's conception of his own work. One of his aphorisms is pertinent here: "When I take up my pen, nothing can happen to me. Fate, remember that."

"Rapid Transit," written in June of 1920 and set by Eugen Auerbach (another of Kraus's accompanists), has the evanescence and perceived meaninglessness of life as its theme and the dichotomy between inside and outside as its focus. The poet's staleness on a dirty, crowded train is contrasted with the lucid yet unspecific and non-concrete landscape outside which tends to blur and blunt his perceptions. Though he is forced to stay aboard with the aimless multitude of his traveling companions, his disgust at his situation is a kind of rebellion. Being locked into his life of devotion and self-abnegation, he is fated to yearn for integration into the vanishing scenery.

"To an Old Teacher," one of several poems Kraus wrote about his childhood and youth, is dedicated to his favorite teacher, Heinrich Sedlmayer. In a brief memoir of his former pupil (published in *Die Mutter*, Vienna, in February of 1925), Sedlmayer points out that Kraus had used poetic license in the poem he wrote years previously in "flawless Horatian form" to create a unity of place and time. Actually, Sedlmayer had found Kraus a satisfactory student of German in the lower classes of secondary school, and he had not taught him Latin until several years later — in the *Oktava*, the graduating class. The old teacher recalled that in the spring of 1887 Kraus had called on him to ask whether he could recommend a book for the improvement of his German style. Though Sedlmayer made the point that true style was a matter of character and experience and could not be learned from a book, he did recommend Greistorfer's Manual. Sedlmayer believes that Kraus's style blossomed when he no longer had to

21

write on set topics and opines that the learned but inhibited German teacher Kraus had in the upper classes may have stirred satirical impulses in the young man.

Annie Kalmar, to whom "The Actress" is a late tribute, was the first of several women of great physical and spiritual beauty in Kraus's life. Kraus met the talented young actress in the summer of 1900, but she died of tuberculosis in Hamburg in May of the following year, aged twenty-three. Kraus's one-act play *Traumtheater* (Dream Theater, 1924) is dedicated to her memory, which Kraus cherished for the rest of his life.

Kraus evidently needed an idealized private sphere of wholeness, purity, and love to provide a counterpoint (and counterpoise) to the numerous evidences of decay he perceived all around him. Such a sphere was provided for him from 1913 to the end of his life by a Czech aristocrat, Baroness Sidonie Nádherný von Borutin, and her family estate at Janovice (Janowitz) near Prague became Kraus's *buen retiro*, a Garden of Eden six and a half automobile hours from Vienna which he had to share only with his beloved, her twin brother, and a brace of friendly dogs. A modern mythology about a Tristan and Isolde living through the last days of mankind is multifariously expressed in Kraus's letters to "Sidi" (over a thousand missives to her were long believed lost but were rediscovered in 1969 and published in 1974), in many of Kraus's poems addressed to her or inspired by shared experiences, and in the dedication of several volumes to the woman who, as Kraus once put it, had a true appreciation of only two books: "the railroad time-table and *Worte in Versen*." Kraus proposed marriage to Sidonie Nádherný on several occasions, but class differences and possibly Kraus's Jewish birth seem to have stood in the way of such a union. His beloved's conflicting emotions, her indecision, and her infidelity must have been excruciating for Kraus, and Sidi for her part must have found it increasingly difficult to cope with Kraus's perfectionism, absolutism, and ill-concealed jealousy, to dance on an emotional volcano, as it were, to be the counterweight to the satirist's heavy burden, and to represent beauty and worth in an ugly, unworthy age. "He is a great load on my life," she wrote in her diary on 18 August 1918 (the same day on which Kraus wrote "Unter dem Wasserfall" at Janovice), though four years earlier she had called Kraus "the glory and crown of my life."

Of the approximately fifty "Sidi poems," those included here are, in addition to "Under the Waterfall," "Lawn in the Park," "To a Wrinkle" (set by Dora Pejacsevich and by Franz Mittler), "Rapid Transit," "Your Flaw" (January 1922), "Distant Light with Glow So Near" (January–February 1922), and Kraus's last poem (dated Janovice, 13 September 1933, and bearing the dedication "to Sidi"). A brief note on "Lawn in the

Park," a poem with tragic undertones, must suffice here. Kraus's wartime description of a sad Sunday is dated 16 November 1915. The poet wants to relieve the darkness of the times by recapturing the timeless past, in particular his childhood. But his firm footing and reposeful communion with nature vanish, the spell is broken, and the present bleakly reasserts itself in the form of a "dead day."

Two of the other wartime poems in this book, "With Stopwatch in Hand" (written on 19 November 1916) and "Prayer," are spoken by the *Nörgler* (Grumbler), the Kraus figure in *The Last Days of Mankind* — in act 3, sc. 36 and act 5, sc. 28 respectively. "With Stopwatch in Hand" is mentioned and quoted in part by the late Jacob Bronowski in his book *Science and Human Values.*

The word "Ursprung" (origin, or source) figures prominently in Kraus's writings, including two poems presented here, "My Ambivalence" and "Two Runners," so a brief elucidation of this characteristic Krausian concept is indicated. In his orphic epigram "Two Runners," written in 1910, Kraus depicts two antithetical forces alive in the human spirit — one that he loves and one that he hates. The world is perceived as a circuitous route back to the *Ursprung*; intellectuality may be the wrong road, but it does lead back to immediacy; satire is a roundabout way to poetry, and poetry, to Kraus, is a philosophical or linguistic detour on the way to a lost paradise. Kraus saw himself as being midway between *Ursprung* and *Untergang*, the origin or source of all things and the end of the world (or of the human spirit) as conjured up by his satiric vision, and he viewed language as the only means of going back to the origin — the origin that was forever the goal. This *Ursprung* represents a kind of naive realism, a secular idea of Creation diametrically opposed to speculative philosophy's tendency to make cerebral man the center of reality. In contrast to this Kraus posits the unity of feeling and form from which all art, morality, and truth spring. This world of purity constitutes a timeless counterpoise to the world against which Kraus the satirist struggled, and such an inviolate nature stands in mute yet eloquent contrast to a contemporary world and society which Kraus, in a sardonic pun fully comprehensible only to those familiar with German synonymous prefixes, perceived not as a *Gegenwart* but a *Widerwart*.[6]

---

6. The prefixes are *gegen* and *wider*. *Gegenwart* means "present" (time or tense); *Widerwart* is Kraus's coinage, derived from *widerwärtig* (repulsive).

The Play

Die letzten Tage der Menschheit is Karl Kraus's *magnum opus*, an enormous dramatic repository of most of his satiric themes and techniques. In the history of European drama this powerful pacifist play occupies a very special place. While it is in the mainstream of the German expressionistic theater, it also foreshadows the genre of documentary drama which achieved international prominence through the works of Bertolt Brecht and has held the German-speaking stage during the past two decades through the writings of Rolf Hochhuth, Peter Weiss, Heinar Kipphardt, Tancred Dorst, and others. Kraus wrote *The Last Days of Mankind* during World War I; one world war and several lesser wars later, the stupidity, malice, and worthlessness of his villains may have paled into relative insignificance in the face of Auschwitz, Lidice, Coventry, Hiroshima, Biafra and Vietnam; alongside the Krupps and their ilk as well as the Strangeloves of the East and West. Yet Kraus's satiric vision is as fresh and as relevant today as it was six decades ago.

To adapt Clausewitz's phrase, Kraus's monumental play represents a continuation of his satiric writing by other means. While the entire orbit of the Central Powers becomes one giant pillory here, Kraus's satire is concentrated on "Kakania" ("Kakanien," Robert Musil's term for *k. k.* Austria-Hungary, a conglomeration of peoples totaling fifty million which caused constant clashes and conflicts of an ethnic, political, economic, and social nature). In Kraus's view, this empire, "all this national variety-store stuff which has plunged us into cultural disgrace and material misery," bore the blame for the war, and Emperor Franz Josef, the "Habsburg demon incarnate," became a prime target for his satire ("Never before in world history has a stronger non-personality put his stamp on all things and forms").

Most of the 209 scenes of the 5 acts of *Die letzten Tage der Menschheit*, originally subtitled "Ein Angsttraum" (A Nightmare), were sketched during the summers of 1915, 1916, and 1917. The 10-scene Prologue dates from July 1915 and the Epilogue from July 1917. Parts of the play appeared in several special issues of the *Fackel* as well as in *Worte in Versen*, and were read by Kraus at numerous wartime recitals, censorship apparently having been but a minor problem in those days ("Satires which the censor understands are rightly prohibited"). The complete play was first published in book form in 1922 and amounted to almost 800 pages. In the author's lifetime, only the Epilogue, "Die letzte Nacht" (The Last Night), was performed on the stage, the satirist having refused offers by Max Reinhardt and Erwin Piscator to put on this essentially unperformable play.

But Kraus later read his own "stage version" of the drama in Vienna and elsewhere, and long after the author's death Heinrich Fischer and Leopold Lindtberg staged their adaptation of the play, similar in many respects to the English rendering by Max Knight and Joseph Fabry in this volume, a collaborative effort that bears Fischer's stamp of approval.

The play begins with the voice of a newspaper vendor and ends with the voice of God (though in the present version, the Grumbler — that is, Kraus himself — has both the first word and the last). It is set in public rather than private places: in the streets of Vienna and Berlin, in offices and barracks, churches and cafés, amusement places and military hospitals, railroad stations and army posts. The play's many hundreds of characters include emperors and editors, journalists and jesters, poets and prostitutes, soldiers and sycophants, inspectors and innkeepers, politicians and professors, chauvinists and showmen, profiteers and policemen, teachers and tradesmen, children and churchmen. There are many actual as well as fictitious persons, and through their speech patterns, captured with consummate linguistic mimicry, they reveal and judge themselves. This dramatic typology of man's inhumanity to man is basically documentary in nature; about one-half of it consists of authentic (though artistically presented) newspaper editorials and articles, war communiqués, court judgments, advertisements, letters, and other documents. Even the scenes and texts invented by Kraus reproduce with uncanny accuracy and authenticity the language of the "great times," which becomes the index of the Nietzschean vision of the disintegration of European culture and of a dying way of life.

"A sorcerer's apprentice seems to have utilized the absence of his master," wrote Kraus in reference to Goethe's poem; "but now there is blood instead of water." Kraus's wartime waxworks of "Goethe's people" and his fellow Austrians includes such characters as the two fatuous privy councilors who vie with each other in mangling one of the glories of German poetry, Goethe's "Wanderer's Night Song" ("O'er all the hilltops is quiet now . . ." in H. W. Longfellow's translation — though in the Knight-Fabry version this has been ingeniously changed to a brutal "updating" of Austria's Christmas gift to the world: "Violent night, victory night . . ."); the Bavarian storyteller Ludwig Ganghofer, who yodels his way along the front, writes war reports for the *Neue Freie Presse*, and swaps jokes with an appreciative Kaiser; the "patriotic" pastors of the "praise-the-Lord-and-pass the-ammunition" variety to whom Kraus gives the names of birds of prey; a judge who celebrates his hundredth death sentence; the two fat Berlin profiteers who disport themselves in the snows of the Swiss Alps; Alice Schalek, the first woman accredited to the Austrian army as a correspondent, whose gushy effusions in a denatured language about the emotions of the common man, "liberated humanity," and "the fever of the adventure" and whose search for "human-interest" material amidst degradation, destruction, and death made her a macabre joke and a frequent Krausian target; the grocer Chramosta, whom followers of the contemporary Austrian scene will recognize as an ancestor of the cabaret character "Herr Karl"; and the "happy hangman," another all-too-familiar type, who appears on a picture postcard (used by Kraus as an illustration) holding his paws over the head of an executed man while the grinning or smug-looking bystanders gather around the lifeless, dangling body. Another prime target of Kraus's satire was Moriz Benedikt ("Maledikt"), the editor of the *Neue Freie Presse*, whom Kraus depicts as the "Lord of the Hyenas" and the "Antichrist," but who is also referred to — less apocalyptically but quite reverently — as "he" in the conversations of newspaper readers and other patriots. Old Man Biach, one of Kraus's fictitious characters and an assiduous mouther of Benedikt's editorials, dies, as it were, of linguistic convolution and spiritual poisoning when even he can no longer reconcile the harsh reality with all the journalistic double-talk and governmental double-think.

The scenes in Kraus's play are by turns lyrical and prosaic, comic and tragic; but even what seems to be light-hearted and purely humorous acquires a certain grimness from the context and more often than not appears as gallows humor. There is no hero or plot in the conventional Aristotelian sense. The scenes range in length from one-line "blackouts" in the tradition of the cabaret (what is blacked out tends to be the human spirit) to lengthy dialogues or monologues, dramatized editorials, and phantasmagoric tableaux. The *couplets* hark back to the nineteenth-century Viennese comedies of Johann Nestroy and Ferdinand Raimund. The 23 conversations between the Grumbler and the Optimist function as the choruses of a tragedy; they represent oases of relative repose and reflection. In his running commentary the Grumbler constitutes the ever-present anguished conscience of the times and the voice of reason, presenting eschatological views rather than espousing *Realpolitik*, and displaying the kind of conscience, compassion, and consistency that might have saved European civilization.

While the Prologue — ranging, in the original, from 28 June 1914, the day on which the successor to the Austrian throne, Archduke Franz Ferdinand, and his wife were assassinated, to their third-class funeral — shows with grim realism what lies underneath the veneer of Austrian *Gemütlichkeit*, surrealistic touches are introduced as the tragedy (and the war) rush toward their cataclysmic conclusion. "Corybants and Maenads" spew forth word fragments, and there are choruses of Gas Masks, Frozen Soldiers, 1200 Drowned Horses, and the Dead Children of the *Lusitania*. The rhymed Epilogue is a harrowing poetic satire raised to a supernatural plane in which many motifs of the play are recapitulated in cinematographic or operatic form. After the silence that follows utter destruction, God's voice is heard speaking the words of Kaiser Wilhelm II at the beginning of the war: "Ich habe es nicht gewollt" (I did not will it so) — possibly a final glimmer of hope that man can yet redeem himself and work toward a better destiny.

Even though these final scenes could not be included, the translators have made a skillful abridgment and rearrangement of Kraus's massive work; and this has resulted in a three-act drama which not only has a continuity and an integrity of its own but is also eminently readable and performable.

A final, personal word from the editor. No translation should ever be regarded as an adequate substitute for the original. Any literary translation is successful only if it directs attention to the original and makes access to it seem desirable. The editor still remembers a *bar mitzvah* present he received almost five decades ago in the city where Karl Kraus had died but a few months previously: a selection from the Hebrew poetry of Chaim Nachman Bialik in German translation. Let an adaptation of the final message of that book's translator conclude these remarks: "Learn German, gentle reader, and read Karl Kraus in the original!"

Selected Prose

translated by

Harry Zohn

Torture in Austria

Has torture been abolished in Austria ?
It is still permissible to torture geniuses to death.
In full view of the public!
Smetana was tortured until he died demented.
His crime ?
Progress.
Smetana's life was a slow death by starvation.
When he was no longer able to hear it, definitely unable to hear it, they called him the Mozart of our time.
How much good that does a man when he is already lying between boards that are not associated with all the world being a stage!
Smetana is finished . . .
Anton Bruckner is placed in the dock. The penal process continues.

Hanslick[1] asks:

Do you plead guilty to having written symphonies?

Bruckner is silent and creates.

The chief judge gently applies the small thumbscrews.

He declares that he leaves the Musikvereinssaal [concert hall] before a Bruckner symphony is played in order not to witness the desecration of the Musikvereinssaal.

The crowd hoots. They leave the Musikvereinssaal before every Bruckner symphony.

Bruckner's bones crack.

But Bruckner has a strong constitution.

Assistant Dömpke rolls up his sleeves.

The chief judge asks:

Anton Bruckner, do you plead guilty to having written a quintet?

Bruckner is silent and creates.

Assistant Dömpke steps forward: "Anton Bruckner composes like a drunkard!"[2]

The crowd hoots.

Bruckner's bones crack.

But Bruckner has a strong constitution.

Assistant Kalbeck is called. He presses his slouch hat down over his face.

The chief judge asks:

Anton Bruckner, do you plead guilty to writing symphonies against us to this day and to enticing foreigners?

Bruckner is silent and creates.

Assistant Kalbeck begins to "tighten" Bruckner.

The crowd hoots.

Bruckner's bones crack.

But Bruckner has a strong constitution.

He is declared insane.

But he does not want to go insane. He has faith in God and believes in art.

He writes his Ninth and dies.

Assistant Kalbeck is still "tightening" him . . .

Now Hugo Wolf is captured.

The chief judge asks:

Hugo Wolf, do you plead guilty to having invoked, through your songs, the spirit of Moerike that was already asleep in literary history?

---

1. Eduard Hanslick, Max Kalbeck, and Gustav Dömpke, the most prominent music critics of Vienna in the second half of the nineteenth century, were all opposed to Bruckner (and Wagner) but favored Brahms.

2. Dömpke made this statement in the pages of the *Wiener Allgemeine Zeitung*.

Hugo Wolf rants, raves, and creates.

He has to be softened up.

Hugo Wolf is killed with silence.

The living man is deleted from life. A vacuum is created around the creative man.

Hugo Wolf suffers.

So he is still alive.

The chief judge asks:

Hugo Wolf, do you believe in Brahms ?

Hugo Wolf curses the clique.

He does not get soft.

In the meantime, Assistant Dömpke has left.

Assistant Kalbeck is prepared to "tighten" Hugo Wolf as well.

The chief judge asks:

Hugo Wolf, do you confess that you still believe in Richard Wagner ?

Hugo Wolf rages, thrashes about, and creates.

The chief judge loosens the thumbscrews: "Undoubtedly a man of spirit and talent, but he must beware of 'good friends' and arrogance."

The good friends feed Hugo Wolf.

Let him beware of eating.

The good friends shelter Hugo Wolf.

Let him beware of resting in the beds of good friends.

He is no longer starving. So let him beware of arrogance, says the chief judge.

Hugo Wolf bewares, goes to the insane asylum, and dies.[3]

The people wake up and send their condolences to Doctor Michael Haberlandt.[4]

Hugo Wolf has become ripe for anecdotal obituaries.

He died of his Goethe and Moerike songs.

If he had set to music the poems of Rudolf Lothar,[5] his name would never have disappeared from the columns of the daily press; he would have been called "our immortal Hugo Wolf" twice a day; he would have been interviewed like a haberdasher or a hatmaker.

In two hundred years some historian will study Viennese culture at the end of the nineteenth century from yellowed daily journals.

He will write:

3. Wolf died on 22 February 1903, a few days before this piece appeared in the *Fackel*.
4. Dr. Haberlandt, a noted scholar, befriended Wolf in his last years and founded a Hugo Wolf Society in Vienna.
5. Once a famous dramatist, essayist, storyteller and editor, now almost forgotten.

"At the end of the nineteeth century Richard Wagner, Anton Bruckner, and Hugo Wolf made futile attempts to gain the recognition of small circles in Vienna. Their names paled before the fame of an artist whose presence could not be expunged from the memories of the Viennese. If we may trust the sources at our disposal, Charles Weinberger[6] must be regarded as the most important composer around the year 1900."

"Ist die Folter in Österreich abgeschafft ?"   (1903)

6. Weinberger (1861–1940) was a prolific but decidedly minor composer of operettas.

In Praise of a Topsy-Turvy Life-Style

For a time I tried a normal life-style, but all too soon I came to feel its sad consequences on my body and my soul, and I decided to start leading an unsensible life before it was too late. Now I see the world again through one of those veils which not only help one get over the reality of earthly misery, but to which I also owe many an exaggerated vision of the possible pleasures of life. In my case, the sound principle of a topsy-turvy life-style in the framework of an upside-down world order has stood every test. I too once accomplished the feat of rising with the sun and retiring with it. But the insufferable objectivity with which the sun shines on all my fellow citizens, without regard to person or general deformity and ugliness, is not to every-one's taste; and anyone who can betimes escape the danger of taking a clear-eyed view of this earth does the wise thing and experiences the plea-sure of being avoided on that account by those he avoids. For when my day was still divided into morning and evening, it was a joy to awaken with the cock's crow and go to bed with the nightwatchman's call. But then the other division came into vogue: there was morning paper and there was evening paper — and the world lay in wait of events. Anyone who has observed for a time how disgracefully these events debase themselves before curiosity, how cravenly the course of the world adapts itself to the increased need for information, and how in the end time and space become forms of perception of the journalistic subject, turns over in bed and goes on sleeping. "Take vantage, heavy eyes, not to behold this shameful lodging."[1]

Hence I sleep in broad daylight. And when I wake up, I spread the whole paper shame of mankind before me so I might know what I have missed, and this makes me happy. Stupidity gets up early; that is why events are accustomed to happening in the morning. True, many things can happen by eveningtime; but generally speaking, the afternoon does not have the noisy bustle through which human progress attempts to prove itself worthy of its good name until feeding time. A true miller gets up only when his mill has stopped turning, and anyone who wishes to have nothing in common with people whose being here is being there gets up late. But then I go out on the Ringstrasse and watch the preparations for a parade.[2] For four weeks there is noise; it's like a symphony on the theme of money circulating. Mankind gets ready for a holiday; carpenters raise grandstands and their prices; and when I consider that I won't get to see that magnificence, *my* heart begins to beat faster, too. If mine were still the normal life-style, that festive procession would have forced me to leave town; but now I can stay and still see nothing. An old king in Shakespeare cautions: "Make no noise, make no noise, draw the curtains . . . . we'll go to supper i' the morning."[3] A fool who confirms that this world order is upside down adds: "And I'll go to bed at noon." But in the evening, when I have breakfast, everything will be over, and from the newspapers I shall learn in comfort how many cases of sunstroke there have been.

All the more important accidents happen in the morning. I know about them only from hearsay, and by dint of being late I preserve my faith in the excellence of human institutions. The evening papers report not only what happened but also who was present; thus one feels at a safe distance from the scene of a fire and still has a chance to count the heads of those loved

1. The Earl of Kent in Shakespeare's *King Lear*, act 2, sc. 2.
2. A mammoth event in commemoration of Emperor Franz Josef's sixtieth anniversary on the throne in 1908. The parade was the subject of Kraus's "Der Festzug," which appeared in the *Fackel* of March 1908, a few months before the publication of the present piece.
3. *King Lear*, act 3, sc. 6.

36

ones who (among others) were spotted in time — so that not a single head is missing.[4] Utilize as best you can the transformation of the universe into a local section; use the process by which time is canned and called a newspaper. The world has become uglier since it began to look into a mirror every day; so let us settle for the mirror image and do without an inspection of the original. It is uplifting to lose one's faith in a reality which looks the way it is described in a newspaper. He who sleeps away half a day has won half a life.

All major stupidities happen before noon; a person should wake up only when office hours are over. Let him step out into life after lunch, when it is free of politics. To be sure, he will not learn from the evening papers that assassinations, too, happen in the morning, for usually even the reporters are asleep then. There is a newspaper which sent one correspondent after another to Paris in order to learn in time about attempts on the life of the president; and lo and behold, one president after another lost his life, and each time a president's death was the twin brother of a correspondent's sleep. When recently the German princes were in our city and everyone was up and doing, I knew nothing about it. Nor did this incident have any adverse consequences for me in other respects — except that for the first time I could not get my accustomed beef for breakfast, which meant that I could not satisfy a taste by which I had hitherto demonstrated my affiliation with the city in which I live. The waiter made his excuses, and by way of consoling me he referred to the consolidation of the Triple Alliance. This I had slept away. If a theologian brings himself to believe no longer in the immaculate conception, this happens in the morning; if a nuncio makes a fool of himself, it happens in the morning; and truly, it is better for a farmers' march on a university or the cry "Stop universal suffrage!" to disrupt our morning sleep than to disturb our afternoon rest. Only once did I happen to be around when a minister tendered his resignation after lunch. But how messy things were then! At three o'clock the police flailed away at a crowd that had yelled "Out with him!" and by a quarter to four they said: "Go on home, folks; Badeni's gone, too!"[5]

What about justice? It is blind only in the morning, and if, by way of exception, a judicial murder takes place at a late hour, it is surely a particularly important case. Or it could happen in German-speaking countries

4. A reference to a line in Friedrich Schiller's poem "Das Lied von der Glocke": "He counts the heads of his loved ones, and lo! not one dear head is missing."

5. Count Kasimir Felix Badeni (1846–1909) was forced to resign as prime minister of Austria-Hungary in 1897 over the question of the language ordinances (he attempted to place Czech on a par with German in Bohemia and Moravia).

that in a sex case truth is on the march (for twenty-five years), and then it probably has to use afternoons as well. To escape such an event it does no good to withdraw to one's bedroom, for, as everyone knows, a bedroom has proved to be the least safe place *vis-à-vis* the quest for truth. But even though it is one of life's comforts that one can sleep away life's discomforts, I must unfortunately admit that there is one area in which I have had no luck at all with my practice: the arts. For it is an old experience that most theatrical flops occur in the evening.

Still, in all areas of public activity it is quiet at night. Nothing stirs. There is no news. Only the street-sweeping machine moves through the streets like the symbol of an upside-down world order — so the dust left by the day may be spread; and when it rains, the streetsweeper is followed by the sprinkling truck. Otherwise there is peace. Stupidity is asleep, and I go to work. From the distance comes a noise like the sound of printing presses: stupidity is snoring. I sneak up on it and even derive enjoyment from my murderous intentions. When the first morning paper appears on the eastern horizon of civilization, I go to bed. . . . These are some of the advantages of a topsy-turvy life-style.

"Lob der verkehrten Lebensweise"   (1908)

The Good Conduct Medal

In Austria there is a climax of culpability for young girls who embrace vice. A distinction is made between girls who are guilty of the unauthorized practice of prostitution; girls who falsely state that they are under the supervision of the morals division of the police; and, finally, girls who are licensed to practice prostitution but not to wear a good conduct medal. At first glance this classification is confusing, but it is thoroughly in keeping with the actual situation. A girl who seemed suspicious to a detective (nothing seems more suspicious to a detective than a girl!) stated that she was under the supervision of the morals division of the police. She had only been kidding, but the matter was investigated. Since her statement proved to be false, the police launched an investigation for unauthorized practice of prostitution. But since this suspicion also proved to be unjustified and it turned out that the girl was not practicing prostitution at all, the public prosecutor brought action for making false statements. The girl was charged with "having arrogated to herself a social position that she was not entitled to." Since she was practicing neither licensed nor unlicensed prostitution, she was a swindler; and she escaped being sentenced only because during the hearing she answered the judge's question as to what had been in her mind by saying, "Nothing." To recapitulate, then: The girl had claimed that she was under the supervision of the morals division of the police. Because this was an untruth, an investigation was launched on suspicion of immoral conduct. She was able to prove that she was not immoral enough to engage in immoral conduct, but she could not prove that she was moral enough to be under the supervision of the morals division of the police. So the only thing to do was to accuse her of making false statements — which in Austria, after all, is the basis for sentencing even murderers if it cannot be proved that they have committed a murder.

Let us now go a step further. If a girl is licensed to practice prostitution, it could happen that she suppresses that fact and fraudulently states that she is not licensed to practice prostitution. She would then be arrogating to herself an immoral conduct in which she engaged not because she is authorized to do so but though she is not authorized to do so, whereas in reality she is authorized only to engage in the immoral conduct that she is authorized to engage in. Such cases rarely occur in practice, and the judgments of the Superior Court fluctuate. But the most difficult case recently occurred in Wiener-Neustadt. In a local brothel there is a girl who is licensed to practice prostitution and who has not previously run into trouble. She never arrogated to herself any immoral conduct that she does not engage in, and she has not even been shown to have falsely stated that she does not practice a prostitution which she is licensed to practice. But the devil was riding this girl of the clean record, and one evening she walked around the parlor of the house wearing a good conduct medal on her chest. "By so doing she aroused in the customers . . ." Well, what do you suppose she aroused in the customers ? Not what you might think, but the opposite: annoyance. And when a *fille de joie* arouses annoyance in the customers of a bawdyhouse, it is presumably high time for the public prosecutor's office to take action. In point of fact, the girl was charged with an arousal for which she was not licensed. The lower-court judge acquitted her, saying that a good conduct medal was not a military decoration and the annoyance was merely of the kind that should be dealt with by the police. This, to be sure, was an admission on the part of the judge that the girl would have been guilty if she had worn, say, the Takowa medal. It is obvious that the unauthorized wearing of a medal might have made a journalist culpable, but not a prostitute. But in Wiener-Neustadt the women's movement seems to have progressed to the point where both sexes are deemed equally capable of medal-hunting. In any case, the lower-court judge did say that a good conduct medal was not a military decoration. The public prosecutor was of a different opinion, however: he appealed the verdict, and the Superior Court imposed on the defendant a fine of twenty crowns. The Superior Court said that a good conduct medal was a badge of honor equivalent to any military decoration. And the Court regarded "the wearing of the medal in a brothel" as a particularly aggravating circumstance. When the defendant was asked what she could have been thinking of, she answered, "Nothing." But this time that answer did her not one bit of good, for it is better that a respectable girl presume to be a prostitute than that a prostitute presume to wear a good conduct medal. What was her excuse? She said that a civilian had given it to her; he was a generous man and gave her the medal as her "wages of shame." But then she should have stuck it in her stocking. Only customers are entitled to wear a badge of honor in a bawdyhouse, and if this should arouse the annoyance of the girls, the girls would be guilty of a culpable action. But if a customer gives a girl a good conduct medal instead of twenty crowns, she is not allowed to wear the medal, or else she has to give the twenty crowns to the court. For justice is a whore that won't let herself be stiffed, and collects the wages of shame even from the poor!

"Das Ehrenkreuz"   (1909)

The World of Posters

Even as a child I was less intent upon deriving life from the great works of art than upon supplementing it with its own little realities. Unconsciously I took the right road to life by conquering it with every step instead of taking possession of it as a tradition for which a young mind has no use. Adults who still derive childlike pleasure from hanging the gifts of a ready-made education on the Christmas tree of a child waiting outside the door to life do not realize how unreceptive they are making children to everything that constitutes the true surprise of life. My curiosity always overrode such gratification. Instinctively I shunned the temptation to absorb what wiser people had thought; and while my schoolmates were receiving bad marks in conduct because they were reading books under their benches, I was a model pupil because I paid attention to every word of my teachers in order to observe their ridiculousness. At an early age I was bent upon receiving information about people from people, and I really recognized only one form of artistic communication which seemed to me to get across unobtrusively what was worth knowing: the advertising poster. A sentimental hit tune played by a hurdy-gurdy in front of our country house on a summer Sunday powerfully affected my mind and heart, too; I stopped catching flies, and the mysteries of love opened up to me. (Others who boast that *Tristan und Isolde* had a similar effect on them are still catching flies.) I was always unpretentious when it was a matter of choosing outward impressions to get at inward experiences, and I disdained those strong stimulants which weak souls need to purchase an illusory effect with greater damage. In short, the numerous libraries and museums which I have passed in my life have had no cause to complain about my obtrusiveness. On the other hand, street life has always attracted me, and listening to the noises of the day as though they were the chords of eternity has been an occupation at which my craving for pleasure and my thirst for knowledge have been amply gratified. And truly, anyone who is born with the triply dangerous idealism which seeks confirmation of beauty in its antithesis can be moved to reverence by a placard.

I owe valuable information to the posters of a time when the first attempts were made to draw the attention of intellectual life to the sources of supply of outer life. For the endeavor became more and more distinct to offer the observer whose thought was distracted by higher interests a full substitute in the posters. He was supposed to find the intellectual values to which he had become disaccustomed in the very place where he had least expected to encounter them again, and he was bound to be all the more surprised to find the shoe polish to whose contemplation he had just sacrificed art and literature presented in connection with precisely those indispensable possessions of life. Up to that time, awareness of the usefulness and cheapness of a pants hanger was a matter which had nothing to do with painting, gnomic wisdom, or emotional life. But if we receive a pants hanger wrapped in artistic or intellectual values, why should we object? Why should we make two trips if happiness can be attained on one? Why should we pay for cultural ideals that do not cost a penny as the wrapping of a pants hanger? When the possessions of life were monopolized by businessmen, the plastic and graphic arts could occasionally assert their freedom to be commodities themselves rather than serve commodities, but it seemed certain that the words of a writer would have to lose their *raison d'être* outside industrial advertising. It is not that commercial interests are threatening to crowd out intellectual life. This life, rather, will be forced out of its unprofitable contemplativeness and into a social occupation, and many an artistic talent which would have been smothered in the fog of thankless problems will live to serve the conviction that there is only one silverware "for eternity" — and astonishingly cheap, too.

When they started banishing intellectual life to the world of posters, I missed hardly a lesson in front of billboards. And long before I recognized that the nature of the poster was the recommendation of some merchandise, I perceived it as a warning against life. I soon knew about the status of the intellect. It affected me with the revelatory power of an experience when one day I saw in a shopwindow the representation of two men, one of whom had trouble with his necktie while the other stood next to him triumphantly, pointed to his finished job, and gloated: "But my dear friend, why get hot under the collar ? Buy Schlesinger's Collar Support; it will keep your collar and your cravat in place!" I did not stop to think that mankind needed visual education in this field; rather, I assumed that it was a realistic presentation, that in good society such dialogues were carried on every day, and that there must be many whose lives are centered about that problem and are only a pretext for achieving the final consolidation of collar and cravat. And suddenly I saw the streets full of such people; I saw these faces everywhere, the surly struggler with life and the cheerful victor over it, and I learned to distinguish the choleric from the sanguine type, though both had waxed moustaches and pointed shoes. So I received from that picture my first and decisive impression of a humanity which in its overwhelming majority consists of counter-jumpers, and all of a sudden it was I before whom they all coalesced into the question: But my dear friend, why get hot under the collar ?

This again drove me to the posters, which at least offered me the horror-content of life in extract form. I liked to imagine that all intellectuality had been taken over, that everything literature had to offer in the way of quotations, language in the way of sayings, and the heart in the way of emotions was used only in posters, and that life outside advertisements was mere show and at most an effective advertisement for death. One day the flood of mercantilism came rushing in; the butcher, the baker, and the candlestick maker acted like the executors of a divine will, and it became the fashion to depict the heads of these people at street corners. For years I was pursued by a face in whose features I thought I could detect at least pride in a victorious battle. I grew older, but the face had no wrinkles, and I knew that it would outlive me and that the century would bear its imprint. Once it was the physiognomy of Napoleon which had such enduring effect on pregnant women that even the faces of their great-grandchildren were cause to suspect marital infidelity. The face which today leaves a similar impression on the souls of the contemporary world belongs to a watchmaker. Because he boasts of having the best watches, he also has the courage of a personality; he gives his head as security and his honest eyes as a guarantee. . . . Where have I seen this face before? This is what many people have asked themselves, thought about, and been unable to remember. They met a man, greeted him like an old acquaintance, and yet did not know who he was. But at the next street corner their greeting was returned by a poster. It was an innkeeper or a hatmaker or the lubricant manufacturer of whom we have all grown so fond, though we would not have expected to meet him in person because, after all, Beethoven does not climb down from his pedestal either. Is there life beyond the posters? When a train takes us outside the city, we do see a green meadow — but this green meadow is only a poster which that lubricant manufacturer has concocted in league with nature in order to pay his respects to us in the country as well.

There is no escape, so let us close our eyes and flee to the paradise of dreams. . . . But even there we have reckoned without our host, who regards dream life as a most appropriate opportunity to bring his face close to us. Terrible things become apparent. Mercantilism has been bold enough to use even the threshold of our conciousness as a plank. The everyday world did not offer room enough, and so the horrible possibility the very thought of which made us choke has become a reality: advertising faces have been used for those hypnogogic figures that surround our beds when we are half-asleep. And since there are also hypnogogic sounds, auditory hallucinations to which drowsy senses are prone, they have chosen—I shudder to think of it — all those slogans and summonses which fill our consciousness by day. What an exhortation! We lie there and atone for Macbeth's guilt. One by one the kings of the day appear: the Button King, the Soap King, the Textile King, the Picture-Postcard King, the Carpet King, the Cognac King, and finally the Rubber King. His eyes remind us of our sins, but his features bespeak the untearability of human trust. And yet, and yet! . . . A shaggy head appears and moans: "I used to be bald!" And again: On this side there are still pimples, on that side they have disappeared after use. Oh, there is a face *before* use and another face *after*. . . . A "clear head" appears; it is the one that uses Dr. Oetker's Baking Powder. The air hums with "Where is there good food and drink?" and already there is an open mouth swallowing goulash and another to show us how to drink beer. Who is coming in now? William Tell with his son? "From the head of my child I am to . . ."[1] At that point he wavered, but he does lend himself nonetheless to being a trademark of a chocolate firm. . . . Look, look, who is bursting in? A woman whose hair is longer than she is — thus a woman who has reason

1. "Ich soll vom Haupte meines Kindes . . .," a line from act 3, sc. 2 of Friedrich Schiller's play *Wilhelm Tell.*

to emphasize her personality. She cries: "I, Anna . . ." But what she says is drowned out by the rattling of a car whose driver calls out to me: "You're on the right road if you drink our coffee . . ." But he is interrupted with "Distance is no obstacle!" by a wordly wise man who wishes to bestow upon the world old clothes that have seen better days. And now the maelstrom of maxims bursts forth unrestrained: "Be sure to ask for . . . Beauty is wealth, beauty is power . . . Astonishingly rapid relief . . . A woman's delight . . . Throw your suspenders away! . . . Give a shilling . . . Once you try it, you will buy it . . . How are you fixed for baby clothes ? . . . The confirmation present with a future . . . The world-famous, prize-winning Limburger cheese . . . It's just what the doctor ordered . . . For acid indigestion . . . Would you like to be strong and healthy ? . . . Any woman can be beautiful . . . If you suffer from the consequences . . . This is how I look in one of my corsets; it's so light I don't even know I'm wearing it . . . The Rare Bird says . . . You can shave in the dark! . . . If a mother is incapable of . . . 10,000 shillings free . . . To all who feel tired and listless . . . Bedbugs and insects of all kinds . . . Music hath charms . . ." Yes, music wants to lull me to sleep and entices to erotic dreams. I hear a song: "Ich liebe die Eine, die Feine, die Kleine . . ."[2] But I am fooled; it is only an advertisement for a lozenge. What's that dancing up in the air ? "I am a rubber glove! Don't you know me yet, ma'am ?" Romulus and Remus appear under an umbrella. What ?! The founding of Rome has been cancelled due to inclement weather ? "A crime!" somebody roars. "Everyone commits a crime who does not use . . ." I feel feverish. But already a government counselor and five physicians are standing around my bed and giving expert testimony. "Lack of virility!" mumbles one of them scornfully. "One touch and the bed pops out!" is the knowing response. "Drink mineral water!" counsels an unauthorized source. "It's the good Krondorfer; our table wouldn't be complete without it!" is the response. "Drink Old Gessler's Liqueur!" I hear, and feel a beard tickling me. "Are you chewing Ricci yet ?" asks a gnome. "How do I acquire vim and vigor ?" moans someone who is getting scared stiff in this room. And the gremlin hunched up on my chest stares at me and has but one wish: "If I could only speak with you in person!" Help, help! Who's calling for help there ? Who is running his head through the wall ? Who is tearing his hair out ? Who is despairing and jubilant, cheerful and depressed, who is jumping around and banging on the window with his fists ? Oh, it's someone who is unhappy because they don't

2. "I love the only one, the fine one, the little one . . ." — a line (misquoted) from "Die Rose, die Lilie, die Taube, die Sonne" by Heinrich Heine, the third song in Robert Schumann's song cycle *Dichterliebe*.

let him buy his clothes at Gerstl's and who finally gets his will. "I'll kill myself ... !" he cries if he is restrained. "Whaaaat ?! Can it be ? ? ?!!!" he cries because he finds the prices too low. "Freedom of choice!" he roars, getting the democrats on his side, though it quickly turns out that he means only the choice of material. And now there is a cacophony of voices; I can no longer tell the products apart; a hundred grotesque faces appear and a hundred cries can be heard. I can make out only advice like "Cook with gas!", "Wash with air!", and "Bathe at home!" And since life is surging around my bed of pain in such profusion, offering all the conveniences and all the automatic joys that can be obtained at this point in time, a gun dealer notices I no longer know what is going on and drowns out the din with his own slogan: "Be your own murderer!"

"Die Welt der Plakate" (1909)

The Discovery
of the
North Pole

The discovery — or, as it has also been called, the conquest — of the North Pole occurred in 1909. It was the work of a daring American, and it was hailed with all the greater satisfaction because in the same year his country's national reputation had been considerably tarnished by the cession of numerous American women to Chinese waiters.[1] Cultural self-respect was given a boost not only in America but all over the world. People felt encouraged again and began to trust a providence which evidently wished to compensate the civilized world for the disagreeable discoveries of the same season with the discovery of the North Pole. Even

---

1. The reference is to certain erotic situations and criminal occurrences in Chinatown, New York, including the murder of Elsie Siegl, which Kraus discussed in his prose piece "Die chinesische Mauer" (The Great Wall of China), published in the *Fackel* in July 1909, a few months before the appearance of "The Discovery of the North Pole."

one solitary missionary of science who returns from the Eskimos safe and sound is ample compensation for a dozen female researchers of faith who stay behind in Chinatown. It was not regarded as accidental but as a special kindness of fate that the German national consciousness had a share in the conquest of the North Pole in the person of a man whose original name is said to have been Koch,[2] just as this national consciousness had participated in a different sense in the murder of Elsie Siegl. People did not hesitate for one moment as to which of the two was the greater event; after all, the more recent occurrence had an advantage over the earlier one: people could at last wag their tongues again. In this respect it felt almost like relaxation. For when the news went around the world that the yellow peril was the taste of white women, white men — oh, accursed opalescence! — became whiter still and had just enough presence of mind to pull out morality, without suspecting that it was precisely this morality which had got them into that situation. And now shame and fear contended for the chance to shut the world's mouth. There ensued that icy silence which was finally pierced by the saving cry: The North Pole has been discovered! Then it seemed as if the whiteness of that region were the found background against which color once again appeared in the countenances of white creatures. The frozen world came to life, warmed up, and thawed out in the realization that the Eskimos are finer human beings after all. You have only to understand their language, people said, bring them something or press something into their hands, and they will readily show a stranger the way to the North Pole. The Eskimos left some grounds for hope; the Chinese left every ground for fear. They give no answer if they are asked about developments, and just grin if a polite stranger asks which of them murdered his wife.

It was in the year 1909 that Christian civilization began to retreat from the East and to concentrate on the North. Yes, people counted on the Eskimos, for they considered the discovery of the North Pole not only as a way out of an embarrassing situation but also as the fulfillment of an old heart's desire. For centuries mankind had lacked a final something in order to be happy as it constantly marched forward and, despite the bunions of progress, did not take a rest. What could it have been? What was it that feverishly filled days and dreams? What kept in suspense a world whose pulse is counted by its records? What was the paradigm of all desire? The

2. Dr. Theodor Albert Koch emigrated to the United States from Hamburg ca. 1849, married Magdelena Long, and settled in Calicoon, New York. He changed his name to Cook while serving in the army during the Civil War. His son, Frederick Albert Cook, was born at Calicoon on 10 June 1864 and became a physician.

trump of ambition? The Ultima Thule of curiosity? The substitute for paradise lost? The big sausage on which science sicked all sled dogs at the earthly fair? Alas, mankind was not content to stay at its daily labors; the idea that up there there were a few square miles on which human feet had never trodden seemed unbearable. Before people had finally succeeded in finding that "desolate area," life was more desolate than said area. It was a disgrace that we, the owners of the world, should have let ourselves be deprived of its last little slice. Since the discovery of America we had been ashamed, and all that time we had hoped that America would reciprocate. It was no pleasure to live in a world about which one was not completely informed, and many a suicide out of unknown motives may have happened because even on earth there is an undiscover'd country from whose bourn no traveler returns. And in the nursery of mankind the question "What would you like to be when you grow up?" always drew this resounding answer: "The discoverer of the North Pole!" But a child learns to discard his ideals, whereas a grown-up never wears out his short pants. He really has to have the North Pole! His favorite dream, that the North Pole is discovered, does not suffice him; he presses for fulfillment of that dream. But with all the ingratitude of an idealist whose wishes are gratified he does not hesitate to deny his respect to virgin nature as soon as it has surrendered to his wooing. Mr. Cook cries "I was disappointed!" and calls the idol of mankind a desolate area. For the only valuable thing about the North Pole was that it had not been reached. Once it has been reached, it is just a pole from which a flag waves — thus worse than nothing, a crutch of fulfillment and a barrier to imagination. The modesty of the human spirit is insatiable.

The discovery of the North Pole is one of those realities which could not be avoided. It is the wages which human perseverance pays itself when it thinks that something is taking too long. The world needed a discoverer of the North Pole, and as in all areas of social activity, merit was less important here than opportunity. Never was the moment more propitious than in the days when the spirit strove earthward and the machine rose to the stars; when lifeless progress, followed by a merry widow, went to its grave. When only those jokes were understood on earth which were carved of the crudest material, the discovery of the North Pole occurred. It is an effective extemporization of a past development. It happened and made a hit. A North Pole discoverer was needed, and he was there. The world would not have let itself be talked out of him for all the money in the world — the world which loves *faits accomplis* and lulls itself to sleep over the scruples of science: Let's be glad we have a discoverer of the North Pole! Only a rationalistic nursemaid would try to wrest a tin soldier from a

50

child's clasped hand with the motivation that the soldier can't march. Does one have to be able to discover the North Pole to discover the North Pole? But the doubts of science are part of the child's play it seeks to disrupt. When Mr. Cook related where he had been, the world became divided into idealists and skeptics. Never before had there been so many representatives of both intellectual camps, and they deserved one another. The idealists were primarily the men who are in charge of writing newspaper editorials and have to see to it that the last long-eared subscriber and loyal ass of our paper gets to wear the dignity of being a contemporary. The skeptics were the men of science: that is, the gentlemen of the North Pole competition. For as in all areas of social activity, merit was less important here . . . — in a word, the idealists were the more likeable group. It was edifying when their leader, the editor of the financial section, enthusiastically cried that the discovery of the North Pole was a matter that concerned everybody, when he called it a moral gain for mankind and praised the idealism which was present after all in a world dominated by material interests. But unfortunately he had second thoughts and began to concern himself with the very last still-unsolved problem of an age that has arrived, to wit: Who owns the North Pole? You see, the Attorney General in Washington had immediately done what attorneys general always do automatically: he had appropriated the North Pole. The idealist from the financial section thought that this was not valid, however, for the occupation must be "actual," and he began to dream of a time when financial interests would gain a foothold in the region of permanent ice. The skeptics, not to be outdone, concentrated on investigating the background of Mr. Cook, since they realized that among the greatest human difficulties is not only the reaching of the North Pole but the proof of the opposite. For the occupation of North Pole explorer not only deserves the highest credit but also receives it, and in no field can science count on such popular currents and favorable winds as in this one. There are times when the claim to have reached the North Pole is a stroke of genius compared to which the reaching of the North Pole can only be considered a finger exercise, and when a person's claim that he has been to Oslo finds skeptics and his assurance that he has been to the North Pole, idealists. So it is a futile effort to discover in the Arctic background of a man a dubious scaling of Mount McKinley; and once the world has a North Pole discoverer, no doubt, however well founded, would be likely to wrest him from it.

Only if there are two of them does stupidity get suspicious. This is where politics begins. Then the dividing line between idealists and skeptics gets blurred. In its place two purposeful parties form, one of which swears by — no, bets on — Cook, and the other, Peary. And from the solved problem of the North Pole the human spirit begins to soar to the heights of the world-historical turf scandal. The duplicity of events is a beneficial institution which helps the capacity of brains by giving them time to spell out the "Ah" of astonishment. Two heads are better than one, said a good-humored fate when it clinked glasses with the hero at the banquet and told him that he had missed a rendezvous up there. Mr. Cook was aghast, and so were his contemporaries in the face of an audacity that blazed a trail for the idea of unfair competition right into the region of polar ice, where a person is dependent on another person's provisions and has to start using someone else's Eskimos and dogs. But reason gradually prevailed, and people decided to distribute the laurels in such a way as to award unqualifiedly the priority of North Pole discovery to one of the two men.

Could Peary's achievement have counted on the joy which Cook's claim had aroused? Could a plain North Pole discoverer pass muster next to a man who had discovered the world's need for a North Pole discoverer? The honors that were left for the former were Chinese lanterns when compared to the flames of enthusiasm which a timely word had kindled. Thus the world reduces the merit of having reached the North Pole to its deserved dimensions. After all, people were enthusiastic about the discovery, not the person. Whether one man unjustly boasted of a favor that another man was enjoying; whether Mr. Cook reaped the victory that Mr. Peary had won — the good reputation of the North Pole was gone. The ideal was done for, and all interest now concentrated on the scientific brawling. Cook was dishonest enough to call "Cheers!" to the other man, and Peary was honest enough to tell him, "Disgusting!" Cook was so good-natured that he believed every other discovery of the North Pole after his own. He had long since done all he could to offer scientific proof. For he had not contented himself with assuring people that he was not a swindler and asking them to believe his assurances, because then they would believe that he had discovered the North Pole. He had not contented himself with furnishing samples of a feuilletonistic talent which had to convince even the most sober-minded newspaper reader that he had really scaled the "summit of the world." No, he had done more; he had virtually challenged the skeptics to go to the North Pole themselves! They had not expected such an answer, and they sat up and took notice. On the North Pole, so he said, they could find an American flag, and buried beneath it a metal tube in which he had deposited a document about his expedition. When the timid question was asked whether the ice on the North Pole did not drift, he replied that of course it did, but that he had already told everything. He was evidently trying to say that the floating ice on the North Pole was none of his business, and there he would

52

certainly have been right. In response to this explanation the people shouted hurray, and even Mrs. Cook no longer had any doubts. She cried: "I knew he would succeed; he was so sure of it when he left, I knew he couldn't fail!" Whereupon the director of a vaudeville theater offered the explorer 16,000 marks for ten weeks. But since an American publisher offered twice that amount for a wire report, Mr. Georg Brandes[3] opined that Cook would be a fool to go on the vaudeville stage. The idealists had not yet viewed the North Pole from that angle, and the liberal paper with an international readership which is directed by the financial expert began to get interested in the family situation of the discoverer. Mrs. Cook, so it said, had shared his ambition and her wealth with him. Another report painted a gloomy family picture: "During her husband's absence, Mrs. Cook had to struggle with material difficulties, and she had to sell valuables and art objects to feed herself and their children" while the harum-scarum was off discovering the North Pole. Now his fate had caught up with him. Mrs. Peary, so the newspapers reported, had disputed his ability to make scientific measurements, and if Mrs. Rasmussen had not come to his defense at the last moment, the ladies living next door to the Arctic zone would not have believed that he had discovered the North Pole.[4]

Some nice things were brought up. About Peary it was said that he had "had the bad taste to permit too many people to go along," and the only reason he did not get there first was that "he took his wife and a midwife to the North Pole." When the child arrived, there was no wetnurse, of course.[5] Cook was shrewder in this respect as well. He said he did not need any old wives; he knew that people would believe his tales about the North Pole even without one, and he did find a publisher who offered him a million and a half marks for them. In the profusion of winning moves which permitted us to share in the family life of two polar explorers, we must not forget the speech which Mrs. Peary made from the balcony of her villa to the visitors of a seaside resort and in which she announced her intention of henceforth keeping her husband to herself. This at least seemed to settle the question as to whom the discoverer of the North Pole

3. Danish-Jewish literary historian, 1842–1927.
4. The Danish explorer and anthropologist Knud Rasmussen was a passenger on the ship that brought Cook from Greenland to Denmark. At first he supported Cook, but after talking with Cook's Eskimos (who are reported to have said that they had never been out of sight of land) he changed his position and endorsed Robert E. Peary's claim.
5. Peary took his wife, Josephine Diebitsch Peary, along on his second and third expeditions (1891 and 1893). Their daughter Marie Ahnighito Peary, the "Snow Baby" (later Mrs. Stafford of Brunswick, Maine), was born on 12 September 1893, the first white child to be born in such an extreme northern latitude.

belongs to for all time. But after such a touching confession from a woman's lips, the statement unexpectedly made by a rear admiral sounds quite harsh. He called Peary "the greatest swindler America has ever produced." Again two men fighting to carry off the palm ? Who was first in not discovering the North Pole ?

One really begins not to know what's what and hopes daily to hear the decisive word from science. For science carefully follows the newspaper accounts and pays attention to all contradictions in order to appropriate them. As soon as a fabricated or distorted wire report is held under its nose, it gives expert opinions. It is aware of its responsibility to reporters, and it knows that in order to garner honors it really need not have reached the North Pole but only the desolate area of a newspaper office at night. And the world owes it only to a lucky chance that science did not endorse the report that Mr. Cook had succeeded in discovering "eine von Wilden reich bevölkerte Gegend" [an area densely populated by savages]. This report appeared in a paper less read by science, while the leading organ of science carried the correct version — namely, that the expedition had discovered "ein wildreiches Gebiet" [an area rich in game]. And that must be true, for Jules Verne said so. Nevertheless, in such a difficult matter as the North Pole and in view of the fact that it definitely had not been discovered prior to Messrs. Peary and Cook, science can do no more than alternately give or take credit. Science staunchly maintains the viewpoint that it is not inclined to skate on thin drift-ice with two Eskimos and one flag. For the Eskimos are even more unreliable than the flag. Cook had invoked Messrs. Itukisut and Avila as eyewitnesses to his discovery of the North Pole,[6] and they were supposed to frame his martyrdom like the thieves in the flesh when someone asked, "What is truth ?" Cook vehemently rejected Peary's objection that Eskimos were known to be liars. When Peary wired that Cook's two companions had told him that Cook had not covered any appreciable distance in a northerly direction, Mr. Cook had no choice but to refer to the axiom that Eskimos are liars (though Peary had already declared it to be a prejudice), and again we faced the question, "What is truth ?" For it is the specific secret of this secret that it is not the midnight sun which brings it to light. In general, this sun does not seem to promote truth as much as it promotes rudeness. While Cook was still pretending to be proud of Peary, Peary was already being advised by another arcticologist to keep his mouth shut. But people let the learned geographers wrack their brains over whether Mr. Cook was a provisions

6. The Eskimos' names are spelled variously Etukishook, Ahwelah (Cook), and Etookashoo, Ahpelah (Peary).

thief or Mr. Peary a baggage burglar, and the district court was supposed to decide who had discovered the North Pole. Let the courts look for the truth between *Ehrendoktorat* [honorary doctorate] and *Ehrenbeleidigung* [defamation of character]. The idealists rejected that side of the North Pole. The whole affair, whose daily revelations punctually came up to the satirical expectations of the day before, promised no further surprises. People were sated with the North Pole, and never before had they been disillusioned so suddenly and so painfully. They had been invited to a festival of humanity, and it turned into a family brawl at which the heroes threw ideals at each other's heads. A church fair had ended with the beating up of the saints. The crowd dispersed, the North Pole was such a compromised matter that no one wanted to have anything to do with it anymore, not even the President of the United States,[7] and many people began to turn their attention to the South Pole. . . . Science will make one last attempt and send out its arbiters. It is hoped they will establish that there really is a North Pole, because they know it from hearsay, and the Pole will be pleased if it comes out of this affair without a scratch, this self-satisfied spot "from which everywhere is south" and everywhere meanness — a desolate area since it came into contact with things human.

For it is written that the world becomes greater every day. Is it so inwardly contented that it can go out conquering ? Or is it not led on this course by the inner enemy, stupidity ? The press, that goiter of the world, swells up with the desire for conquest and bursts with the achievements which every day brings. A week has room for the boldest climax of the human drive for expansion: from the conquest of Lower Austria by the Czechs via the conquest of the air to the conquest of the North Pole. Combinations are possible, and if it had not been Mr. Cook's turn, the North Pole would surely have been conquered by the zeppelin through the newly-conquered air. The general readiness to wag one's tongue is receiving unprecedented cooperation from the events themselves, and with the dimension of admiration, the dimension of realities increases until the gapers and fate run out of breath in the race. And a jacking up of all values and meanings begins, an inflation which those who once had value and meaning cannot even imagine. "The greatest man of the century" is the title of the hour; the next hour bestows it upon someone else. "We've done it!" is no sooner the slogan of a type of moustache that points *ad astra* than it is a greeting offered to bolder, though no less controversial, inventions. Progress, with its head down and its legs up, kicks away in the atmosphere

7. Theodore Roosevelt.

and assures all crawling spirits that it dominates nature. It annoys nature and says it has conquered it. It has invented morality and machinery in order to rid nature and man of nature, and it feels sheltered in a structure of the world which is held together by hysteria and comfort. Progress celebrates Pyrrhic victories over nature. Progress makes purses out of human skin. When people were traveling in mail coaches, the world got ahead better than it does now that salesmen fly through the air. What good is speed if the brain has oozed out on the way? How will the heirs of this age be taught the most basic motions that are necessary to activate the most complicated machines? Nature can rely on progress; it will avenge it for the outrage it has perpetrated on it. But nature does not want to wait, and it shows that it has volcanoes to rid itself of troublesome conquerors. It mates its women with the mortal enemies of civilization, enflames lust through morality and fans it into a world conflagration through racial fear. People console themselves and conquer the North Pole. But nature knocks on the gates of the earth and undermines their usurped overlordship. People console themselves and conquer the air. Against slippery ice there still is no remedy but "sanding," and when it rains the only thing to do for the time being is to open an umbrella. But otherwise people have learned to impress nature in the most ingenious way. Nature does not read editorials and thus still does not know that people are currently engaged in "transforming the world of elemental forces into a realm of reason." If nature knew that the news about the reaching of the North Pole has "heightened a feeling of superiority over nature" in all errand boys, it would split its sides laughing, and cities and states and department stores would then be thrown somewhat out of kilter. As it is, nature twitches a bit more frequently than is good for the superiority of its inhabitants. In a matter of weeks the elemental forces have so clearly evinced their readiness to meld into a realm of reason that even the masses must understand. They did so by destroying hundreds of thousands of lives and untold millions in property in America, Asia, and Australia by means of earthquakes, flash floods, typhoons, and torrential rains, leaving only European newspaper editors with the hope that "the human will" will shortly "move all levers of nature." Every parasite of the age is left with the pride of being a contemporary. They print the newspaper column "Conquest of the Air" and ignore the adjoining heading "Earthquakes"; and in the year of Messina and daily tremors of the earth man proved his superiority over nature and flew to Berlin. In 1909 the idealists sacrificed macaroni to the ungracious elements and created a substitute for their lost ideals on the North Pole. For it is the style of idealism to console itself for the loss of something old with the ability to gape at something new;

and if the world goes to ruin, man's feeling of superiority triumphs in the expectation of a spectacle to which only contemporaries are admitted.

The discovery of the North Pole was inevitable. It is a light seen by all eyes, especially blind ones. It is a sound heard by all ears, especially deaf ones. It is an idea grasped by all brains, especially those no longer capable of grasping anything. The North Pole had to be discovered some day, because for centuries the human mind had penetrated the night and the fog in a hopeless struggle with the murderous elemental forces of stupidity. The road is marked with the blood of those countless people who again and again dared to battle a torpid humanity for the sake of an intellectual deed. How many pioneers of thought have starved to death and been consumed by those real beasts of the polar sea whose very existence signifies the limit of the intellectual zone? Human imagination has not wrested one inch away from the realm of the white death at a place where even the hope of transforming the world of human forces into a realm of reason foundered. Poems were read to walruses until they finally accompanied the discovery of the North Pole with knowing nods. For it was stupidity that reached the North Pole, and its banner waved victoriously as a sign that it owns the world. But the ice fields of the intellect began to grow, and they moved and expanded until they covered the whole earth We who thought, died.

"Die Entdeckung des Nordpols"   (1909)

The
Beaver Coat

My life in Vienna has now been enriched once again. That constant
sneaking along the wall of life to keep from being accosted on the sidewalk
by some idiot is at an end, and every day brings me fresh adventures. In all
those years no party, no theater, no parade of flower-bedecked carriages —
how can anyone stand that? My supply of the most valuable impressions
had been cut off, and who knows how long my inner resources might have
lasted? Even the catastrophes of the season — the comet and the hunting
exhibition — seemed powerless to change this state of affairs. Sure, I can't
conceal the fact that I expected the end of the world to provide me with
some stimulation. But what if that had turned out to be just another dud?
So one goes on following the same path which always leads from the same
desk to the same restaurant where one always eats the same foods and always
avoids the same people. One doesn't get any more cheerful that way. The
world around one is colorful, and one would like to rub up against it to see

58

whether the color will come off. One doesn't like to give up so much without finding out how little one is losing. To sit just once more at a fully occupied table; to hear once more all the belches of *joie de vivre;* to squeeze the sweaty hand of love-thy-neighbor — this is what I used to dream of, and a good fairy (presumably the one who sings songs at the cradles of operetta composers) fulfilled my wish. I'm in the thick of it, the earth has me again[1] — for someone has stolen my fur coat!

Nothing could have brought me closer to my fellow men than the theft of my coat. Now I would have to resort to the methods of a Caracalla if I wanted to resist associating with them. Now there no longer is any way of escaping from life; it is necessary to swallow the bitter pill and be someone who loves people. I have incurred their hatred long enough; but now they forgive me for the sins they have committed against me. They forgive me, they love me, they pity me, they admire me, for there can no longer be any cover-up or denials — someone has stolen my fur coat! And in an unguarded moment, sociability took me by the scruff of the neck. I used to live quietly and innocently; I was a private gentleman, for I had been active in literature for many years. I had no idea that I was above all the owner of a fur coat. I wrote books, but people understood only the coat. I sacrificed myself, and people meant the fur. When I no longer had it, general recognition followed. By losing the fur I justified the attention of the public which I had aroused by owning the coat.

In the café where it happened, the first effect of the discovered theft was a chaotic confusion in which several upset customers forgot to pay their checks. I was thrust into the center of this confusion with such suddenness that I had to take the roundabout route of reflection to be certain that *I* had not stolen the coat. People reacted as though they wanted to tear the clothes I was still wearing off my body, and from all sides I was showered with reproaches on account of my carelessness. In this way they seemed to vent their anger at the thief who had escaped the consequences of his action. For they did have *me*, they could hold on to me; and whenever I leaned back, exhausted from the investigation of the case, in the right frame of mind to read a newspaper at last, the chorus of my fellow men walked past me and cried: "Well, what on earth!"

I felt the sting of reproach. I realized too late that a man who owns a fur coat has certain duties toward the world, and I now had no choice but to fulfill that last duty toward the world which one still has when one no longer has a fur: the duty to answer questions. For even though in such cases it is

1. "Die Träne quillt, die Erde hat mich wieder"—Faust's line from the "Nacht" scene of Goethe's *Faust*, Part 1.

no longer possible to ascertain where the fur has gone, you must at least tell the public and the police where it came from, how much it cost, how much it is worth today, whether the collar had long or short hairs, and whether the loop was of cloth or of leather. The police ask you, in addition, whether you have any suspects. If you have no fur coat, a suspicion warms you, and the suspicion you may have is, in the view of the police, always sufficient compensation for the certainty which you have lost and which it will never retrieve for you.

Why this meddling through an official action? I had always thought that the police concerned themselves with public morality and not with private affairs such as a stolen fur coat. But such curiosity! No sooner had my coat been stolen than three representatives of the police appeared in the café, pushed their way through the usurers standing around my table and expressing their indignation at the theft, and asked me whether I had any suspects. By now the whole neighborhood had been mobilized, for the rumor had spread through the metropolis like wildfire, and numerous passers-by, among them personalities known for their presence at premieres and earthquakes, witnessed the police action. If the theft of the fur had been accomplished with tact and dignity, the sympathy of the public was expressed loudly and ostentatiously. For while fur thieves don't like to make a stir, bank robbers attach the greatest importance to being noticed everywhere and written about in the newspapers. In this case, to be sure, they had miscalculated. For the newspapers would not take cognizance of a comet if its tail had touched my head. For the same reason I had to fear that the chief of the police's Bureau of Public Safety would not pursue my case with the same vigor that he is used to expending when the prospect of journalistic support spurs him on to feverish activity. But of course a genuine expert interest cannot be denied by such considerations. Thus, while the representatives of the authorities asked me about my age, occupation, and criminal record, some customers kept voicing their regret that they had not been watching when the fur coat was stolen, and they expressed the view that the thief must have chosen a moment when he felt himself unobserved. The employees of the café were plied with questions; but the head waiter, the waiter, the apprentice waiter, and the busboy had but one wish: "If I was to get my hands on such a creature, I'd brain 'im!" I asked them not to get carried away and make such dangerous threats in the presence of police detectives. Then I begged the latter to see to it that I was not called in to testify, for all I could possibly say was that I had neither a fur nor a suspect. I escaped the ovations of the crowd by taking my hat, which was still there, and heading for the exit — past the cashier, who was wringing her hands. Outside I was greeted by the fiacre coachmen, who somehow hoped that the events of the day would bring them some special benefit. But one of the policemen caught up with me and suggested that I go with him and look through the rogues' gallery. I declined this suggestion, because I had not seen the thief of my fur coat and thus had no basis for comparison. But if the police produced him, I would be prepared to identify him on the basis of his photograph. Then one of the waiters suddenly claimed to have a suspect, and he seemed determined to accompany the policeman. As I learned later, this investigation did not materially aid my case, though it did have gratifying results in another direction. The waiter is said to have recognized several former habitués of the café, and never before had such a joyous mood of reunion prevailed at a police station. Since cries of "Jeepers, it's Herr von Kohn!" and "Oh, no — Herr von Meier!" wouldn't cease, they finally had to tear the picture album out of the good man's hands. On the next day I received a summons, but I ignored it. I had always managed to avoid having anything stolen, for there is nothing I fear more than trouble with the police, and they have really never been able to prove the least thing against me. Should I now have saddled myself with such an embarrassing investigation because of this one *faux pas?* Never! So I did not present myself to the police. At least I was determined not to do so until they had retrieved my fur coat. For the rest, I hoped they would hush up the case and let me quietly pursue my accustomed occupation.

Consequently, when I went to the café again and was about to go to my reading corner, I faced some gentlemen who normally were interested only in trotting races but this time had bet on whether or not I would get my fur coat back. Those who were of the opinion that I would get it said, "He won't get it nohow!" while those who were of the opinion that I would not get it kept crying, "He will *so* get it!" In this way I was able to distinguish the two groups without, however, being able to decide on the merits of the opposing views. I sat down, and from the billiard room I heard shouts like "A genuine beaver, I tell you!" and "I'm telling you, mink!" — whereupon a third person plunged into the debate with a crude "Astrakhan, you should be so lucky!" I sent someone to ask the gentlemen if my reading a newspaper disturbed them. They said it didn't and changed to an entirely different subject — that is, one of them claimed he could still remember how old Loew's fur ("worth a thousand guilders, one thousand") was stolen. When someone interjected "What Loew?" he was reprimanded: "The one who later went bankrupt, of course." At that point I felt that attention had been diverted from me, and I was pleased. I picked up the newspaper which for years had managed to sustain the interest of its readers by never printing my name, and looked for a notice saying that a fur coat was stolen from a gentleman and that "one of our reporters had occasion to speak with the thief, a widely known personage." Thereupon an unknown lady came up to me, rebuked me for my carelessness, and asked me whether I still associated with the T. family. I replied that I did not associate with *anyone*, and asked for my check. Outside I was greeted by the coachmen, who invitingly pointed to their fiacres and yelled something like "Take care you don't catch cold!" after me.

But I still haven't related what happened when I saw my cleaning woman on the day after the theft. It was really her fault, for after a snowfall in a very severe May she had talked me into wearing the fur coat which had been in storage at a furrier's all winter. I had resisted the idea, for I had had a vague premonition that new snow makes fur thieves sprout, whereas the snow shovellers don't get any work because the municipality favors their competition, the spring thaw. But although the thaw had already set in, the cleaning woman prevailed. and sure enough — half an hour later the fur coat was gone. Now, nothing is more embarrassing to me than arguments about household matters, and so, after the misfortune, I had only one worry: How am I going to break it to my cleaning woman? There was a stormy scene, and I got a good talking-to. A woman's heart is attached to earthly frippery, and women find it hard to part even with someone else's belongings, whereas *I* felt relieved to be able to leave the café during the thaw without my fur coat. In general, the loss of my fur had left me cold, and the only thing that bothered me was the loss of my peace and quiet. That I was the center of attention, that I had become a celebrity in Vienna overnight, and that people pointed me out to one another ("There he goes" — "Do you know him?" — "Sure, beaver" — "He really didn't get it back") — *that* is what grieved me and gnawed away at me the way moths chew a fur that has not been stolen. I decided to avoid going out in the street until I could hear grass grow over the matter. But a week later, when I ventured to sneak into my customary café through the back door, the toilet attendant came up to me and said, "I'm terribly sorry it happened!" When I entered, all eyes were on me and my overcoat, and when I hung the latter on the clothes stand someone in a corner called out, "But now you've got to be doubly careful!" And from another corner: "An ounce of wit that is bought is worth a pound that is taught." When a waiter appeared and said, "Never mind, the gentleman is careful anyway," a voice rang out from the game room: "Once bitten, twice shy!" The waiter said: "If I was to get my hands on such a creature, I'd . . ." I immediately asked for my check and resolved to frequent the café only at night, when different people would be there. No sooner had I taken my seat under altered circumstances than an English trainer turned around to face me, pushed his chair forward, and propping his arms up on the arm rest, said: "One time, old chap, someone stole my horse blanket . . ." I could see that my experience had transcended the communicative needs of the Viennese population and had aroused international interest. Fearing that the promotion of tourism might begin right then and there, I locked myself in and did not emerge until it seemed to me that the hot season had burned out any thought of a fur coat. But at that point I had a novel experience: A black man came up to me and asked in perfect German whether I had ever got my fur coat back. I went to a different café, but its owner not only annoyed me by greeting me but also told me: "This will not happen to you in *my* café."

I realized that there was no road back. For a Viennese problem had been born. This was an event of such a plausible appeal and such an immediate popularity that no consideration for the person affected could keep people away. A solidarity had been created here by the realization, astonishing in its simplicity, that this sort of thing could happen to anyone. I had been drawn into the circle of a community that guarded the fur coat which had been stolen from me, a community whose eyes seemed to be taking my measurements for a new coat without donating one to me. Now the only people who had yet to take an interest in my case were the income-tax collectors, and they might soon enough determine that I was sufficiently affluent to have owned a fur coat. I began to envy the thief — not because he had the fur, but because he had not been caught, because he was a free man, while people behind me kept yelling "Stop thief!" and I, like a man robbed and then caught, had stupidity as an escort. . . . I decided to withdraw from private life. But I still had one hope left: By publishing a new book I might manage to make the Viennese forget me.

"Der Biberpelz"   (1910)

I have never denied the fact

that contraceptive ads are the only decent, sensible, and tasteful contribution which the daily press makes year in and year out. But since the press does not share this view and disavows gratis on the front pages what it presents for money on the back pages, that "certain" ad, as moralists put it, is a repulsive sight — particularly when it has as a trademark an officer who, in order to make things more palatable, strokes his moustache. This product is called Olla. A problem of social usefulness is magnified into the exceedingly ugly vision that the subscribers to the *Neue Freie Presse* will make use of the recommendation. And indeed, it says in bold type:

> **10,000 samples of Olla free! To make Olla available to all
> intelligent strata of the population and convince the
> users . . . that no other brand even comes close to it . . .
> we have decided to send one sample, free and postpaid, to
> everyone who sends us his name, address, and occupation . . .**

This is a breathtakingly graphic vision. Now everybody looks as though he has taken advantage of that offer — the gentlemen who ride in carriages, occupy orchestra seats at the theater, and who may be found wherever *joie de vivre* reigns. Added to this is the certainty that if the firm invests a little more money it will be permitted to print the name of each of the ten thousand delighted recipients in the columns where they used to be able to print their expressions of sympathy. For the only reason morality holds forth on the front pages is that hiring these columns would be too expensive for the rubber firms. But it may suffice them to get their message across to the intelligent classes of the population and to compensate them for the loss of the Mona Lisa[1] in the most appropriate manner. . . . When they perform their devotions like that, the only kind they are still capable of, at that one moment when their intelligence is off duty, in the incestuous pleasure of their bed, where the Rubber King kneels to pray   I would be the Hamlet to make short work of them!

"Ich habe nie ein Hehl daraus gemacht"   (1911)

1. In August 1911 Leonardo da Vinci's famous painting was stolen from the Louvre. Kraus commented on this occurrence in "Mona Lisa und der Sieger," *Die Fackel*, September 1911.

Interview with a Dying Child

I happened to see the following news item:

THE TRAGEDY OF A SICK MOTHER

Jumps from Fourth-Floor Window with Two Children; Mother and Children Dead

The terrible family drama that took place yesterday morning at 2 Stefaniestrasse in Vienna's second district aroused universal sympathy. While her husband, a traveling salesman, was on the road, thirty-year-old Paula Deixner jumped out of a window of her fourth-floor apartment together with her three-year-old son Egon. Her older son, nine-year-old Paul, followed his mother immediately thereafter. The mother and children are dead.

The only account of what happened in the apartment of the family was given by poor Paul, who survived his mother and his brother by only a few hours. At a little after half-past six in the morning, police officer Karl Aiginger found Frau Deixner and her children lying in the street in a pool of blood. Frau Deixner and little Egon were unconscious, but Paul, the older boy, was fully conscious despite his multiple wounds and gave the following account of the horrible deed.

LITTLE PAUL'S STORY

Mother had been sick for some time and under the care of a nurse since last night. This morning she woke up earlier than usual. She complained of pains and asked the nurse to make her some tea. While the nurse was busy in the kitchen, Mother said: "Paulie, I'm going to jump out of the window with Egon. Come jump with us!"

I asked: "Why should I, Mother?"

She said: "We don't want to live anymore!"

Interrupted by constant sobbing, the boy then told how he had planned to call for help. But his mother threatened that she would jump out of the window with Egon immediately. Then she tried to persuade him again, saying, among other things: "Paulie, what are you going to do all alone with Dad when Egon and I aren't here anymore?"

Before the boy could give her an answer, the mother opened the window, pushed little Egon from the windowsill, and at the same time hurled herself down. Without knowing what he was doing, Paul also climbed up on the windowsill and with the cry "Mother!" jumped out of the window.

The mother and the two children plunged to the ground almost simultaneously, and when a moment later passersby and neighbors tried to attend to them, Frau Deixner and the younger child no longer showed signs of life.

NOTHING NOTICED IN THE APARTMENT

A minute later, when Officer Aiginger rang the bell of the Deixner family's apartment and the servant girl answered, neither she nor the nurse had any idea of what had just happened. Soon thereafter an ambulance arrived with Dr. Silber, and the injured were taken to First Aid Station Number Two. A short time after they were admitted, Frau Deixner died; a half-hour later little Egon expired, and at noon Paul followed them into death. . . .

Like the telegraph operator on the *Titanic*, Paul remained on duty until the last moment. But his case is more horrible. He was already drowning, but he still had to answer the questions of the human sharks that had an opportunity to ask them. He was lying in a pool of blood and had to give information to the police reporters and the representative of an illustrated Viennese newspaper about the sequence of events and about his impressions. The account is authentic; it is first-hand and they boast about it. It is beyond comprehension. A child tells an interviewer how he jumped out of the window. A stenographic report of Hannele's feverish visions.[1] "She said: 'Come jump with us!' I asked: 'Why should I, Mother?' . . . With the cry 'Mother' I jumped out of the window, too." The press struggles with Death in order to beat it to the deathbed of a bleeding child for

---

1. The chief character in Gerhart Hauptmann's early play *Hanneles Himmelfahrt* (The Assumption of Hannele, 1893) which Kraus frequently performed in his one-man "Theater of Poetry."

the sake of getting information. Before this spectacle all hatred and contempt for the press fall silent. Nothing is left but sadness. I miss these people on the casualty list of the *Titanic*.

"Interview mit einem sterbenden Kind" (1912)

I Believe in the Printer's Gremlin

"A hitherto unknown tragedy by Shakespeare was recently announced in the advertising columns of a St. Gallen newspaper. It said that the municipal theatre of St. Gallen was going to perform 'King Lehar,[1] a tragedy in five acts by W. Shakespeare.' "

This is no laughing matter. It's horrible. The printer was not trying to make a joke. The word that he was not supposed to set, the association that got into his work, is the measure of our time. By their misprints shall ye know them. What may be read here *is* a Shakespearean tragedy.

"Ich glaube an den Druckfehlerteufel"   (1912)

1. The Hungarian-born operetta composer Franz Lehár (1870–1948) was a frequent target of Kraus's satire as a foremost practitioner of the Viennese operetta in its "silver age" which Kraus, in programmatic contrast to his appreciation of Jacques Offenbach's works, regarded as false, inane, and harmful.

In these great times

which I knew when they were this small; which will become small again, provided they have time left for it; and which, because in the realm of organic growth no such transformation is possible, we had better call fat times and, truly, hard times as well; in these times in which things are happening that could not be imagined and in which what can no longer be *imagined* must *happen*, for if one could imagine it, it would not happen; in these serious times which have died laughing at the thought that they might become serious; which, surprised by their own tragedy, are reaching for diversion and, catching themselves redhanded, are groping for words; in these loud times which boom with the horrible symphony of actions which produce reports and of reports which cause actions: in these times you should not expect any words of my own from me — none but these words which barely manage to prevent silence from being misinterpreted. Respect for the immutability, the subordination of language before this misfortune is too deeply rooted in me. In the realm of poverty of imagination where people die of spiritual famine without feeling spiritual hunger, where pens are dipped in blood and swords in ink, that which is not thought must be done, but that which is only thought is unutterable. Expect no words of my own from me. Nor would I be able to say anything new, for in the room in which one writes there is such noise, and at this time one should not determine whether it comes from animals, from children, or merely from mortars. He who encourages deeds with words desecrates words and deeds and is doubly despicable. This occupation is not extinct. Those who now have nothing to say because actions are speaking continue to talk. Let him who has something to say come forward and be silent! Nor may I bring out old words as long as deeds are committed that are new to us and spectators say that they were not to be expected of them. My words were able to drown out rotary presses, and if these were not brought to a standstill, this is no reflection on my words. Even the greater machine has not managed to do it, and an ear that hears the trumpets of the Last Judgment is by no means closed to the trumpets of the day. All that blood has not made the muck of life congeal in flight, nor has it made printer's ink blanch. The maw, rather, swallowed up the many swords, and we looked only at the maw and measured greatness only by the maw. And "gold for iron" fell from the altar into the operetta,[1] bombing was a music-hall song, and fifteen thousand prisoners were put in a special edition of the newspaper which a soubrette read from the stage so that a librettist might take a curtain call. For me (the insatiable one who does not have sacrifices enough), the line commanded by fate has not been reached. For me it is war only if only those who are unfit are sent off to it. Otherwise my peace has no peace; I secretly prepare for the great times and think thoughts that I can tell only to the Good Lord and not to the good state which now does not permit me to tell it that it is too tolerant. For if the state does not now have the idea of choking off the so-called freedom of the press, which does not notice a few white spots, then it never will; and if I were to put this into its head, the state would do violence to the idea, and my text would be the only victim. So I shall have to wait, though I am the only Austrian who cannot wait but would like to see the end of the world replaced by a simple auto-da-fé. The idea which I should like to put into the heads of the actual holders of nominal power is only an *idée fixe* of mine. But an unstable state of ownership, that of a state and of a civilized world, is saved by such fixed ideas. A

---

1. People were urged to aid the war effort by surrendering objects made of gold, jewelry, and other valuables in return for rings and other items made of various lesser metals, including iron.

general is not believed when he talks about the importance of swamps — until one day Europe is viewed only as the surroundings of swamps.[2] Of a terrain I see only the swamps, of their depth I see only the surface, of a situation I see only its manifestations, of these I see only a reflection, and even of that I see only the outlines. And sometimes an intonation or even a hallucination suffices me. Do me the favor, just for fun, of following me to the surface of this problem-deep world which was not created until it became cultured, which revolves around its own axis and wishes the sun revolved around it.

Above that exalted manifesto,[3] that prose poem which initiated a time full of action, the only poem this time has produced till now, above the most humane poster which the street was able to offer our eyes there hangs the head of a vaudeville comedian, larger than life. Next to it a manufacturer of rubber heels desecrates the mystery of creation by saying of a kicking infant that this is the only way a human being ought to come into the world, using this particular brand. If I am of the opinion that, things being the way they are, it would be better if people did not come into the world at all, I am an eccentric. But if I maintain that under such circumstances no one will come into the world in the future and that at a later date boot-heels may come into the world but without the persons to go with them, because they were not able to keep pace with their own development and stayed behind as the last obstacle to their progress — if I maintain this sort of thing, I am a fool who deduces the whole condition from a symptom, the plague from a bubo. If I were not a fool but an educated man, I would draw such bold conclusions from a bacillus and not from a bubo, and people would believe me. How foolish to say that one should confiscate the bubo to rid oneself of the plague! But I am truly of the opinion that in this time, however we may call it or evaluate it, whether it is out of joint or already set right, whether it is accumulating murder and rottenness before the eyes of a Hamlet or is already becoming ripe for the arm of a Fortinbras—that in its condition the root lies at the surface. This sort of thing can be made clear by a great confusion, and what was once paradoxical is now confirmed by the great times. Since I am neither a politician nor his half-brother, an esthete, I would not dream of denying the necessity of anything that is happening or of complaining that mankind does not know how to die in beauty. I know

2. A reference to Paul von Hindenburg, whose *idée fixe*, the strategic importance of the Masurian swamps in East Prussia, was derided. Important battles were subsequently fought at the Masurian Lakes.

3. *An meine Völker* (To My Peoples), Franz Josef's proclamation of August 1914. This was the solitary apex of Kraus's appreciation of the Austrian emperor whom he henceforth lampooned as "the Hapsburg demon incarnate."

full well that cathedrals are rightfully bombarded by people if they are rightfully used by people as military posts. "No offence i' the world," says Hamlet.[4] But the jaws of hell gape at this question: When will the greater period of the war begin, the war of cathedrals against people ? I know very well that at times it is necessary to transform markets into battlefields so that these might turn into markets again. But one cloudy day people will see things more clearly and ask whether it is right to miss not a single step on the direct road away from God, and whether the eternal mystery from which man originates and the mystery into which he enters really encompass only a business secret that gives man superiority over man and even over man's maker. Someone who wants to expand ownership and someone who merely defends it — both live in a state of ownership, always below and never above ownership. One declares it, the other one explains it.[5] Are we not afraid of something superior to ownership when unparalleled human victims have been seen and suffered, and when behind the language of spiritual uplift, after the intoxicating music has died away, this confession breaks through between earthly and heavenly hosts one grey morning: "What the traveling salesmen must do now is keep putting out their feelers and feeling out their customers!"[6] Mankind consists of customers. Behind flags and flames, heroes and helpers, behind all fatherlands an altar has been erected at which pious science wrings its hands: God created the consumer! Yet God did not create the consumer that he might prosper on earth but for something higher: that the dealer might prosper on earth, for the consumer was created naked and becomes a dealer only when he sells clothes. The necessity to eat in order to live cannot be disputed philosophically, though the public nature of this function evidences an ineradicable lack of modesty. Culture is the tacit agreement to let the means of subsistence disappear behind the purpose of existence.[7] Civilization is the subordination of the latter to the former. This is the ideal that progress serves, and to this ideal it supplies its armaments. Progress lives to eat, and at times supplies proof that it can even die to eat. It endures hardship so that it may prosper.

4. Shakespeare, *Hamlet*, act 3, sc. 2.

5. Kraus's terms are *fatieren*, which means to declare something for purposes of taxation, and *erklären*, which means both "declare" in the above sense and "explain." The two words can be used synonymously, and Kraus probably used them to indicate — from within and from without, as it were — the essential sameness of the political idea of imperialism (for which Kraus employs the metaphor *Besitzstand*, or ownership).

6. The term *Reisende* — "traveler" or "traveling salesman" — here seems to be equated with war correspondents, and the unidentified quotation may be an editor's instruction to reporters to turn themselves into commercial travelers and examine battlefields for their suitability as markets.

7. Kraus's pun involves *Lebensmittel* (foodstuffs) and *Lebenszweck*.

It applies pathos to the premises. The utmost affirmation of progress has long since decreed that demand be governed by supply, that we eat so that another person might get his fill, and that a peddler interrupt even our thinking when he offers us what we do not happen to need. Progress, under whose feet the grass mourns and the forest turns into paper from which newspaper plants grow,[8] has subordinated the purpose of life to the means of subsistence and turned us into the nuts and bolts for our tools. The tooth of time is hollow; for when it was sound, there came the hand that lives on fillings. Where all energy has been expended to make life frictionless, nothing remains that still needs such care. In such a region individuality can live, but can no longer be born. With its emotional desires it may be a guest where it will be surrounded by automata pushing past and forward in comfort and prosperity without face and greeting. As a referee between natural values it will make a different decision. It will certainly not opt for this country's supineness, which has saved its intellectual life for the promotion of its merchandise, has surrendered to a romanticization of foodstuffs, and has placed "art in the service of the businessman." The decision is between spiritual power and horsepower. After the hustle and bustle of business no breed will realize its full potential; at best it will be fit for pleasure. The tyranny of necessity grants its slaves three kinds of freedom; opinion free from intellect, entertainment free from art, and orgies free from love. Thank God there are still goods that get stuck when freight is supposed to be constantly rolling. For in the final analysis, civilization does live on culture. If the horrible voice[9] which these days is allowed to outshout the commands urges traveling salesmen in the language of its obtrusive phantasm to put out their feelers and feel out their customers through the gunsmoke; if in the face of unheard-of things it brings itself to make the heroic decision to claim the battlefields for the hyenas, then it possesses some of that dreary sincerity with which the *Zeitgeist* grins at its martyrs. All right, we are sacrificing ourselves for ready-made goods; we are consumers and live in such a way that the means may consume the end. All right, if a torpedo is useful to us, let it be more permissible to curse God than to curse a torpedo! And necessities which a world gone astray in the labyrinth of economics has set for itself demand their martyrs; and the ghastly editorial writer of

8. ". . . der Wald zu Papier wird, aus dem die Blätter wachsen" — Kraus plays on the dual meaning of *Blätter*: "leaves" and "newspapers" (or "sheets" in both English senses). In his prose and poetry he repeatedly deplored the defilement of nature by the transformation of trees into newsprint.

9. Presumably the voice of commerce, here equated with the voice of a press in league with it, which in the midst of the carnage urges its salesmen (or correspondents) to go out in search of new markets.

passions, the registering Jewish plutocrat, the man who sits at the cash register of world history collects victories and daily records the turnover in blood.[10] The tenor of his couplings and headlines which shriek with greed for profit is such that he claims the number of dead and wounded and prisoners as assets; sometimes he confuses mine and thine with mines and tines;[11] but gently underlining his modesty and perhaps in keeping with impressions gleaned from circles in the know, and without abandoning his power of imagination, he permits himself to make a strategic distinction between "laymen's questions and laymen's answers." And if he then ventures to pronounce a blessing on the so very gratifying upsurge of heroic feelings, to send his greetings and best wishes to the army and to cheer up his "good soldiers" in the jargon of efficiency as though it were the end of a satisfying day at the stock exchange, there is allegedly "only one voice" which takes umbrage at it, truly only one that is uttering it today — but what good is it when there is just this one voice whose echo ought to be nothing less than a storm of the elements rebelling at the spectacle of a time which has the courage to call itself great and does not issue an ultimatum to such a champion!

The surface is at the root and sticks to it. The subjugation of mankind to the economy has left it only the freedom of hostility; and if progress sharpened its weapons, it created for mankind the most murderous weapon of all, one that relieved it, beyond its sacred necessity, of its last concern about its spiritual salvation: the press. Progress, which also has logic at its disposal, replies that the press is nothing but one of the professional associations that subsist on an existing need. But if this is as true as it is correct, and if the press is nothing other than an imprint of life, then I know what the score is, for I know what this life is like. And then it happens to occur to me, it becomes clear to me on a cloudy day, that life is only an imprint of the press. If I learned to underestimate life in the days of progress, I was bound to overestimate the press. What is it? Just a messenger? One who also bothers us with his opinion? Who torments us with his impressions? Who brings the mental image along with the fact? Who tortures us almost to death with his detailed reports about the atmosphere or with his perceptions of observations of minute details, and with his constant repetition of the whole? Who drags behind himself a train of informed, knowledgeable, sophisticated, outstanding personalities who are supposed to accredit him and agree with him — important parasites on the superfluous? Is the

10. Probably a reference to Moriz Benedikt, the editor of the *Neue Freie Presse*, whom Kraus excoriated as the "Lord of the Hyenas."
11. The pun in the original is "mein und dein und Stein und Bein."

press a messenger? No, it is the event itself. A speech? No, life itself. It not only lays claim to the real events being its news *about* the events; it also creates this uncanny identity which always makes it seem that actions are reported before they are performed, often the mere possibility of an action, and in any case it produces a situation in which war correspondents are not permitted to observe, but warriors are turned into reporters. In this sense I do not mind if people say that all my life I have overestimated the press. It is not a messenger (how could a messenger demand and receive so much?); it is the event itself. Once again the instrument has got the better of us. We have raised the person whose job it is to announce a conflagration — and who probably ought to play the most subordinate role in the state — above the world, above the fire and above the house, above reality and above our imagination. But we, like Cleopatra, curious and disappointed, ought to beat the messenger for his message. The man who informs her of a hated marriage and who embellishes his report she holds responsible for the marriage. "Ram through thy fruitful tidings in mine ears that long time have been barren. . . . The most infectious pestilence upon thee! . . . What say you? Hence, horrible villain! or I'll spurn thine eyes like balls before me; I'll unhair thy head. Thou shalt be whipt with wire, and stew'd in brine, smarting in lingering pickle."—"Gracious madam, I that do bring the news made not the match."[12] But the reporter does make the match, sets the house on fire, and turns the horrors that he fabricates into truth. Through decades of practice he has produced in mankind that degree of unimaginativeness which enables it to wage a war of extermination against itself. Since the unlimited promptness of his machinery has made it unnecessary for mankind to have any ability to experience and to extend experience intellectually, the reporter can only just manage to instil into it that death-defying courage with which mankind is rushing into this war. He has the reflected glory of heroic qualities at his disposal, and his misused language beautifies a misused life—as though eternity had saved its apex for the age in which the reporter lives. But do people have any idea what life the newspaper expresses? A life that has long been an expression of *it!* Do people realize just what half a century owes to this loosed intelligence in the way of murdered intellect, plundered nobility, and desecrated holiness? Does anyone know what vital resources the Sunday belly of such a rotary beast has swallowed up before it can appear 250 pages thick? Do people stop to think how much had to be systematically spent on telegrams, telephones, and photographs to teach a society which was still open to inner possibilities that broad astonishment at the tiniest fact which finds its clichés in the

12. Shakespeare, *Antony and Cleopatra*, act 2, sc. 5.

76

horrid language of these messengers when "groups formed" somewhere or the public began to "mass"? Since all of modern life has been subsumed under a quantity which is no longer measured but has always been attained — a quantity that finally will have no other recourse but to swallow itself — since the self-evident record leaves no more room for doubt and the painful completeness makes any further calculation unnecessary, the consequence is that, exhausted by this multiplicity, we no longer have any use for the result. Accordingly, at a time when twice a day and in twenty repetitions we are served up impressions of the impressions of all externals, the great quantity breaks down into individual fates which only the individuals perceive, so that suddenly the unbegrudged hero's death, even in the vanguard, is declared a cruel fate. But some day people might find out what a trifling matter such a world war was as compared to the intellectual self-mutilation of mankind by means of its press and how at bottom it constituted only one of the press's emanations. A few decades ago, Bismarck, who also overestimated the press, was still able to recognize that "what the sword has gained for us Germans is spoiled by the press" and impute to the press the blame for three wars. Today the connections between catastrophes and editorial offices are far more profound and hence less clear. For in the age of those who live through it, deeds are stronger than words, but the echo is stronger than the deed. We live on the echo, and in this topsy-turvy world the echo arouses the call. In the organization of the echo, weakness is capable of a wondrous transformation. The state can use it, but the world derives no benefit from it. At a time when progress was still in its infancy and did not as yet crawl through culture on rubber heels, Bismarck sensed it. "In the long run and at some time," he said, "every country is responsible for the windows broken by its press." Further: "The press in Vienna is worse than I had imagined; in fact, it is worse and has a more deleterious effect than the Prussian press." He came right out and said that in order to avoid the reproach of not having good connections, a correspondent printed either his own fabrications or those of his embassy. Certainly, all of us are primarily dependent on the interests of this one business. If one reads a newspaper only for information, one does not learn the truth, not even the truth about the paper. The truth is that the newspaper is not a statement of contents but the contents themselves; and more than that, it is an instigator. If it prints lies about horrors, these turn into horrors. There is more injustice in the world because there is a press which fabricated it and deplores it! It is not nations that strike one another; rather, it is the international disgrace, the profession which rules the world not despite its irresponsibility but by virtue of it, that deals wounds, tortures prisoners, baits foreigners, and turns gentlemen into rowdies. Its only authority is its unprincipledness, which, in association with a rascally will, can change printer's ink directly into blood. O last, unholy wonder of the times! At first everything was a lie, and they always lied so that lies might be told only elsewhere; but now, thrown into the neurasthenia of hatred, everything is true. There are various nations, but there is only one press. The newspaper dispatch is an instrument of war like a grenade, which has no consideration for circumstances either. You believe, but they know better, and you have to pay dearly for your belief. The heroes of obtrusiveness, people with whom no soldier would lie down in the trenches, though he has to submit to being interviewed by them, break into recently abandoned royal castles so that they can report, "We got there first!" It would be far less shameful to be paid for committing atrocities than for fabricating them. The bravoes of this sphere of activity sit at home, unless they have the good fortune to tell anecdotes in the correspondents' quarters or be pushy right up to the front, and they teach fear to the nations day after day until these have some justification really to feel fear. Of the quantity which is the substance of this time each of us gets a share that he processes emotionally, and the telegraph wires and the cinema screen make what we have in common so graphic to us that we go home contented.

But if the reporter has killed our imagination with his truth, he threatens our life with his lies. His imagination is the cruelest substitute for the imagination we once had. For if one side claims that the other side kills women and children, both sides believe it and do it. Don't people yet feel that the word of an undisciplined creature, usable in the days of military discipline, carries farther than a mortar and that the spiritual fortresses of these times are structures that will collapse in an emergency? If the states had the discernment to settle for universal conscription and do without wire dispatches, a world war, truly, would be milder. And if before the outbreak of such a war they had the courage to drive the representatives of the other trade together at an internationally agreed upon carrion-pit, who knows — the nations might be spared it. But before journalists and the diplomats they use disarm, human beings have to pay the price. "Some of the things printed in newspapers are true after all," said Bismarck. There is, after all, something in the cultural section, and that is where our fine feuilletonists work. They say prayers in battles for a fee, kiss confederates on the mouth, praise the wonderful "tumult" of our days, admire order as they once adored *Gemütlichkeit*, compare a fortress with a beautiful woman or vice versa (it depends), and in general behave in a manner worthy of the great times. Under the heading "Days of Terror" an alien serially described his experiences in a capital city which he had been obliged to leave.[13] The greatest terror was that he was urged to leave town, offered only 1200 francs for 1000 marks, and especially that no taxicab was to be had — something that is said to happen in other traffic centers even *before* a general mobilization. For the rest — one can hardly believe one's eyes — he cannot heap sufficient praise on the calm, considerateness, and even compassion of the local population. And yet dispatches led us to believe that these people had behaved like freed panthers and wolves from a menagerie damaged in a railway accident. In short, the situation there before the war was something like the situation elsewhere after a concert. Wire dispatches are instruments of war. Feuilletons are not monitored that closely; the truth may slip through there. But by the time a feuilleton appears, it may be untrue again, because in the meantime wire reports have appeared and done their share to confirm other wire reports and to correct reality. Or does anyone think that this Nordau glossed over things because he was already trying to assure himself of being able to return to that place in peacetime? In that case journalism manipulates life, depending on whether it seeks only its advantage or also the disadvantage of others. In general it can be said that in wartime there are, in addition to the work done by solid weapons, the accomplishments of words and opportunities. Atrocities perpetrated by the population of enemy countries are of low or very base — that is, cultured— provenance. The mob and the press are above national interests; the former pillages and the latter wires. When the latter wires, the former feels encouraged, and nations repay and atone for what editorial offices have decided. "Reprisals" is what the press is answered with.[14] It exaggerates the condition of the world after it has created it. It would be terrible enough if it were only the expression of this condition; but it is its creator. In Austria it invented and preserved the sterile pastime of "strife among the nationalities" in order to promote the business activities of its shameful intellect unobserved. Once it has reached the desired goal, it puts its patriotism out to board for future profit. It buys up securities that are collapsing — a Phoenix colorfully rising from someone else's ashes. Let me overestimate

13. The reference is to Max Nordau (1849–1923), a physician, writer, and longtime associate of Theodor Herzl in the leadership of the Zionist movement, and his writings in the *Neue Freie Presse* ("Through the *Neue Freie Presse* he had the ear of Europe. . . . His annual summary of events was eagerly awaited" — Anna and Maxa Nordau, *Max Nordau: A Biography*, New York, 1943, p. 209). In September of 1914, Nordau, an Austrian national, had to leave France and took refuge in Spain. He did not return to Paris, where he had settled in 1880, until 1920. Kraus repeatedly commented on Nordau — "Die Feinde Goethe und Heine" (*Die Fackel* no. 406, 5 October 1915), for example, about Nordau's defense of Heinrich Heine when Goethe and Heine were maligned in wartime France.

14. Kraus plays with the words *Repressalien* and *Presse*.

the press! But if I wrongly maintain, if it is not true that in an epoch which is so prone to regard the special edition as the event and which with inflamed nerves lets itself be misled from fabrications to facts, more blood has flown from wire dispatches than they claimed to contain, then let this blood be on my hands!

"May it be the last time," cried Bismarck, "that the achievements of Prussian arms are given away with an open hand to satisfy the insatiable demands of a phantom which under the phony name of *Zeitgeist* or public opinion stuns the good sense of princes and peoples with its screaming until everyone is afraid of everyone else's shadow and all forget that under the lion's skin of the specter there is an entity that may be noisy but is not very terrifying." He said this in 1849. What terrifying dimensions this harmless entity has assumed in sixty-five years! The fact that it does not grow silent in the face of deeds it has instigated shows for whom it hopes these have been done. The machines have declared war on God, and between the performances that *I* have always believed them capable of they still are at no loss for words, while the times measure themselves and are astonished at how great they have become overnight. But they have probably always been great, and I simply did not notice it. Thus it was an optical fault of mine to perceive them as small. However, to clean up "evils" that are rampant on the surface behind which there is something great would be too small a task for me, and I would not be up to it. The other day someone asked me where I was and begged me, with a view to the new times, to rid us of the old filth. I can't. Great and elemental forces must have the strength to cope with evils by themselves and do not need the stimulation and help of a writer. But though the gleam of these great and elemental forces was already dazzling everyone's eyes, they still have not managed it. What do we see? The greatness has concomitants. If the future is on their level, then heaven help us! The great forces have not destroyed the concomitants overnight. That bombs are dropped with jokes and dives announce a 42-Mortar Program shows us how conservative and up-to-date we are. The revealing thing is not the occurrence as such but the anesthesia that makes it possible and tolerates it. We know how the humor ingrained in us accommodates itself to the excess of blood. But what about the intellect? How do our poets and thinkers feel about it? And even if the world stands on its head, it won't be able to think of anything better! Even if the world tears itself to pieces, no intellect will emerge. Nor will it appear later, for it should now have gone into hiding and expressed itself through discreet dignity. But all around us in the cultural sphere we see only the spectacle of the intellect latching onto a catchword when a personality does not have the strength to keep silent and draw on its own resources. The volunteering of the poets for military service is their entry into journalism. We find Hauptmann and Messrs. Dehmel and Hofmannsthal[15] in the front lines with a claim to a decoration, and behind them fights rampant dilettantism. Never before has there been such a rush to join up with banality, and the sacrifice of the leading intellects is so rapid as to give rise to the suspicion that they had no self to sacrifice but acted on the heroic desire to save themselves where it is now safest: in clichéland. But the really sad thing is that literature does not feel its obtrusiveness nor the superiority of the common man who finds in clichés the experience that is his due. To seek rhymes, and bad ones, to express the enthusiasm of others, to welcome troops with whoops, confirm that a mob will rob, and condemn those who pillage a village is surely the paltriest achievement that society can expect of its intellects in hard times. The unarticulated sounds that have reached us from enemy poets at least evidence individual feelings of excitement which reduce an artist to a private person with national limitations. At least they were the poem that the uproar of actualities made of the poets. The reproach of barbarism in wartime was false information. But the barbarism in peacetime which is ready to rhyme when things get serious and which turns some one else's experience into an editorial is an inexpungible disgrace. And after all, a Hodler who is wrong can still pass muster next to a dozen Haeckels who are right.[16] And in the final analysis, an outburst of rage is more cultural than an inquiry which is kind enough to decide the question whether it is all right to perform Shakespeare in his favor. Modern Germany's greatest poet, Detlev von Liliencron,[17] a war poet, a victim of that cultural development that came from victory, probably would not have had the heart to attach himself to the still-smoking actualities with an opinion, and it remains to be seen whether among those who have experienced this war and those who as poets can experience, there will be someone who can fashion an artistic unity out of the substance and the word. What will be shown is whether something organic can grow from the quantity, to which there no longer is a bridge from the spiritual life because this bridge has been blown up. Intellects that nimbly and comfortably bed down

15. Like most German and Austrian men of letters, Gerhart Hauptmann, Richard Dehmel, and Hugo von Hofmannsthal actively and avidly supported the war effort.

16. The reference is to the Swiss painter Ferdinand Hodler (1853–1918), on whom Kraus commented favorably elsewhere, and to the German biologist and philosopher Ernst Haeckel (1834–1919), an agnostic and rightist with a strong pan-German orientation. Hodler condemned the shelling of the cathedral of Rheims by German artillery, and Kraus disagrees with him in the early part of this address. Haeckel advocated the continued performance of Shakespeare in wartime Germany.

17. Kraus liked (and overrated) Liliencron, whose poetry he read on the same evening on which he delivered this address.

in the split in their personalities when danger threatens will be a dime a dozen.

Perhaps even the smallest war has always been an action that cleansed the surface and had an effect on the inside. What effect does this great war have which is great by virtue of the forces against which the greatest war ought to be waged? Is it a redemption or only the end? Or is it only a continuation? May the consequences of this extensive affair be no worse than its concomitants which it did not have the strength to kick away! May it never happen that emptiness throws its weight around even more than before as it refers to the hardships it has endured; that idleness gains glory; that pettiness appeals to the world-historical background; and that the hand that reaches into our pocket first shows us its scars! How was it possible that in the world war a world newspaper could celebrate its anniversary? That a stock-exchange burglar could place himself before a battle of millions and in thunderous headlines demand (and receive) attention for the fiftieth anniversary of his infamous trade?[18] That banks, being in a moratorium, could not serve their customers but did pay that man far more than 400 crowns for each of the hundred advertisements in his anniversary issue? That the homage of news vendors could be heard over the roar of the cannons and the procession of well-wishers marched for weeks like a casualty list of culture? How was it possible that in days when clichés were already bleeding and surrendering their last life to death they were still able to serve as window decoration at a bawdyhouse of liberalism? That flags were raised by writers when they were already in the field and that an account clerk and a freebooter of culture had himself celebrated by a highly placed group of lackeys as "chief of the general staff of culture"?

May the times grow great enough not to fall prey to a victor who places his heel on the intellect and the economy, great enough to overcome the nightmare of the opportunity to have a victory redound to the credit of those uninvolved in it, the opportunity for wrongheaded chasers after decorations in peacetime to divest themselves of what honor they have left, for utter stupidity to discard foreign words and names of dishes,[19] and for slaves whose ultimate goal all their lives has been the "mastery" of languages henceforth to desire to get around in the world with the ability *not* to master languages! What do you who are in the war know about the war?! You are fighting! You have not remained behind! Even those who have

18. The *Neue Freie Presse* was founded in 1864.

19. See act 1, sc. 7 and act 2, sc. 6 of *The Last Days of Mankind* in this volume. Elsewhere Kraus had occasion to give some juicy examples of chauvinistically renamed dishes: *Treubruchnudeln* ("Perfidy Noodles") for "macaroni," *Beiried-Doppelstück* for "rump-steak," *Mischgericht* ("mixed dish") for "ragout," etc.

sacrificed their ideals to life will some day have the privilege of sacrificing life itself. May the times grow so great that they measure up to these sacrifices and never so great that they transcend their memory as they grow into life!

"In dieser grossen Zeit"   (1914)

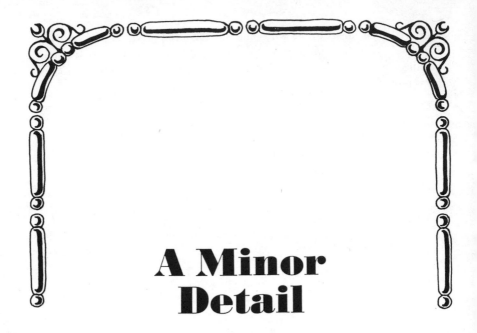

A Minor Detail

Wanted: a father-in-law to go into the women's wear business with me. Am 33 years old and well known as a women's wear salesman. No matchm. Box 3378, Berlin S.W.

I suppose "Cherchez la femme" no longer applies here. Go find mama, boy! Where is she? He doesn't speak of marrying into the business, because the father-in-law himself isn't in business yet. Normally such people at least said they wanted to find a business and were therefore looking for a wife. After all, they needed a living pretext. This is now eliminated; the father-in-law is the vestige of an obsolete stage of development which still had sentimentality and included a wife in the inventory. That's over with. Wanted: a father-in-law. The daughter can be dead if she likes. If she is present at the wedding, fine; if not, that's all right too. He'll just take the father-in-law as his sleeping partner. This is an innovation in women's wear: wear without women. The glow of classical greatness suffuses our time. Where is the woman whom such a fate will befall, who will perhaps read this ad without knowing that in the final analysis it concerns *her?* Where does the women's wear live ? Where does this ready-made apparel of a woman live ? Where is she, that I may implore her to go into hiding and kill herself sooner than become the cadaver of this hyena ? Men are now dying accidental deaths; women will give birth because two men want to go into business. A heroic age is dawning. Do not mourn what has been. Come, O dawn! Two scoundrels will in these great times shake hands over the dead life of a girl.

"Die Nebensache"   (1915)

Yolkwik Egg
Substitute

If the war had brought us nothing but this and Homemaker Egg
Noodles, it could not have been waged. Oh, if some anti-daemon had
whispered "Yolkwik Egg Substitute" in Count Berchtold's and Bethmann
Hollweg's[1] ears on 31 July 1914 (or earlier), they would not have done
it — by God, they would not have done it! And the timely warning, "You
fool, what are you doing? Some day you will have prestige but no Colgate
Shaving Cream," would have caused many a man to press for détente.
Now the only choice is between Yolkwik Egg Substitute and egg substitute made of diluvial chalk and baking powder; and if they don't trust
that and refuse to eat *ersatz* toothpowder, all they have left is Homemaker

1. Leopold Graf von Berchtold, 1863–1912, Austrian foreign minister (1912–15) who
issued the ultimatum to Serbia that touched off World War I; Theobald von Bethmann
Hollweg, 1856–1921, chancellor of the German Reich from 1909 to 1917.

Egg Noodles. And that's why there are robbers and murderers! The blood of ten million dead — *that* no one could imagine. But perhaps it would have sufficed to speak these magic words. You're going to run out of shoe laces! "But what does martial glory have to do with shoe laces ?" So there'll be a shortage of matches. "Oh, no; what do matches have to do with our superiority in artillery ?" So someone ought to have said what we were going to *have*. Oh, the unleashed machine-beast would have stopped in its tracks if someone had had enough imagination and courage to let a call burst forth like thunderpeals[2] from the Baltic to Banja Luka: Yolkwik Egg Substitute!

"Ei-Ersatz Dottofix"   (1918)

2. A reference to "Es braust ein Ruf wie Donnerhall," the opening line of Max Schneckenburger's patriotic poem "Die Wacht am Rhein" (The Watch on the Rhine, 1840).

Promotional
Trips to
Hell

I am holding in my hand a document which transcends and seals all the
shame of this age and would in itself suffice to assign the currency stew
that calls itself mankind a place of honor in a cosmic carrion pit. Even
though any clipping from a newspaper has signified a clipping of Creation,
in this instance one faces the dead certainty that a generation deemed
capable of this sort of thing no longer has any nobler possessions to damage.
After the monstrous collapse of the fiction of culture and after the nations,
by their actions, gave striking proof that their relationship to anything
that ever was of the spirit is a most shameless trickery, perhaps good
enough for the promotion of tourism but never adequate to raise the moral
level of this mankind — after all this it has nothing left but the naked
truth of its condition, so that it has almost reached the point where it is
no longer capable of lying. There is no portrait in which it could recognize
itself so clearly as this one:

But on the other hand, what is that panorama of horror and dread revealed by a day in Verdun, what is the most horrible scene of the bloody delirium into which the nations let themselves be rushed for no reason at all, when compared to the sight of this advertisement ? Isn't the mission of the press — to lead first mankind and then the survivors to the battle-fields — accomplished here in exemplary fashion ?

You receive your newspaper in the morning.

You read how comfortable survival has been made for you.

You learn that 1½ millions had to bleed to death in the very place where wine and coffee and everything else are included.

You have the decided advantage over those martyrs and dead men of first-rate accommodations and food in the Ville-Martyre and at the Ravin de la Mort.

You ride to the battlefield in a comfortable automobile, while those men got there in cattle cars.

You hear about all that is offered you by way of compensation for the sufferings of those men and for an experience whose purpose, meaning, and cause you have not been able to discover to this day.

You understand that it was organized so that some day, when nothing is left of the glory but bankruptcy, there might at least be a battlefield *par excellence*.

You learn that there is something new at the front after all, and that today one can live better there than one once could in the hinterland.

You realize that what can be offered by the competition, which has only the dead of the Argonne and Somme battles as well as the charnel houses of Reims and St. Mihiel at its disposal, is a bagatelle compared to the first-rate offerings of the *Basel News*, which will undoubtedly succeed in using the casualties of Verdun to augment its subscription list.

You understand that the destination has made the promotional trip worthwhile, and that the promotional trip was worth the world war.

You receive, even if Russia starves to death, an ample breakfast as soon as you decide to take in the battlefields of 1870-71 as well; it's all one package.

You have time after lunch to watch the remains of the unidentified dead being delivered, and after you have checked off this number on the program, you feel like having dinner.

You learn that the states whose victim you are in wartime and in peacetime will even save you the passport formalities — which is quite a bit — if you take a trip to the battlefields and obtain a ticket from the newspaper before the deadline.

You realize that these states have criminal laws which expressly protect the lives and even the honor of press pirates who make a mockery of death, make money on a catastrophe, and especially recommend an excursion to hell as an autumn trip.

You will have trouble not violating these laws, but afterwards you will send the *Basel News* a letter of appreciation and thanks.

You receive unforgettable impressions of a world in which there is not a square centimeter of soil that has not been torn up by grenades and advertisements.

And if then you still have not realized that your birth has taken you to a den of cutthroats and that a mankind which desecrates even the blood it has spilled is composed of knavery from top to bottom and that there is no escape from it or remedy against it — then the Devil take you to a battlefield *par excellence!*

"Reklamefahrten zur Hölle"   (1921)

The Sorcerer's Apprentices

The sorcerer's apprentices speak:

> *... The action of the authorities seems even stranger when one considers that quackery threatens to get out of hand in the field of psychoanalysis as well.*

Where else ?

> *... Only recently I pointed out the dangers of analysis in a lecture.*

Rightly so.

> *... No matter what the details of this case may be, it showed that often the analyst himself is in very great danger ...*

94

Oh, I see!

. . . and I have repeatedly called my students' attention to this, since impulsive acts may under certain circumstances be directed against the doctor.

Why shouldn't they be, if intelligent acts are directed against the patient?

As in other countries, analysis threatens to become a veritable epidemic here . . .

You're telling me!

. . . in that people who have no real, steady occupation, or half-cured neurotics, suddenly feel within themselves a mission to make people happy by performing as analysts.

In a word, psychoanalysts

In many instances, people who have entrusted themselves to them have suffered severe damage to their organisms and their emotional lives.

Not to mention their pocketbooks.

. . . Psychoanalysis has become a veritable epidemic — not only in Vienna but in all cultural centers of the world. Numerous failures flock to analysis because the public is requesting it and goes wherever it is offered. We know of definite criminal types whom we have analyzed but could not bring to happy conclusion because of their hopeless moral insanity. We were very unpleasantly surprised when we read advertisements by these people in the daily papers.

All this is literally true, especially the remark about moral insanity. I have enough material to write a book about it. But how did all this come about? It is probably the way it was with the Captain of Köpenick,[1] to

---

1. In 1906 the unemployed cobbler Wilhelm Voigt bought an army captain's uniform in an old-clothes shop, commandeered a troop of soldiers, and occupied the town hall of Köpenick, a Berlin suburb, in a futile attempt to procure the documents he needed to get a job or a steady place of residence. The man was later pardoned by an amused Kaiser. The most celebrated among several literary treatments of this incident, which was indicative of the Germans' overwrought reverence for military uniforms and titles, is Carl Zuckmayer's play *Der Hauptmann von Köpenick* (The Captain of Koepenick, 1931).

whom the world ought to be grateful for unmasking a profession that exerted a fetish-like fascination upon it for an even longer period, and the idolatry of which also filled an emotional gap. The false military patrols by whom the citizen was taken in have taught him to be on his guard against the genuine ones. The false psychoanalysis has a merit which the genuine one does not yet possess: to convince people of the falseness of the genuine one. There are real psychoanalysts about whom one does not know, for one thing, whether they are doctors or patients: and it is part of the nature of the illness and its therapy that the illness has the therapy and the therapy the illness, that the healthy emerge from the doctor's office as patients and the patients as doctors. Constant confusion prevails there, and it is the same with genuine and false psychoanalysts. There is magic — the magic of neurosis as once there was the magic of the uniform, and mankind should try to become inured to the fascination that emanates from the regulation of inhibitions. But it is a sorcery that has no master and must keep engendering only apprentices. The professions really have something: namely, that which the false psychoanalysts reveal as effectively as the false military men. They deserve well of mankind. If psychoanalysis has become an epidemic — which it has really always been, from the first observed case — this is healthy in that people will guard against recognizing exceptions because these are supposed to be authorized to have cholera.

"Die Zauberlehrlinge" (1924)

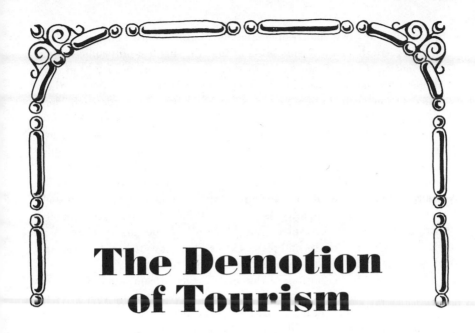

The Demotion
of Tourism

Since I cannot be constructive but only destructive, I am, of course, not in favor of promoting tourism but of demoting it. But with this inclination I do pursue a positive goal, because I am of the opinion that as tourism has gone up — due, that is, to the exclusive concentration of Viennese intellectual life on this ideal — the intellectual level has dropped beneath point zero. In my youth, when I first heard people talk about tourists and about how everyone in Vienna was striving to make life as pleasant as possible for them (unlike Tauris, where in accordance with a somber practice at the altar of Diana every stranger had to sacrifice his life, while in accordance with Vienna's more hospitable customs he has only to sacrifice his money) — in my childhood, then, I had a desire to become a foreigner some day. This desire I still have not abandoned, though I no longer wish to be a foreigner in Vienna but somewhere else. In the course of time, you see, I have found out that tourism in Vienna is quite different from what people imagine (that it is only a chimera, albeit one that entertains the Viennese), and that the slightest hint suffices their imagination. I have discovered that there are not many tourists, and that it is always the same people who keep coming back — not because they like it so much here, but because they have to, having been recruited. They are the people who can be seen moving down the Ringstrasse packed into their private buses and for whom one often feels sorry because they are exposed to the curiosity of the natives and because one has the feeling that the public has been asked to protect their facilities, which means that they are fair game for all sorts of mishaps and attacks, and also because it must really be sad to have to enjoy the advantages of an old civilization in such togetherness. But sympathy is misplaced here, for one immediately realizes that, in the first place, the tourists have no one to blame but themselves, and, in the second place, this is what they are here for, because they are kept for the sole purpose of promoting tourism.

When I got to the bottom of this my youthful dream was finished, for I would never, never lend myself to such a thing. In time this state of affairs led to all kinds of irregularities, for it often happened that Viennese infiltrated the tourists in order to get to know their city. The trust of the population was abused when persons claimed to be foreigners in order to get some courteous information. Fortunately, however, motherly eyes recognized these impostors right away and they were dealt with with the proper rudeness, while on the other hand strangers who wished to act as though they were at home here had to suffer humiliations. Such unpleasant mistaken identities, however, were no distraction from the real endeavors of tourism; and in order to increase the number of tourists — which, after all, is what really matters — the most daring ideas were resorted to. Thus it is rumored that next summer people will not be content to lure the foreigners with song (as the dolphins did with the members of the Vienna Men's Choral Society, and vice versa),[1] but that every Viennese is to be asked to procure "at least one tourist" by his own efforts. If this project is carried out with any vigor at all, it will lead to the displacement of the natives or to a catastrophic housing shortage. But there is hope that such consequences of an overwrought patriotism will be reconsidered at the last moment and that the natural attractiveness of the music festival will be deemed sufficient. A peculiar proposal which was abandoned in

1. The reference is to the Vienna Men's Choral Society's voyage to America which Kraus commented upon satirically in his prose piece "Fahrende Sänger" (Traveling Minstrels) in the *Fackel* of May 1907. It seems that the men were fascinated by the dolphins they encountered, but that the dolphins were less enthusiastic about the men's singing.

time was to have a party of American tourists met in Paris by an equal number of Viennese tailors. At the railroad station these tailors were supposed to measure each American for a custom-made Styrian outfit, and then they were going to hand the finished garments to the Americans upon their arrival in Vienna, bowing and curtseying like the village tailor in the fairy tale. The reason why this undoubtedly sensible idea was not carried out was probably that Styrian garb had in the meantime become too notorious to give pleasure to American business types. So the powers that be refrained from taking their measurements in Paris and contented themselves with stripping them in Vienna. For they are convinced that it is possible to provide a lasting memento of Vienna in this fashion, too, and they would certainly decide to accommodate the tourists with small kindnesses like soap in railroad toilets if Austria did not have natives who walk away with the soap. For even though these natives greatly care about foreigners coming into the country, they are not prepared to make any sacrifices in their behalf. Though there may be no toilet articles on the train, efforts are in good train to effect a radical change and see to it that benefits to which foreigners may lay legitimate claim do not benefit the natives. A sharp line of demarcation is to be drawn, and in order to guard the institution of tourism against falsification and immediately identify each tourist as a tourist, congresses were instituted a few years ago.

The congresses are one of those progressive achievements which one can accentuate simply by saying that we used not to have them. Since that exemplary Congress of Vienna people have expected congresses to promote tourism, and so I believe that the best way for me to contribute to the destruction of this illusion is to reveal the secret of the composition of these congresses. Week after week we now read that a Europe already united in this respect has decided to send the representatives of its most important cultural interests to Vienna; they are to convene here alternately as sociologists, British hotelkeepers, German writers and journalists, members of cultural associations or P.E.N. Clubs, pan-Europeans or even plain Europeans, and to be fed here at the public expense. If this were really the case and if it were true that German writers and journalists in particular — people who have missed any other congress-worthy occupation — are wined and dined at Schönbrunn as guests of the Austrian government and that members of cultural associations — people who don't even know what mischief they are up to — are entertained at City Hall, I would not hesitate to urge people to refuse to pay their taxes. However, I am convinced that the reports about these banquets and receptions, about all the fuss and feathers of a broken-down dignity and this claptrap of a dubious culture, are fabrications.

Of course, I can well believe that Herr Ramek,[2] the head of a strongly alcoholic government, is capable of all sorts of things in this area. But a socialistic municipal government saddled with the victims of the war and the postwar period has more important things to do than to patronize such entertainments, which it ought to tax rather than subsidize. But I don't believe that these congresses exist. Rather, I am convinced that it is simply the old institution of tourists who are now apparently being handled in herds — in congresses, that is — in an effort to simulate profusion (as provincial theaters do with their meager crews of extras who are made to walk on and off the stage continuously) and to use tourists to promote tourism. This suspicion is confirmed by a glance at the photos in the illustrated papers which for weeks have been showing us the participants in the various congresses. They are always the same figures, deliberately shown in blurry photographs, whether they are supposed to be British hotelkeepers or people interested in cultural cooperation (plus their wives). The only difference is that on the upper right we may see either the face of Sukfüll the hotelkeeper (the pioneer who introduced tourists to Austria as Drake introduced the potato) or the face of Hofmannsthal the poet, though it is possible to confuse those faces, too. No matter which trade they may belong to, culture or hotelkeeping pure and simple, the tourist guides change; the tourists remain the same. As regards the British hotelkeepers, they were invited not only because they are tourists but because they in particular must be in a position to give advice on how to deal with tourists. For what the scarab was to the ancient Egyptians, the tourist is to the Austrians. So no matter what congress may convene here, they are simply tourists who have no other occupation and no other interests than to be strangers here and therefore not to know what is in store for them — namely, that they are to serve exclusively for the promotion of their own tourism: tourist-inbreeding. If they realized this, they would not come again. For the Austrian Monroe Doctrine — Austria for the Non-Austrians! — has another side: they are supposed to constitute a sight for the natives. In revealing this secret, I hope to have made a first breach in tourism, for the demotion of which I would long since have started a society if I were a more sociable kind. For if I regard the economic principle that people must support innkeepers as deceitful, I regard the demand that foreigners support innkeepers as disgraceful. I don't know how else it could be done, and I needn't offer more than the results of a congress of economists. A female tourist recently asked me whether it was true that I was incapable of being

2. Rudolf Ramek (1881–1941), Christian-Socialist politician; Austrian federal chancellor 1924–26.

constructive; she had heard this from various sources. After some hesitation, and because it could no longer be concealed, I decided to admit it, but not without at the same time boasting of a positive ability: that I am capable of being destructive.

"Zur Aufhebung des Fremdenverkehrs"   (1926)

Just Like
Home

This is how Hasenclever[1] found life in Hollywood:

"Berthold Viertel[2] picked me up and we drove out to his seaside villa. After three days and four nights I got a decent meal again. There were his wife, the wonderful Salka, her three sons, an enormous shepherd dog, a library, and a picture of Karl Kraus. It was like home." (Does Hasenclever have a picture of me?) Then Greta Garbo came in, and she was followed by an earthquake. Hasenclever took a cat on his arm and consoled it.

1. The German dramatist Walter Hasenclever, 1890–1940 (suicide).

2. Viennese-born essayist, poet, and theatrical and film director (1885–1953). During World War I Viertel wrote an appreciative study of Karl Kraus, and in 1924 he directed the premiere performances of Kraus's one-act plays *Traumtheater* and *Traumstück*. His first wife, Salomea (Salka) Steuermann Viertel, was a close associate and friend of Greta Garbo as head of the MGM Story Department. See her autobiography *The Kindness of Strangers* (New York, 1969).

"'Poor cat,' I said, 'it was only an earthquake.' Greta watched me doing this. 'Me too,' she begged. I put the cat down and took Garbo on my arm." (In front of my eyes!) "'Poor Greta,' I said, 'it's all over now.' Then the cat did the only right thing. It ran to its dish and drank milk. I went to the teatable, poured some cream into a saucer, and handed it to Greta. And she did exactly like the cat. Then we were all happy. That was her best role."

How differently one pictures Hollywood! And yet it's just like home.

"Wie zu Hause"   (1931)

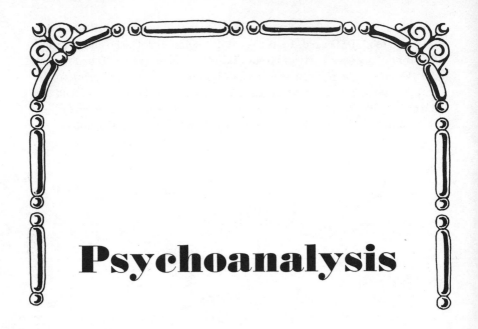

Psychoanalysis

"The well-known psychiatrist Dr. Rudolf Urbantschitsch," who gave a profound lecture on infantile sexuality and made "inspired" (and thus God-given) remarks about "the share of civilization in the origin of the neuroses," and who got himself discussed a bit too much, "coined the aphorism 'Neurosis is the escutcheon of civilization.'"

Very nice; but nowadays we already have far more heraldists running around than aristocrats.

"Psychoanalyse"   (1931)

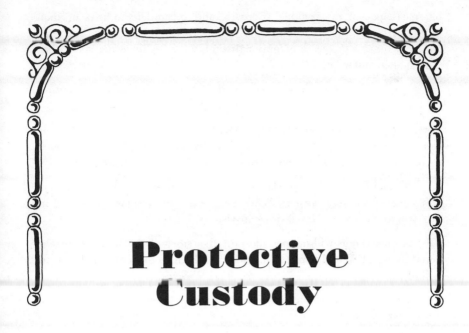

Protective
Custody

The murderer remains without any idea of his deed or its effect, and he has a way of taking it back into the realm of humanity that really ought to gain him mankind's sympathies. Everything, after all, was done in good faith, and therefore this good faith is demanded of the world, too, which learns how a case, presented as one of the most horrible bloody deeds after an outbreak of despair on the part of the murdered man, really happened:

Dr. Ernst Eckstein, who was taken into protective custody as one of the first political functionaries,

—virtually an act of protection, then—

had trouble coping with the conditions of his confinement.

The rumor had been circulated that these conditions were forced labor amidst blows with rifle butts, whiplashings in the face, dosings with castor oil, participation in speaking choruses, and misunderstandings of that nature. After all, there were also occasional tours of the city in an open van, allegedly amidst the jeers of nationalistic fighters, while other spectators were shaken and wept.

> Just two weeks ago he was busy working for the Breslau concentration camp.

Certainly not *in* the concentration camp; a kind of office work. Not, of course, without the physical exercise that the assiduous Heines, who once set an example himself, provides for his charges. One of them states:

> He had to cart heavy rocks, and when we others could relax, he was detailed to clean latrines. While he was forced to rummage around in there, he was displayed to camp visitors.

Yet, as such things will happen, despite diversions of this kind he surrendered to dejection and depression, states to which he evidently inclined. In a fit of

> depression he attempted to commit suicide in his cell. Finally he refused food, so that

— because they wanted to keep him alive and working —

> he had to be fed intravenously.

They spared no efforts. Doctors were sent for. They attribute his death

> primarily to his losing the will to live.

Unfortunately he preferred death to more important tasks that were in store for him. According to conjectures of those prone to believe atrocity stories, he had been taken from Breslau to Oels (the residence of the Crown Prince), "where his lungs and kidneys were damaged in the course of hours of beating." He moaned all night; they said

> he apparently was no longer quite right in the head. . . . They took him to his unfortunate mother. . . . She had him committed to the insane asylum on Einbaumstrasse where he died shortly afterwards.

The low resistance of prisoners often gives rise to complaints. No sooner has a person been in the concentration camp for a few hours than

> he had to be taken to the hospital.

Some prove to be "unfit for protective custody" on the way to the camp and have to be rerouted to the hospital — though they were driven in open

106

cars through streets lined with lively, cheerful crowds. The observation that someone turned out to be "unfit for custody" at this early stage is not made without a certain reproach. In such cases the following official report (of the Bochum police) is issued, based on statements by the escorts:

> He has a number of contusions on his body caused by beating. Also, he was only partially conscious. At present he is critically ill. Up to now it could not be established under what circumstances he received his injuries, since he cannot be questioned at this time.

The authorities who had made the arrest and had not let the man out of their grasp were baffled. He never regained consciousness and the case remained unsolved. Sometimes even the most conscientious investigation produces no results. Business leaders, as we know, must often be taken into protective custody "on suspicion of fraud" — a most reprehensible activity. One such man proved unreliable even in transit, for he

> inflicted injuries on his arm and on his temple, though these are not critical.

That can happen, too. Politicians pose a special problem. Many deputies who are not even on their way to protective custody but simply to the Reichstag have to be hospitalized. This sort of thing is always noted with a certain sympathy. A Bulgarian doctor was released from protective custody but showed traces of the care he had received; as a foreigner he had been treated for only three days and his wife had been allowed to be present. When he was being taken away in the car, his escort asked him solicitously:

> Did they beat you? Oh, how embarrassing!

At times it is announced with some regret that a person's state of health leaves something to be desired. Many cases, to be sure, involved crybabies. A Polish workman, for example, roared so loudly that he was heard all over the camp. Later the cause became known:

> He died of heart failure; in any case, he was stateless.

Most people die of natural causes. Often exhaustion is diagnosed; sometimes there is a fit of faintness which causes someone to plunge three stories into the yard of the administration building, and the guard deplores the carelessness which made the person go near an open window. Not infrequently there is a nervous breakdown, particularly among travelers, on whom suicide is then committed. As far as this manner of death is concerned, it simply appears incomprehensible if it takes place prior to the arrest. In such a case it can only be stated that nothing is known about the motives for the action.

In the case of Oberfohren it is believed that he had taken his possession of a memorandum about the Reichstag fire to heart. But if rumors persist that his death was caused by someone else, the following statement cannot fail to make an impression where revulsion at this world has really caused this action:

It is a clear case of suicide.

An analogous explanation was given of an incident at the Journeymen's Convention in Munich where a priest

succumbed to a stroke because he got excited about a clash in the street.

The following news item would contradict an unnatural interpretation of the death of this priest (who had a fractured skull):

The police chiefs of Krefeld and Mönchen-Gladbach have ordered the abolition of rubber truncheons, saying that this weapon is not worthy of a civilized nation.

While backward Austria still uses it against bomb throwers. Something that is a complete mystery to the investigating authorities and may once again be indicative of a lost will to live are the three waterlogged bodies that were found together and weighed down with stones. In all reported versions of such accidents one can discern honest regret over the fact that many a constitution, particularly those of intellectuals, did not prove equal to the rigors of the new order, or that worry, excitement, and immoderation nowadays lead so many people to cut their natural lives short. But it seems particularly deplorable that the meaning of protective custody is so frequently misunderstood, leading to expressions of displeasure and impatience even though it is solely designed to protect an official or a private person from violence which might befall him in freedom — to protect politicians from an enraged crowd, lawyers and doctors from angry clients and patients, radio station managers from dissatisfied listeners. There may never before have been an age in which the citizenry has been protected so intensively, and in any case, the beneficent intent of this protection deserves to be more appreciated. No reasonable person will deny that a Marxist background or a Jewish birth contains the suspicion of criminal activity. It is the purpose of protective custody to avert the consequences, but this custody is granted only upon the conclusion of an individual examination in the S.A. barracks whose purpose is clearly defined by a police decree:

Those arrested are first to be turned over to a nationalistic organization. It is the task of the nationalistic organization in support of the political police to give those apprehended a thorough preparatory hearing about their criminal offenses.

Then the persons involved are taken either to a hospital or, if they prove to be fit for custody, to a camp where their case is dealt with within a communal framework. From this one can see that a thorough preparation has been ordered and that accordingly the complaints that alleged excesses of the S.A. occur without the approval of the competent authorities are without foundation. The nationalistic organizations are brought in to relieve the political police, which has its hands full issuing false passports to murderers going to Austria, waiving the entry fee (whose harshness is being deplored) in such deserving cases, and, finally, determining that none of this is happening. While these men are exposing themselves to the greatest dangers on the other side of the border, people injurious to the national revolution are afforded protection. Of course, those who abuse this protection risk being shot while trying to escape; such shooting is done in the forehead and keeps an incautious person from repeating the attempt. To be sure, the representatives of the press who were able to convince themselves of the exemplary set-up of the institutions were not shown such measures, which are necessary only in extreme cases, nor were they given an opportunity to attend the other exercises, which are more internal in nature. They were, however, permitted to "sample the prison food and then witness the release of some inmates." But what good is such a release? They will be back! Shortly before it went bankrupt, the *Berliner Tageblatt* was able to print this sensational item:

Quite a few young people who had been given their freedom returned of their own free will and requested continued employment.

Since the day they encountered discipline and learned to appreciate it, they haven't given a hoot for freedom. We had been able to imagine that by its very set-up such a camp serves concentration more than diversion; now we also learned that

with its institutions of religious services and civic instruction, as well as its daily routine, it is comparable to a boarding school.

The official line was that "in accordance with the existing regulations, they are real educational institutions," and that it was the task of the press to look into the pedagogical factor, for

from the viewpoint of domestic policy, the important question is above all whether educational work is being done in these camps.

I'll say it is:

> On the basis of the experience up to now, an unqualified affirmative answer can be given to this question.

This is printed in the press which otherwise ought to observe certain qualifications concerning itself. That is why it chooses the simple definition that a concentration camp is

> a temporary curtailment of liberty with an educational aim. But in many cases one may also speak of a spiritual rehabilitation.

Oh, one practically must. In Dachau it was even noticed

> that the Communists, who came to the camp in a grim mood, after some time learned to like good, patriotic songs again. "Ich hatt' einen Kameraden" is particularly popular.[1]

In short, patriotic memories

> are gaining the upper hand

provided this upper hand does not happen to be busy elsewhere, and today the Communists are

> quite different people from what they were when brought here

while

> the fresh arrivals are morose, obdurate, and care-worn.

Of course, this does not mean that they are still fresh when brought in and become morose later, but the other way around.

> After an educational cure of a few weeks, they too will be different persons.

Sometimes one day is said to be enough. These people, obviously, cannot testify to this themselves — for one thing because they are not allowed to, and for another because the spiritual transformation which often occurs at a stroke not infrequently results in unconsciousness or at least an impaired memory, and because astonishment at unaccustomed things may result in

---

1. "I once had a buddy; a better one you won't find . . ." — Ludwig Uhland's poignant poem (1809) about a fallen soldier has become one of Germany's most beloved folk songs. The marching tune was arranged in 1827 by Friedrich Silcher after a Swiss folk melody.

speech disorders. But we shall content ourselves with the statement of the representatives of the press that they received the distinct impression

> that Germany has nothing to hide in this area either and that the prisoners have nothing to complain about.

Everything goes like clockwork, occasionally like lock work. Every activity has its appointed time.

> Rise at five-thirty, make beds till six.

Of course, the beds are unmistakably of straw, but the straw is changed at least once a week.

> Roll call at six. Until six-thirty, degassing and ventilation.

Hygiene leaves nothing to be desired. Work, exercise, tattoo (nine o'clock) fill the day. The educational cure and the other tricks take place in between; the civic instruction comes from *Mein Kampf*. Here there is still order; out there in freedom things are at sixes and sevens; there everyone leads and is led at the same time and does on his own hook whatever occurs to the hook. There a man faces the irrational; here he only faces the guards. Here the weak are to be "toughened up to make them useful members of human society again"; there the scum of society predominates. Consequently, since Dachau, Dürgoy, and Sonneburg not only equal boarding schools but practically reach the level of sanatoriums (though what is striven for is more a *mens sana*), an order has been given to fix an appropriate charge for the benefits which the state confers upon its charges via such institutions, the costs of which would otherwise be a burden on the community.

> Stuttgart, 23 June. Competent authorities have announced that those in protective custody are jointly responsible for the cost of this custody. This means that every individual in protective custody is responsible for the total costs of protective custody. If this custody is utilized, the state has the right of recourse to the other inmates by way of an assessment. . . . Hence a number of wealthy persons in protective custody have been billed the amount of approximately 100,000 marks to defray the costs of protective custody

If a wealthy prisoner — who is entitled to be in first class — refuses to sign a check, he is threatened with third class; but usually one interrogation suffices to make him sign. It is said that in some cases an appropriate additional payment resulted in release from the institution, though without any guarantee for a person's future progress. One can see how this branch of government, too — in line with a social policy which determines all measures of the state — is intent upon favoring the impecunious, who still enjoy their stay including room and board as well as treatment gratis or at moderate cost at the expense of the rich, who pay sanatorium prices. The representatives of the press have been able to convince themselves that these prices are decidedly in keeping with what is offered. Sums of money which the inmates may still have on them when admitted are converted into "camp money" with which they can buy so-called "sundries" at the canteen — food substitutes and such — and whose bills bear, in addition to the emblem of barbed wire, the signatures of three torture-chamberlains. A widely noticed innovation was the continuous exchange of inmates among the camps — an effort to redress complaints about the monotony of the environment and particularly to offer the staff a certain variety and thus an opportunity to enrich their experience with the personalities of their charges. This, to be sure, is an arrangement which might appear to a layman whose stomach turns easily as one of the most artful figments of a hangman's imagination. We have read that Göring, who takes pity on animals, has proscribed vivisection because "it could no longer be tolerated that an animal be equated with an inanimate object." Anyone who disregards this prohibition is taken where the technique is practiced without anesthesia, and not so much for the purpose of scientific knowledge as for the entertainment of the orderlies. In fact, what goes on there frequently seems to be connected with the fields of music or lecturing. The hangman leans against the doorpost and sings "Morgenrot, Morgenrot, leuchtest mir zum frühen Tod."[2] Fire on a person's soles causes the Horst Wessel song to be struck up.[3] In addition to patriotic songs, hit tunes are practiced. Instruments provide the accompaniment. There is a number called "playing the zither" or "playing the phonograph" in which a person lying on a plank bed is the phonograph. Of course, things are not always as lively as they were in the beginning, when Count Helldorf came to the Brown House at Annaberg to watch two hundred men with bandaged heads standing at attention and singing a variation on a popular song:

> Where did I get those nice black eyes?
> From the S.A. They're all great guys.

2. "Rising sun, you shine on my way to an early grave" — the beginning of the folk song based on Wilhelm Hauff's "Reiters Morgengesang" (Cavalryman's Morning Song, 1824).

3. "Make way for the brown battalions . . ." — the marching song of the S.A. and, next to "Deutschland, Deutschland über alles," the semi-official national anthem of Nazi Germany. Horst Wessel, a street brawler and pimp, became a martyr and folk hero in the "Thousand-Year Reich."

On the other hand, there is a report from a different camp that an Austrian who worked in Hamburg as a chief stoker on ships was won over to the idea of *Anschluss* with Germany in the following manner:

> Each morning he had to empty and rinse the garbage pails in his cell and then step forward together with a Jewish businessman. A match was placed between the index and middle fingers of each man's right hand, and then they had to raise the hand in the Hitler salute.

With the salute went a half-hour's instruction in alternately reciting the following lines "clearly, distinctly, and rhythmically":

> The Jew: "I am a stin-king Jew!"
> The Austrian: "And I de-sire to be-come a Ger-man!"

Every time one of them faltered, a German named Gaborinski helped him along with a rubber truncheon (which is still in vogue in those parts). After a so-called "rub-down" with this truncheon, which netted him loose front teeth, the Austrian managed to secure his deportation through the intervention of the Austrian consulate. He had come with sixty marks and some clothes and left with the suit on his back and as much as twenty-two marks.

But one should certainly not imagine the S.A. spirit in action as following only the straight line of thrashing. Rather, it has variants of treatment whose very improbability refutes those atrocity stories. If, for example, one reads that prisoners have to pull out grass with their teeth (before it turns into a metaphor); that the beast of Breslau, the murderer and police chief Heines, has old men whipped, that he lets a former Prussian governor be spat upon by his former employees and forces him to sew the Socialist fighting emblem on the seat of his pants and display it to visitors, then one is surely justified in not believing any of it — especially when the *Manchester Guardian* claims that the same man has prisoners taken to a pig sty and makes them "shake hands with the pigs and address them as their comrades" while the guards stand around and guffaw. Is it not understandable that the *Neue Freie Presse* does not print such news items but prefers to feature love affairs? At any rate, Europe has learned via London and Paris that many prisoners in Dürgoy, where those amusements take place, have broken ribs and every two weeks are

> escorted to Breslau and dragged through the streets. While they march they have to sing — they stagger along with hollow cheeks and dim eyes, a procession of starved, beaten wretches who are not even recognized by friends waiting to exchange a glance with them.

But what use does Europe make of this knowledge ? And of the fact that "nothing in the movement happens without my knowledge and without my will" ? And of a satrap's words, "Nothing may be done which the supreme commander cannot approve" ?

from *Die Dritte Walpurgisnacht*   (1933)

Selected Poems

translated

by

Max Knight and Karl F. Ross

Nächtliche Stunde

Nächtliche Stunde, die mir vergeht,
da ich's ersinne, bedenke und wende,
und diese Nacht geht schon zu Ende.
Draussen ein Vogel sagt: es ist Tag.

Nächtliche Stunde, die mir vergeht,
da ich's ersinne, bedenke und wende,
und dieser Winter geht schon zu Ende.
Draussen ein Vogel sagt: es ist Frühling.

Nächtliche Stunde, die mir vergeht,
da ich's ersinne, bedenke und wende,
und dieses Leben geht schon zu Ende.
Draussen ein Vogel sagt: es ist Tod.

Nocturnal Hour

Nocturnal hour that passes away
as I, considering, weighing and grading,
note that this night is already fading.
Outside a bird proclaims: it is day.

Nocturnal hour that passes away
as I, considering, weighing and grading,
note that this winter is already fading.
Outside a bird proclaims: it is spring.

Nocturnal hour that passes away
as I, considering, weighing and grading,
note that this life is already fading.
Outside a bird proclaims: it is death.

Der Tag

Wie der Tag sich durch das Fenster traut,
schau ich auf den Platz,
staunend, dass der Nacht
noch ein Morgen graut,
die ich so durchwacht
ohne Freudenlaut,
aber immer bauend Satz auf Satz.

Wie der Blick sich durch das Fenster traut,
geht ein Wagen, geht,
langsam geht er hin
ohne Klagelaut.
Liegt ein Toter drin,
eine arme Haut.
Und ich geh zurück an mein Gebet.

The Day

Through the window dares the breaking day;
down the square I gaze,
awed that such a night
yields to morning gray.
No glad sounds betray
sleepless vigil's flight
as I go on piling phrase on phrase.

Through the window dares my glance to stray;
rolls a wagon there,
slowly rolls ahead.
No sad sounds betray
that some wretch lies dead,
being hauled away
as I am returning to my prayer.

Schnellzug

Auf dieser Lebensbahn
rattert es drauf und dran
in schnellem Zug.
Und meine Melodie
macht es, ich weiss nicht wie,
zu einem Trug.

Draussen das liebe Land,
das noch nicht stille stand,
wie es sich dreht!
Alles bleibt mir versäumt,
alles bleibt ungeträumt,
alles vergeht.

Man wird vom Schauen stumpf,
hier drin die Luft ist dumpf,
draussen ist's schön.
Dann wird die Zeit mir lang,
dann wird mir wieder bang
vor dem Vergehn.

Welch eine Menschennot
schlägt sich die Zeit hier tot
auf ihre Art.
Hier drin ist nichts wie Schmutz,
und ich bin voller Trutz.
Welch eine Fahrt!

Doch was auch quält und närrt,
ich bleibe eingesperrt
bis an das End'.
Wollte mich gern befrein,
wollte die Landschaft sein,
die rückwärts rennt!

Rapid Transit

Along this lifetime track
with noisy clickety-clack
speeds my express.
Its din drowns out my song
and somehow makes it wrong
and meaningless.

And when I look outside,
I see the landscape slide
forever past.
My dreams are dreamt in vain,
for nothing on this train
is meant to last.

My eyesight seems to fail.
The air in here is stale —
out there it's clear.
At times I am distraught
and feel with anxious thought
the end is near.

An aimless multitude
in every kind of mood
parades inside.
There's lots of dirt and dust,
which fills me with disgust —
aw, what a ride.

Aboard I'm doomed to stay
until my final day —
how sad a plight!
If only I could flee
and join that scenery
in backward flight.

An einen alten Lehrer
(Henricus Stephanus Sedlmayer)

Da neulich sah ich wie in der Jugendzeit
Dich weissen Hauptes, irgendwohin den Blick
    Gerichtet nach einer Vokabel,
        Welche ein Schüler verloren hatte.

Ein andrer musste, nicht auf den Ruf gefasst,
Eh er sich fassen konnte, sie fassen schon,
    Und war auch er es nicht imstande,
        Nanntest du es eine Seelenroheit.

Von strenger Milde war dieser Unterricht.
Du guter Lehrer hattest den Schüler gern.
    Doch näher deinem reinen Herzen
        Lag wohl das Wohl eines armen Wortes.

Latein und Deutsch: du hast sie mir beigebracht.
Doch dank ich Deutsch dir, weil ich Latein gelernt.
    Wie wurde deutsch mir, als ich deinen
        Lieben Ovidius lesen konnte!

Denn jenes wahrlich machte mir Schwierigkeit.
Mir fehlten Worte, und es gelang mir nicht,
    Den Frühling, den ich erst erlebte,
        In einem Aufsatz auch zu beschreiben.

Ovid ja selber hätte es nicht vermocht,
Und Goethe länger als eine Stund gebraucht —
    Wie sollte es ein Schulbub treffen,
        Wenn er nicht grade ein Journalist war?

Du guter Lehrer wusstest das nur zu gut.
Du übtest Nachsicht und weil ich in Latein
    Doch vorzüglich bestanden hatte,
        Gabst du in Deutsch mir nicht nichtgenügend.

To an Old Teacher
(Henricus Stephanus Sedlmayer)

I saw you lately, as in the days of youth;
your hair was snow-white; you cast about your glance
as though you sought a word in Latin
that had been lost by a luckless student.

Another student, not ready for the call,
was meant to catch it ere he could catch himself,
and if he also failed to do it,
you used to call it a "mental cruelty."

Benignly stringent were you in teaching us;
you, kindly teacher, you liked the students well.
But closer to your sterling spirit
was your concern for a poor word's welfare.

Not Latin only — German you also taught,
I learned my German thanks to your Latin class.
How wonderfully unfolded German
when I had learned to read your dear Ovid.

For German, truly, proved very troublesome.
I lacked the words and had no ability
to turn the Spring I had just tasted
skillfully into a German essay.

Ovidius, even, he would have floundered here
and Goethe would have needed an hour for this.
How, then, should a schoolboy have done it,
were he not also by chance a journalist?

You, kindly teacher, knew all this well enough.
You were so lenient, and since I did succeed
and passed my test with A's in Latin,
you never gave me an F in German.

So kam ich durch und besserte später mich,
Weil ich es fühlte, dass ich dir schuldig war,
  Im deutschen Aufsatz nach der Schule
    Deinen Erwartungen zu entsprechen.

Hätt' ich schon damals gleich zwischen acht und neun
So Deutsch geschrieben, wie zwischen zehn und elf
  Latein ich las, wär' diese Ode,
    Diese horazische, nicht entstanden.

Nimm diese Fleissaufgabe als Jugendgruss.
Denn du stehst milde heute wie einst vor mir.
  In Bild und Wort bist du mir nahe,
    Als ob ich heute noch vor dir sässe.

Ich sehe dich, wie du mit der feinen Hand
Die Stirn dir streichst, die sorgende, als ob du
  Ein krankes Wort betreuen müsstest —
    Heilige Pflicht vor profanen Zeugen.

Schneeweiss wie damals, neigend den Kopf, doch hoch
Den Sinn wie damals, traf ich dich auf dem Weg
  Zur Schule neulich und es war mir,
    Dass ich mit dir in die Schule ginge.

Wohin verlor sich, sag mir, dein Altersblick,
Mir unverloren? Lehrest du immer noch
  Verlorner Gegenwart die Sprache?
    Folg mir und lasse die Klasse fallen!

And so I finished, grew and improved in time,
because I felt that this much I owed to you:
    to meet your standards after high school
        when I was writing a theme in German.

If I in those days, right between eight and nine,
had written German as, between nine and ten,
    I read my Latin — then this ode in
        Horace's meter would not be written.

Accept this offering as a salute from youth.
You stand before me, kindly today as then;
    in word and picture you are near me
        just as if still I sat there before you.

I clearly see you, passing your tender hand
across your forehead, worriedly, as if you
    were asked to tend an ailing idiom —
        reverent task before soulless listeners.

Snow-white, as then, your head was bent low, but high
your spirit, as then, when we met as you went
    to school that morning and I fancied
        that we were going to school together.

Where did your aging glance, tell me, lose itself,
not lost to me? And are you now teaching still
    the language to a lost, forsaken present?
        Take my advice, sir, and flunk the students.

Die Schauspielerin

Das Stichwort fällt, gleich trittst du auf,
es drängen Partner sich zuhauf,
und stets gebeten, nie bedankt
spielst du, was man von dir verlangt,
und wie den vielen es gefiel,
stehst du und alles auf dem Spiel,
und oft gespielt und immer neu
und jeder will, dass er es sei,
und jeder durch die Maske spricht,
der nicht erkennt das Urgesicht
der monotonen Vielgestalt
und Wechselblicks Naturgewalt;
blickst insgeheim dich um und um,
spielt mit das ganze Publikum
und jeder fragt, wer heut sie wär',
man flüstert, Eros sei Souffleur;
süss schwindet diese Stimme hin,
die sich verlor von Anbeginn,
es lebt sich, bis der Vorhang fällt —
Applaus, versunken ist die Welt.

The Actress

There goes your cue, you're stepping out,
the other players mill about,
requests are many, thanks are few,
you play what they demand of you
and what the critics do and say
is critical for you and play
which, often staged, is ever new
and each one wants to be it, too,
and each one talks as through a mask
who fails to recognize the task
of picturing life's many moods
with changing facial attitudes;
and as you cast a furtive glance
you see the audience in a trance,
they wonder who she is today,
Eros is prompter, so they say;
that voice keeps fading, sweet and low,
from the beginning of the show,
there's action till the curtain drops —
applause, the world around you stops.

Dein Fehler

Dein Fehler, Liebste, ach ich liebe ihn,
weil du ihn hast,
und er ist eine deiner liebsten Gaben.
Seh' ich an andern ihn, so seh' ich fast
dich selbst und sehe nach dem Fehler hin,
und alle will ich lieben, die ihn haben!

Fehlst du mir einst und fehlt dein Fehler mir,
weil du dahin,
wie wollt' ich, Liebste, lieber dich ergänzen
als durch den Fehler? Ach ich liebe ihn,
und seh' ich ihn schon längst nicht mehr an dir,
die Hässlichste wird mir durch ihn erglänzen!

Doch träte selbst die Schönste vor mich hin,
und fehlerlos,
ich wäre meines Drangs zu dir kein Hehler.
Ihr, die so vieles hat, fehlt eines bloss
und alles drum — ach wie vermiss' ich ihn —
ihr fehlt doch, Liebste, was mir fehlt: dein Fehler!

Your Flaw

That flaw of yours, that want — I love it, dear;
its's part of you
and ranks with me among your finest features.
When I find out that others have it, too,
I look for it and almost see you near
and love all similarly wanting creatures.

If I, for want of you, that want should miss —
were we to part —
where would I better find my consolation
than in that flaw I love with all my heart?
And when you're gone, with such a want as this
the homeliest would win my admiration.

Yet if there came the fairest of the fair,
and flawless she,
my thoughts of you would linger and keep haunting.
No matter what her charms and virtues be,
her fault would be the flaw that wasn't there —
I would not want her if your want were wanting.

An eine Falte

Wie Gottes Athem seine Fluren fächelt,
so wird es leicht und licht
in diesem klaren Angesicht.
Es hat die Erde gern
und schwebt ihr fern
und liebt und lächelt.

Und Gottes Finger bildete den Bug
vom Ebenbilde.
Es zieht so milde
hin über alles Leid,
und es verzeiht
der edle Zug.

In dich, o unvergesslich feine Falte,
betend versanken
meine Gedanken.
Dass diese letzte Spur
seiner Natur
mir Gott erhalte!

To a Wrinkle

Just as God's breathing fans his plains,
so does your face appear,
candid and clear.
And as it floats above
the earth, in love,
it smiles, sustains.

God's finger, from his image, formed the crease.
It passes gently,
benevolently,
across all past distress.
It promises
forgiving peace.

In you, O tender, well-remembered line,
praying I sought
to rest my thought,
so that this final trace
of godly grace
may remain mine.

Wiese im Park
(Schloss Janowitz)

Wie wird mir zeitlos. Rückwärts hingebannt
weil' ich und stehe fest im Wiesenplan,
wie in dem grünen Spiegel hier der Schwan.
Und dieses war mein Land.

Die vielen Glockenblumen! Horch und schau!
Wie lange steht er schon auf diesem Stein,
der Admiral. Es muss ein Sonntag sein
und alles läutet blau.

Nicht weiter will ich. Eitler Fuss, mach Halt!
Vor diesem Wunder ende deinen Lauf.
Ein toter Tag schlägt seine Augen auf.
Und alles bleibt so alt.

Lawn in the Park
(Janowitz Castle)

Time's standing still. In stopping back I stand
firmly, and as if dreaming, on the lawn,
like in the green reflection here the swan.
And all this was my land.

The many bluebells! Look, and listen too!
Upon the rock is sitting quietly
the butterfly. A Sunday it must be
and everything rings blue.

I won't go farther. Foolish foot, keep hold!
Faced with this marvel, terminate your stride.
A dead day looks at you, eyes open wide.
And everything stays old.

Fernes Licht mit nahem Schein

Fernes Licht mit nahem Schein
wie ich mich auch lenke,
lockt es dich nicht da zu sein,
wenn ich an dich denke?

Wo du bist, du sagst es nicht
und du kannst nicht lügen.
Nahen Schein von fernem Licht
lässt du mir genügen.

Wüsst' ich, wo das ferne Licht,
wo es aufgegangen,
naher Schein, er wehrte nicht,
leicht dich zu erlangen.

Fernes Licht mit nahem Schein
mir zu Lust und Harme,
lockt es dich nicht da zu sein,
wenn ich dich umarme?

Distant Light with Glow So Near

Distant light with glow so near,
close to all I do,
don't you wish that you were here
when I think of you?

You won't tell me where you are
and you cannot lie.
Glow so near from light so far
has to satisfy.

If I knew the distant spot
where the light was lit,
nearby glow would keep me not
from attaining it.

Distant light with glow so near,
light that cheers or harms,
don't you wish that you were here
when you're in my arms?

In diesem Land

In diesem Land wird niemand lächerlich,
als der die Wahrheit sagte. Völlig wehrlos
zieht er den grinsend flachen Hohn auf sich.
Nichts macht in diesem Lande ehrlos.

In diesem Land münzt jede Schlechtigkeit,
die anderswo der Haft verfallen wäre,
das purste Gold und wirkt ein Würdenkleid
und scheffelt immer neue Ehre.

In diesem Land gehst du durch ein Spalier
von Beutelschneidern, die dich tief verachten
und mindestens nach deinem Beutel dir,
wenn nicht nach deinem Grusse trachten.

In diesem Land schliesst du dich doch nicht aus,
fliehst du gleich ängstlich die verseuchten Räume.
Es kommt die Pest dir auch per Post ins Haus
und sie erwürgt dir deine Träume.

In diesem Land triffst du in leere Luft,
willst treffen du die ausgefeimte Bande,
und es begrinst gemütlich jeder Schuft
als Landsmann dich in diesem Lande.

Here in This Land

Here in this land no one gets ridicule
but he who tells the truth. He then must stand
defenseless and attract some smirking, cool
disdain. Nothing dishonors in this land.

Here in this land a person's wickedness,
which elsewhere would lead straight to prison's door,
mints him pure gold, brings glory and success,
and garners honor for him evermore.

Here in this land a gauntlet you must run
of petty thieves with deep contempt for you,
who wish to steal your purse and, when it's done,
will try to win, besides, your handshake too.

Here in this land you never will find rest
when fleeing from contaminated schemes,
for to your house the post comes like the pest
and mercilessly kills your pleasant dreams.

Here in this land you strike an idle blow
if you attempt to hit this wily band,
and every knave will grin and let you know
you're his compatriot here in this land.

Kriegsberichterstatter

Wie? Es gibt Krieg? Wir wissen es von solchen,
die noch ihr dreckiges Ich haben, das erzählt,
in welcher Stimmung sie den Krieg besichtigt?
Ein Schlachtross fänd' es unter seiner Würde
mit seinem linken Hinterhuf die Krummnas'
von sich zu stossen — und die oben sitzen,
empfangen sie, und stehn ihr Red' und Antwort,
verköstigen an ihrem eigenen Tisch
den Auswurf? Wie, war das Ereignis denn
nicht stark genug, den innern Feind zu schlagen?
Er dringt zur Front, macht sich ums Blatt verdient?
Stellt uns den Krieg vor, stellt sich vor den Krieg?
Er wird nicht untergehn? Er lebt? Er dient nicht?
Nicht exerzieren müssen die Gemeinen?
Ist es ein Krieg? Ich denk', es ist der Friede.
Die Bessern gehen und die Schlechtern bleiben.
Nicht sterben müssen sie. Sie können schreiben.

War Correspondents

What? There is war? We get the news from those
who're still their abject selves as they report
to us the mood in which they watched the war?
A war horse would consider it beneath
its dignity to kick that creep aside
with its left hind hoof, yet the men on top
receive him, answer meekly what he asks,
and even wine and dine at their own table
the scum? What? Was what happened not enough
to overcome the enemy within?
He presses to the front? Wins credit for the press?
Presents the war to us, and puts his presence
before the war? He lives, won't perish, doesn't serve?
No base camp is set up to drill the base ones?
Is this a war? It looks to me like peace.
The good ones go. The bad ones need not fight.
We cannot let them die, for they can write.

Mit der Uhr in der Hand

Berlin, 22. September 1916:
Eines unserer Unterseeboote
hat am 17. September im
Mittelmeer einen vollbesetzten
feindlichen Truppentransport-
dampfer versenkt. Das Schiff
sank innerhalb 43 Sekunden.

Dies ist das Aug in Aug der Technik mit dem Tod.
Will Tapferkeit noch Anteil an der Macht?
Hier läuft die Uhr ab, aller Tag wird Nacht.
Du mutiger Schlachtengott, errett uns aus der Not!

Nicht dir, der du da dumpf aus der Maschine kamst,
ein Opfer war es, sondern der Maschine!
Hier stand mit unbewegter Siegermiene
ein stolzer Apparat, dem du die Seele nahmst.

Dort ist ein Mörser. Ihm entrinnt der arme Mann,
der ihn erfand. Er schützt sich in dem Graben.
Weil Zwerge Riesen überwältigt haben,
seht her, die Uhr die Zeit zum Stehen bringen kann!

Geht schlafen, überschlaft's. Gebt Gnade euch und Ruh.
Sonst sitzt euch einst ein Krüppel im Büro,
drückt auf den Taster, hebt das Agio,
denn grad flog London in die Luft, wie geht das zu!

Wie viel war's an der Zeit, als jenes jetzt geschah?
Schlecht sieht das Aug, das giftige Gase beizen.
Doch hört das Ohr, die Uhr schlug eben dreizehn.
Unsichtig Wetter kommt, der Untergang ist nah.

Entwickelt es sich so mit kunterbunten Scherzen —
behüte Gott den Gott, dass er es lese!
Der Fortschritt geht auf Zinsfuss und Prothese,
das Uhrwerk in der Hand, die Glorie im Herzen.

With Stopwatch in Hand

Berlin, 22 September 1916.
On 17 September one of our
submarines sank a fully
loaded enemy troop transport
in the Mediterranean. The
ship went down in 43 seconds.

This is how Death confronts Technology.
Can bravery contribute still to might?
The clock has stopped. The days have turned to night.
O spare us, god of war, this agony!

That was a sacrifice to the machine
and not to you who hurtled from its hole.
Here stood an instrument without a soul —
your proud accomplice — with victorious mien.

There stands a mortar. He who built that gun
seeks shelter in a trench, a wretched coward.
While giants fall, by midgets overpowered,
the clockwork fights with time to stop its run.

Take heed, and take it easy. Otherwise
you'll see a cripple sit behind a desk
and push a button with a grin grotesque —
and London disappears. Surprise, surprise!

The stormclouds gather with destructive power.
What was the time when all this came to pass?
The eye sees dimly in the poison gas —
but hark the striking of the zero hour.

With pranks like that to blow our world apart,
keep God that god from picking up the pieces
as Progress stalks with warhead and prosthesis,
stopwatch in hand, and glory in its heart.

Gebet

Du grosser Gott, lass mich nicht Zeuge sein!
Hilf mir hinab ins Unbewusste.
Dass ich nicht sehen muss, wie sie mit Wein
zur Not ersetzen ihre Blutverluste.

Du grosser Gott, vertreib mir diese Zeit!
Hilf mir zurück in meine Kindheit.
Der Weg zum Ende ist ja doch so weit,
und wie die Sieger schlage mich mit Blindheit.

Du grosser Gott, so mach den Mund mir stumm!
Nicht sprechen will ich ihre Sprache.
Erst machen sie sich tot und dann noch dumm,
es lügt ihr Hass, nimmt an der Wahrheit Rache.

Du grosser Gott, der den Gedanken gab,
ihr Wort hat ihm den Rest gegeben.
Ihr Wort ist allem Werte nur ein Grab,
selbst Tat und Tod kam durch das Wort ums Leben.

Du grosser Gott, verschliess dem Graus mein Ohr,
die Weltmusik ist ungeheuer!
Dem armen Teufel in der Hölle fror,
er fühlt sich wohl in diesem Trommelfeuer.

Du grosser Gott, der die Erfinder schuf
und Odem haucht' in ihre Nasen,
schufst du die Kreatur zu dem Beruf,
dass sie dir dankt mit ihren giftigen Gasen?

Du grosser Gott, warum beriefst du mich
in diese gottverlassene Qualzeit?
Strafst du mit Hunger, straflos setzte sich
der Wucher zu der fetten Totenmahlzeit.

Prayer

Almighty God, avert these eyes of mine!
Grant me a merciful forgetting,
lest I must witness how they take to wine
as mock replacement for the blood they're letting.

Almighty God, dispel this evil day!
To childhood take me back in kindness.
The end is still so very far away,
so strike me — like those conquerors — with blindness.

Almighty God, so let my tongue go numb!
Keep me from mouthing their expressions.
They make themselves not only dead but dumb,
with Truth the victim of their hate-obsessions.

Almighty God, Creator of the thought —
they killed it off by their conniving.
Their word has turned all earthly worth to naught,
with neither deeds nor even Death surviving.

Almighty God, obstruct my ears as well!
The music's pitch is climbing higher.
Poor Satan got the shivers down in Hell —
now he feels cozy in this cannon fire.

Almighty God, Who gave the living breath
to men of science and invention:
that they should pay You back by dealing death
with toxic gases — was that Your intention?

Almighty God, why did You call me here
at just this time so godforsaken?
You smite with famine, yet the profiteer
enjoys his meal unpunished and unshaken.

143

Du grosser Gott, warum in dieser Frist,
wozu ward ich im blutigen Hause,
wo jeder, der noch nicht getötet ist,
sich fröhlich setzt zu seinem Leichenschmause?

Du grosser Gott, dies Land ist ein Plakat,
auf dem sie ihre Feste malen
mit Blut. Ihr Lied übt an dem Leid Verrat,
der Mord muss für die Hetz' die Zeche zahlen.

Du grosser Gott, hast du denn aus Gemüt
Vampyre dieser Welt erschaffen?
Befrei mich aus der Zeit, aus dem Geblüt,
unseligem Volk von Henkern und Schlaraffen!

Du grosser Gott, erobere mir ein Land,
wo Menschen nicht am Gelde sterben,
und wo im ewig irdischen Bestand
sie lachend nicht die reiche Schande erben!

Du grosser Gott, kennst du die Mittel nicht,
die diese Automaten trennten,
wenn sie sich trotz dem letzten Kriegsgericht
bedrohen mit Granaten und Prozenten?

Du grosser Gott, raff mich aus dem Gewühl!
Führ mich durch diese blutigen Räume.
Verwandle mir die Nacht zu dem Gefühl,
dass ich von deinem jüngsten Tage träume.

Almighty God, why did it have to be
this era and this blood arena
where he who still lives on sits down with glee
to feast upon the dead like a hyena?

Almighty God, this country is a scroll
on which with blood they are inscribing
their merry parties. Murder pays the toll.
Their songs make sorrow target of their gibing.

Almighty God, did You perhaps in rage
create the vampire generation?
Then save me from this breed and from this age,
this parasites-and-hangmen type of nation!

Almighty God, find me a land on earth
where money is no lethal tender,
and where a man inherits rights at birth
which he may not for shameful gain surrender!

Almighty God, have You no means at all
to stop these robot politicians
who, fearing not the final trumpet call,
pursue their war with cannons and commissions?

Almighty God, remove me from this scheme
and from this bloodstained path I tread on.
Convert this nightmare into just a dream,
a vision of Your coming Armageddon!

Unter dem Wasserfall

Wer vor mir liess von diesem Wasserfall,
von dieser Sonne sich begnaden!
Wer vor mir stand, das Haupt im All,
stolz an der Ewigkeit Gestaden!

Von Gott bin ich hier eingeladen,
so hoch in Gunst wie jedes Tier,
und hier ist niemand ausser mir,
hier will ich frei von mir mich baden!

Was ich mir selbst schuf, nahm mich selbst nicht auf,
und Wort und Weib, sie wiesen nach den Schatten
und alles Leben wurde ein Ermatten,
zurück in mich lief meiner Welten Lauf.

Nun bin ich zu den Wundern heimgegangen
und auf der Gotteswelt allein.
Hier dieser Sonnenstrahl ist mein.
Wie hat die Schöpfung festlich mich empfangen!

Lust ohne Leiden, Liebe ohne Last,
Naturdrang ohne Scham und Schranken —
ich bin an Gottes goldnem Tisch zu Gast
und hab' mir nichts mehr zu verdanken!

Weit hinter mir ist alles Weh und Wanken.
Wie hat der Wasserfall Bestand!
Wie segnet dieses Sonnenland
vor meiner Nacht mir die Gedanken!

Under the Waterfall

When did this sun, when did this waterfall
bestow such blessings on some other mortal
who, gazing at the universe, stood tall
here at eternity's majestic portal?

Co-equal with all creatures large and small
I've come at the Creator's invitation
and, with no other person within call,
I can indulge in self-purification.

I found no comfort in my past endeavor;
with words and women all portending doom,
my life was steeped in unremitting gloom
while flowing back into itself forever.

Returning to these marvels, I surrender
to God's good earth where now I stand alone.
This ray of sunlight is my very own;
Creation welcomes me in all its splendor.

Sans shame and shyness nature's funds I'm spending,
unblemished beauty, bliss without a blight,
God's golden board beneath its bounty bending —
it's not to me I owe so much delight.

The woes and worries of the world are ending
before this waterfall's enduring state.
This sunny land, how does it elevate
my spirits ere my night begins descending.

Mein Widerspruch

Wo Leben sie der Lüge unterjochten,
war ich Revolutionär.
Wo gegen Natur sie auf Normen pochten,
war ich Revolutionär.
Mit lebendig Leidendem hab ich gelitten.

Wo Freiheit sie für die Phrase nutzten,
war ich Reaktionär.
Wo Kunst sie mit ihrem Können beschmutzten,
war ich Reaktionär.
Und bin bis zum Ursprung zurückgeschritten.

An den Bürger

Dass im Dunkel die dort leben,
so du selbst nur Sonne hast;
dass für dich sie Lasten heben,
neben ihrer eignen Last;
dass du frei durch ihre Ketten,
Tag erlangst durch ihre Nacht:
was wird von der Schuld dich retten,
dass du daran nie gedacht!

My Ambivalence

Where lives were subjugated by lies
I was a revolutionary —
where norms against nature they sought to devise
I was a revolutionary;
when someone suffered I smarted within.

Where freedom became a meaningless phrase
I was a reactionary —
where art they besmirched by their arty ways
I was a reactionary,
backing all the way off to the origin.

To the Bourgeois

That in gloom some are despairing
so that sun be yours alone;
that your burdens they are bearing
in addition to their own;
that their nights your days would earn you,
that their chains your freedom built —
that this never did concern you,
who can rid you of that guilt?

Zwei Läufer

Zwei Läufer laufen zeitentlang,
der eine dreist, der andre bang:
Der von Nirgendher sein Ziel erwirbt;
der vom Ursprung kommt und am Wege stirbt.
Der von Nirgendher das Ziel erwarb,
macht Platz dem, der am Wege starb.
Und dieser, den es ewig bangt,
ist stets am Ursprung angelangt.

Kriegswelt

Sie waren bei Laune, es ging ihnen gut,
nur unser Leben hatten sie über.
Tags waren sie schon betrunken von Blut
und gossen des Nachts noch Wein darüber.

Sie lebten und lachten in Saus und Braus
und konnten nicht über Langweile klagen.
Und gingen ihnen die Menschen aus,
so haben die Zeit sie totgeschlagen.

Two Runners

On the track of time two runners run,
one bold, in fear the other one.
The one from Nowhere his goal acquires,
the one from the Source on the way expires.
The one from Nowhere who reached the goal
makes room for him who paid the toll.
And he who was fearful along his course
has always safely reached the Source.

The Warmakers

They spent their lives in laughter and play
while ours were put on the line.
They got themselves drunk with blood in the day
and chased it at night with wine.

They feasted and threw their weight about,
considering boredom a crime;
and when their supply of people ran out,
they turned to killing time.

Der Flieger

Arsenale zu treffen, wäre nicht ohne,
doch werden nur Kinderzimmer ruiniert.
Vielleicht, wer auf einen Säugling visiert,
zerstört endlich doch einmal eine Kanone!

Expansion

'nen Platz an der Sonne erlangen?
Nicht leicht.
Denn wenn er erreicht,
ist sie untergegangen.

Anschluss

Wenn's zum Anschliessen kommt, bleib' ich verdrossen
und lass meine Hände im Schosse ruhn.
Was hätte ich denn in Deutschland zu tun?
Ich bin an Österreich noch nicht angeschlossen!

The Aviator

Destroying an arsenal would be fun,
but what does he hit? A baby.
Eventually he would hit a gun
if he aimed at a nursery. Maybe.

Expansion

A place in the sun — you want to gain it?
It's hard to get.
For when you attain it,
the sun has set.

Unification

This talk of merger gets me upset —
I care for no Austro-German reunion.
With Germany I have no communion —
I have not even joined Austria yet.

Der Journalist

Die Zeitung ein Mittel,
um etwas zu künden?
Es gilt, zum passenden Titel
das Ereignis zu finden!

Militarismus der Freiheit

Mit ganzem Herzen am Zweck beteiligt,
hab ich vom Mittel mich abgewendet.
Denn jener hätte wohl dieses geheiligt,
hätte nicht dieses jenen geschändet.

Grabschrift

Wie leer ist es hier
an meiner Stelle.
Vertan alles Streben.
Nichts bleibt von mir
als die Quelle,
die sie nicht angegeben.

The Journalist

What paper has yet
sought news to present?
The headline is set —
go, find the event!

Militant Freedom Fighters

They strove for a worthy end, I reckoned,
but then their means my judgment reversed.
The first would have justified the second,
had not the second demeaned the first.

Tomb Inscription

How bare is this place,
the end of my course.
Given up the fight.
There's left no trace
of me but the source,
which they did not cite.

Karl Kraus, 1900
(The dedication is to Annie Kalmar)

I PUT MY PEN TO THE AUSTRIAN CORPSE BECAUSE I PERSIST IN BELIEVING
THERE'S LIFE IN IT.

1908

ARTISTS HAVE A RIGHT TO BE MODEST AND A DUTY TO BE VAIN.

Probably 1915

AT MY DESK AT NIGHT, IN AN ADVANCED STATE OF INTELLECTUAL
ENJOYMENT, THE PRESENCE OF A WOMAN WOULD DISTURB ME MORE
THAN THE INTERVENTION OF A GERMANIST IN MY BEDROOM.

With "Sidi," summer of 1915

TWO PEOPLE DID NOT GET MARRIED. SINCE THEN THEY HAVE BEEN LIVING IN
MUTUAL WIDOWHOOD.

August 1920

I ASK NO ONE FOR A LIGHT. I DON'T WANT TO BE BEHOLDEN TO ANYONE —
IN LIFE, LOVE, OR LITERATURE. AND YET I SMOKE.

Spring of 1929

LET MY STYLE CAPTURE ALL THE SOUNDS OF MY TIME. THIS
SHOULD MAKE IT AN ANNOYANCE TO MY CONTEMPORARIES. BUT
LATER GENERATIONS SHOULD HOLD IT TO THEIR EARS LIKE A
SEASHELL IN WHICH THERE IS THE MUSIC OF AN OCEAN OF MUD.

At Janovice, summer of 1933

I MUST BE WITH PEOPLE AGAIN. FOR THIS
SUMMER — AMONG BEES AND DANDELIONS —
MY MISANTHROPY REALLY GOT OUT OF HAND.

Reading "Promotional Trips to Hell," 1933/34

WHEN I READ, IT IS NOT ACTED LITERATURE;
BUT WHAT I WRITE IS WRITTEN ACTING.

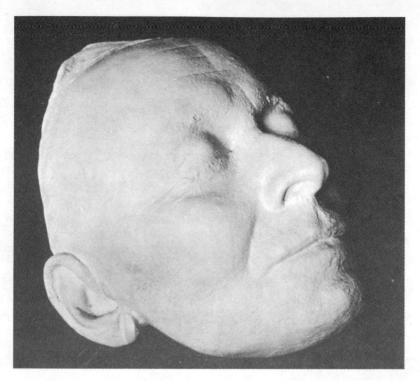

Death mask of Karl Kraus

I DREAMT THAT I HAD DIED FOR MY COUNTRY. AND RIGHT AWAY A COFFIN-LID
OPENER WAS THERE, HOLDING OUT HIS HAND FOR A TIP.

The Last Days of Mankind

Selections arranged and translated

by

Max Knight and Joseph Fabry

Prologue

GRUMBLER: This play, which by earthly standards would take ten evenings to perform, is meant for a theater on Mars. Earthly audiences could not bear it. For it is blood of their blood, and its contents are the contents of those unreal, incomprehensible years beyond the reach of conscious memory, which live on only in nightmares where clowns act out the tragedy of man. The action, running through a hundred scenes and a hundred hells, is improbable, disjointed, and heroless. The events shown in this play, no matter how unlikely, actually took place; the words spoken in this play, no matter how unlikely, are true quotations. News reports stand up as people, and people wither into editorials. Clichés walk around on two legs while men are having theirs shot off. Anyone with weak nerves—even if you were strong enough to live through the period—had better leave the theater. War is a disgrace, but the greater disgrace is that some refuse to hear about it. They can bear the fact that wars exist but not the facts of war. Nevertheless, I am placing these facts on record: this play, my unqualified confession of guilt, the guilt of being a part of mankind, is bound to be welcome somewhere and of use at some time. And "while men's minds are wild," let the high court held among the ruins hear Horatio's message to the future:

And let me speak to the yet unknowing world
How these things came about: so shall you hear
Of carnal, bloody, and unnatural acts,
Of accidental judgments, casual slaughters,
Of death put on by cunning and forced cause,
And, in this upshot, purposes mistook
Fall'n on the inventors' heads. All this can I
Truly deliver.

Act I

Scene 1

Vienna. Ringstrasse next to the Opera House. Summer evening.
Bustle of passers-by coming and going, forming groups.

FIRST NEWSBOY: Extra, extra . . . ! Austria's heir to the throne assaaassinated! Killer arrested!

SECOND NEWSBOY: Extra . . . ! The massacre of Sarajevo! The killer a Serb!

PASSER-BY (*to his wife*): Thank God he wasn't a Jew.

WIFE: Come home. (*She pulls him away.*)

FIRST OFFICER: Hi, Povolny. Well, what do you say ♪ Having dinner at
the Gartenbau ♪

SECOND OFFICER (*with cane*): How can I ♪ It's shut down.

FIRST OFFICER (*perplexed*): Shut down ♪

THIRD OFFICER: Shut up.

FOURTH OFFICER: Touché. Say, that was one helluva good party last night.
Did you notice the unbelievable blonde on the cover of *Muskete?*
A real classic.

SECOND OFFICER: I'll say!

FIRST OFFICER (*to second*): Well, what *do* you say ♪

SECOND OFFICER: Let's eat at Hopfner's instead.

FIRST OFFICER: Good idea—but I meant about politics. Let's hear it from
the political wizard.

SECOND OFFICER: Things are looking great! At last we're going to get a
little action . . . (*Waves his cane.*) It's about time for some excitement
around here.

FIRST OFFICER: You're a real killer. You know who'll get a real kick out of
this ♪ Skunkie.

SECOND OFFICER: Yes, Skunkie is a real patriot. Know what he says ♪
"Doing your duty (*he salutes*) isn't enough. There are times when a
man is called upon to be nothing less than a patriot." Know what I
think ♪ I think we're going to have a crisis. But what do I care.

THIRD OFFICER: How about going to Hopfner's ♪

SECOND OFFICER: You know Slepička von Schlachtentreu ♪ He's such a
highbrow. He reads the *Neue Freie Presse* from front to back. Says we
should read it too. They have a story, he says, that we're for peace, but
not for peace at any price. Think that's true ♪ (*A sexy-looking girl passes
by.*) Look, there's the broad I told you I had for free the other night.

THIRD NEWSBOY: Latest news about the assaaassination! Read all about it!

SUBSCRIBER TO THE NEUE FREIE PRESSE (*talking to Old Man Biach, an inveterate subscriber*): A fine mess.

BIACH: Why mess? Everything's looking up. Glorious times are coming. We've had nothing like it since the days of Maria Theresa. Mark my words!

SUBSCRIBER: But for heaven's sake! Serbia! My son!

BIACH: War is out of the question, remember that. And then—why your son? There are enough other young men. (*Murmuring.*) God is just. Wait till you see tomorrow's editorial in the *Neue Freie Presse*. Only "he" can find the words.* What "he" wrote when Mayor Lueger died will be nothing compared with this! At long last "he" will be able to express himself freely. With caution, of course.

SUBSCRIBER: Maybe the whole story is not true.

BIACH: Pessimist! (*Both leave.*)

DRUNK (*face flushed, voice hoarse from shouting*): Down with Serbia! Down! Hurrah for Habsburg! Hurrah! Hurrah, Serbia!

PASSER-BY (*poking him*): How dare you . . . ?

DRUNK (*stops for a moment, contemplating his mistake*): Down with Serbia! Down! Hurrah! Down with Habsburg! Serbia!

> *In the crowd a hoodlum walks behind a prostitute trying to snatch her handbag.*

HOODLUM: Hurrah! Hurrah!

PROSTITUTE: Let go, you big ape! Let go, or . . .

HOODLUM (*letting go of her handbag*): Why don't you shout "Hurrah"? You call yourself a patriot? A whore, that's what you are—and don't you forget it!

PROSTITUTE: Yeah, and you're a purse snatcher!

HOODLUM: You bitch! There's going to be a war, and don't you forget it!

PASSER-BY: National unity, please! Keep national unity!

THE CROWD (*starting to notice the disturbance*): She's a whore. What did she say?

PASSER-BY: I hear she said something against our most illustrious dynasty!

CROWD: Go and get her! (*The girl manages to duck into a doorway.*) Aw, let her go. The heck with her. Hurrah, Habsburg!

FIRST NEWSPAPERMAN (*to second*): There seems to be plenty of public opinion around here. What's doing?

*"He" refers to Moriz Benedikt, editor of the *Neue Freie Presse*.

SECOND NEWSPAPERMAN: Let's wait and see.

FOURTH NEWSBOY: Extra . . . ! Archduke Franz Ferdinand . . .

INTELLECTUAL: Tremendous loss, this, for the theaters. The Volkstheater was completely sold out, and now has been closed.

HIS WIFE: There's absolutely nothing to do tonight. We should've stayed home, but no, you always have to go out . . .

INTELLECTUAL: I'm amazed at your selfishness. I'd never expected such a lack of social conscience.

WIFE: So you think I don't care. Of course I care. But there's no point eating in a restaurant with a band if the band isn't playing. We might as well eat in a place with good food.

INTELLECTUAL: All you think is food. This is no time to think about restaurants. Great things are about to happen—wait till you see the funeral they'll give him! Never before in history . . . (*Both leave.*)

FIFTH NEWSBOY: Extra . . . !

MAN: Let's have one. How much?

NEWSBOY: Ten hellers.

MAN: That's robbery. The hell with it. Says nothing, anyway. Hey, look at that dame. Gorgeous, eh? Them two fun apples . . . that's where my old lady falls flat.

SECOND MAN: Cool down, Charlie, she's a protestute.

MAN: Hey, look at that crowd in front of the Bristol. Let's go . . . maybe we can see some bigshot. (*They leave.*)

POLICEMAN: Keep moving! Keep moving!

FIRST NEWSPAPERMAN (*to second, as if rehearsing for an editorial*): This is the place to hear the heartbeat of public opinion. Here, at the great square in front of the Opera House, the news spread like wildfire. The gay bustle which ordinarily fills the air at this hour suddenly died down, and mirrored in the faces of the people was dejection, the expression of deep shock, and most of all a quiet sadness. Strangers talked to each other, everybody was buying extras, crowds were forming . . .

SECOND NEWSPAPERMAN: Let's put it this way: Under the chestnut trees of the Ringstrasse at the Opera House groups of people gathered, discussing the news. Policemen kept dispersing the crowd, warning them that the forming of groups was forbidden. Whereupon groups formed, people began to gather . . . look, over there!

A dispute about a fare has arisen between the coachman of a horse-drawn carriage and his passenger. Passers-by take sides; there are shouts of disapproval.

163

SIXTH NEWSBOY: Extra . . . ! Heir to the throne and wife assaaassinated!
COACHMAN: But sir, only five kronen, on a day like this . . . !

Scene 2

Vienna. Terminal of the Southern Railroad. Bathed in pale morning light, a hall from which one can see, through a doorway, the waiting room for members of the court. Black drapes everywhere. In the center of the hall, still visible to those waiting outside, two marble coffins, one standing a step below the other. High candelabras with burning candles. Wreaths. Prayer stools. Black-liveried servants are lighting the last candles and preparing the mourners' reception. In the foreground the crowd is being held back by policemen. Dignitaries, officials in various uniforms appear, remain in the foreground, or disappear toward the waiting room, exchanging silent or whispered greetings. A continuous coming and going. The scene takes place in twilight. The dialogues are those of shadows.

PRIVY COUNCILOR NEPALLECK (*enters deeply depressed, acknowledging condolences from many of those present*): It is a tragedy. His Serene Highness is depressed and too indisposed to attend personally this most illustrious mourning ceremony. What a blow. Here on the right, the most beautiful wreath on the coffin of our Most Serene Duchess was sent by His Serene Highness.

ANGELO EISNER VON EISENHOF (*in deep mourning, steps to Nepalleck and presses his hand*): He was my friend. I stood close to him. For instance, at the opening of the Adriatic Fair. But what is my grief compared with yours, dearest privy councilor.

A door is opened and the hall is filled with representatives of the court, the government, and the church. A master of ceremonies directs each person to his reserved place. People try to enter, present their invitations, and are either admitted or turned away. Ten reporters, in frock coats, are led reverently, without having to show their credentials, past the waiting crowd to the hall where they line up in such a way that they can observe the doorway but block the view for the public. After the reporters have entered, the coffins can

164

no longer be seen. While each of the ten pulls out a notebook, two officials approach the group, and each introduces the other.

ZAWADIL: Spielvogel.

SPIELVOGEL: Zawadil.

BOTH (*simultaneously*): A dismal morning. We've been here since 6 A.M. to make the arrangements.

ANGELO EISNER VON EISENHOF (*steps over to the reporters and speaks gravely to one of them. All begin to write. He points at various people, who then stretch their necks and try to make themselves noticed. Eisner signals to each person that the reporters are taking note of his presence. Meanwhile Privy Councilor Schwarz-Gelber* and his wife have managed to contact the reporters directly and tap one of them on the shoulder.*)

SCHWARZ-GELBER AND HIS WIFE: No power on earth could keep us from being here in person.

ANGELO EISNER VON EISENHOF (*turning indignantly to Dobner von Dobenau, his neighbor in line*): People like that are out of place at a holy ceremony. Probably their first time. What will my friend Prince Lobkowitz think . . . (*He keeps greeting and waving.*) Ah, he noticed me but he didn't recognize me.

DOBNER VON DOBENAU (*with a frozen facial expression, slowly*): As Lord High Steward I would be entitled to stand among the prominent.

DR. CHARAS: The First Aid Service, of which I am president, has come out in force for this occasion but has not yet had many opportunities to assist.

STUKART: As head of the Security Bureau my presence is required as a matter of course, not only because of my social position, but also because of my professional qualifications. No one can blame me — the assassination could not have happened in Vienna.

BUREAU CHIEF WILHELM EXNER: I am here to represent technological interests.

PRESIDENT LANDESBERGER OF THE ANGLO BANK: They call me a business tycoon. Even so, I do not consider it beneath my dignity to take a modest albeit proud place in the line of mourners although the departed pursued ideals different from my own.

HERZBERG-FRÄNKEL: My name is Herzberg-Fränkel. I know that the departed had no particular sympathy for such as us but death reconciles all differences.

---

*Literally Mr. Black-Yellow — the colors of the imperial Austrian flag. Might be rendered as "Mr. Flag Waver" or "Mr. Patriot."

165

The holy ceremony begins. Those gathered in the hall kneel in prayer. In front are the three sobbing children of the murdered couple. At times the voice of the priest can be heard. Organ music.

A REPORTER (*to another*): Write down how they are praying.

Scene 3

South Tyrol, shortly after the start of the war. The approach to a bridge. The car, carrying Grumbler, is stopped by guards. The chauffeur shows his pass.

GUARD: Hello, folks. May I ask . . .

GRUMBLER: At last a civil person. The others are maniacs, ready to shoot.

GUARD: We're looking for a Russian car, full of gold. We stop everybody on the spot.

GRUMBLER: But you cannot stop a car on the spot; it keeps rolling a few feet. Be careful or you'll hurt someone.

GUARD (*furiously*): Christ, if they don't stop, we shoot to kill everybody . . . shoot to kill everybody . . . shoot to kill everybody! (*The car moves on.*)

Scene 4

Across the bridge. Soldiers crowd around the car. The chauffeur shows his pass.

SOLDIER (*gun drawn*): Halt!

GRUMBLER: The car has stopped. Why is the man such a maniac?

CAPTAIN (*furiously*): He's doing his duty. If he's a maniac with the enemy at the front then he's doing all right.

GRUMBLER: But we are not at the . . .

CAPTAIN: War is war! That's all there is to it! (*The car moves on.*)

Scene 5

Optimist and Grumbler in Vienna, talking.

OPTIMIST: You were lucky. In Styria they shot a Red Cross nurse when her car rolled a few feet.

GRUMBLER: The little man has been given power. It's against his nature.

OPTIMIST: In war, one cannot avoid having subordinates overreact when it comes to law and order. That's unfortunate, but in times such as these every consideration must give way to the single thought of winning the war.

GRUMBLER: The new power of the little man will not be enough to finish the enemy, but it's enough to finish this nation.

OPTIMIST: Militarism means more power for the government, and this leads to . . .

GRUMBLER: . . . military dictatorship. In war, everyone pulls rank on everyone else. The military outranks the government, and the government sees no other way out of its humiliation but to turn corrupt. When the government official takes orders from the military man, he accepts the schoolbook myth of heroes whose time is long past, and which, in our time, cannot be allowed to rule over life and death. Military governments make the goat the gardener and the gardener the scapegoat for the resulting destruction.

OPTIMIST: I don't know how you justify such gloom. You generalize just as you did in peacetime. You let a few unavoidable incidents stand for the total picture. You mistake occasional annoyances for serious symptoms. These are great times and you quibble about minor troubles.

GRUMBLER: The troubles will grow with the times.

OPTIMIST: We live in a soul-stirring age that lifts even the humblest man beyond himself.

GRUMBLER: The little thieves who haven't yet been caught will become the big thieves beyond anyone's reach.

OPTIMIST: Even the little man will gain from the war . . .

GRUMBLER: . . . his cut. He will hold out his hand and point to the scars he doesn't have.

OPTIMIST: Just as his government accepts this unavoidable, defensive war for the sake of honor, so also does the individual citizen. Because of the blood that is shed now, the world will one day be covered with . . .

GRUMBLER: . . . filth.

OPTIMIST: Which you always suspect behind everything. Don't you see that you are behind the times? Stay in your corner, if you wish, grumbling. The rest of us are marching forward into an era of reawakened spirit. A great new era has dawned!

GRUMBLER: I knew it when it was *this* small, and it will become so again.

OPTIMIST: How can you still deny greatness? Don't you hear the cheering? Don't you see the enthusiasm? Can any feeling heart remain unmoved? Yours is the only one. Can you really believe that this emotional upsurge of the masses won't bear fruit, that this exciting prelude will have no sequel? Those rejoicing today . . .

GRUMBLER: . . . will weep tomorrow.

OPTIMIST: The suffering of the individual means little. As little as his individual life. The sights of mankind are raised. Man no longer lives only for material gain but also . . .

GRUMBLER: . . . for medals.

OPTIMIST: Man does not live by bread alone.

GRUMBLER: He must also wage war to have it rationed.

OPTIMIST: There will always be bread. But we also live by hope in the final victory, which is never in doubt, and for which we . . .

GRUMBLER: . . . will all starve to death.

OPTIMIST: What lack of faith! How ashamed you will be some day! Don't stand aside when triumphs are celebrated! The gates of the soul are wide open. The memory of the days when we on the homefront were privileged to take part in the feats and sufferings of our glorious army, even if only by reading the daily front reports, will leave in your soul . . .

GRUMBLER: . . . no scars.

OPTIMIST: The nations will learn from this war . . .

GRUMBLER: . . . how to wage more wars in the future.

OPTIMIST: The bullet has left the barrel, and mankind will feel . . .

GRUMBLER: . . . it go in one ear and out the other.

Scene 6

Street in Vienna, in front of a coffee house.

OLD MAN BIACH (*excitedly*): It would be simplest to throw five more divisions against the Russians, and that would be the end of it.

IMPERIAL COUNCILOR: Of course. Attack is the best defense. Look what the Germans have achieved! What force! A thing like that breakthrough in Belgium has never been done before. We Austrians need something like that.

BUSINESSMAN: Tell me, what's the status of your son ?

COUNCILOR: Draft-exempt—one worry less. But the war situation . . . believe me, it doesn't look so good. We do need something like that breakthrough in Belgium . . . a fresh, offensive spirit, that's what we need.

BUSINESSMAN: Give us a second Belgium, and we'll break through, too.

INTELLECTUAL: We need a Bismarck!

BIACH: What's the use of diplomacy ? Let the weapons talk! If we don't break through now . . .

HABERDASHER: Don't worry, they are surrounded.

COUNCILOR: Surrounded, that's it. It means, we have them by the throat.

BIACH (eagerly): By the throat, yes. We must choke off their breath. I wish I could watch such a choking operation.

HABERDASHER: Klein can watch it. He's at army headquarters. Yesterday he reported that we'll bleed them to death. He won't settle for less.

BUSINESSMAN: What luck, to be right in the thick of it! Say, how do you get into army headquarters ? Do you get in only if you're unfit for active duty, or even if you're fit ?

HABERDASHER: What do you mean, fit ? You get in if you can write and don't want to be shot — but want the others to do the shooting.

COUNCILOR: Why doesn't Klein want to shoot ? Because he is humane ?

HABERDASHER: No, because he's cautious. You can't be humane in the army, and being at army headquarters is as good as being in the army.

BIACH: Army headquarters must be a great place! You can see everything. You're near the front, and the front is near the battle, so Klein is almost in combat. He can see everything, but it isn't dangerous.

BUSINESSMAN: They say you don't see anything on a modern battlefield. You can see more at army press headquarters than right in combat.

INTELLECTUAL: True. And you can report about several fronts at the same time.

COUNCILOR: I can't help feeling pessimistic.

BIACH: Why pessimistic ? Lemberg is still ours.

BUSINESSMAN: See ?

INTELLECTUAL: Absolutely no cause for pessimism. If the war were decided now, at worst it would be a draw.

HABERDASHER: The war is as good as won, I have it from a man in the Ministry. We move in from the right, the Germans move in from the left, and we pinch them till they choke to death.

169

COUNCILOR: But what about Serbia ?

BIACH (*wildly*): Serbia ? What *about* Serbia ? We'll wipe Serbia off the map.

COUNCILOR: I don't know. I can't help feeling . . . The news today . . . you have to read between the lines. And if you look at the map, even as a layman you can see that Serbia . . .

BIACH (*irritated*): Forget about Serbia. Serbia is a side show. It only upsets me! Let's go into the coffeehouse, I wonder what the people from the Ministry have to say. Come on, let's listen in from the table next to theirs. (*They enter the coffeehouse.*)

Scene 7

Street in the outskirts of Vienna. A milliner's store, a Pathéphone record store, the Café Westminster, and the dry cleaners Redcotz and Wapp. Four young men enter the street, carrying a ladder, paper strips, and paste.

FIRST YOUNG MAN: Here's one. Look at that: "Salon" Stern, "Dernier Cri" Hüte! Paper it over, all of it!

SECOND YOUNG MAN: Oh, let's leave the name and what kind of store it is. Lemme handle this. Watch. (*He pastes and reads.*) "Sal Stern, Der Hüte." That's it. That's at least German. Let's move on.

FIRST: "Pathéphone." Isn't that French ?

SECOND: No, it's Latin, that's all right. But look, underneath: "German, French, English, Italian, Russian, and Hebrew records."

THIRD: How about that ?

FIRST: It's got to go, all of it.

SECOND: Lemme handle this. (*He pastes and reads.*) "German and Hebrew records." That's it.

THIRD: Hey, have a look at this one. There's one for you. "Café Westminster." Isn't that English ?

FIRST: We can't do anything about this one without checking with the owner. That's a coffeehouse. He may have pull, and we could get into trouble. I'll call him. Wait here. (*He enters the coffeehouse and returns with the owner, who is visibly worried.*) You see the point, dontya ? It's a patriotic gesture.

OWNER: It's inconvenient, but if you gentlemen are from the Volunteer Committee . . .

FOURTH: Say, why did you give your coffeehouse such a name in the first place ? That wasn't very smart.

OWNER: But gentlemen, how could I know ? Now it bothers me, too. The place is near the railroad station where the English lords arrive during vacation time, and I gave it the name so they'd feel at home right away.

FIRST: Did you ever have an English lord in your coffeehouse ?

OWNER: I'll say. Those were the days! Good Lord!

FIRST: Good for you. But now they can't come anyway.

OWNER: Thank God! Down with perfidious Albion! But don't you see, by now people are used to the name. After the war, when, God willing, the English customers will show up again . . . Give me a break!

FIRST: I'm sorry, mister, but public opinion doesn't care about breaks. The public is aroused . . .

OWNER: Yes, of course. I know. We are a public coffeehouse . . . but . . . what shall we call it ?

SECOND: Don't worry, we won't hurt you. (*He scratches off the letter "i" in Westminster.*)

OWNER: Hey, what are you doing ?

SECOND: There. Now you get a painter to put in an *umlaut* u.

OWNER: An *umlaut?* An ü ? Café Westmünster ?

SECOND: Right, an ü. Westmünster means the same as Westminster, and it's German. Perfect. No one knows the difference but still everyone sees it's something else. How do you like that ?

OWNER: Great! Absolutely the greatest! I'll call the painter. And thank you for your consideration, gentlemen. I'll leave it that way for the duration. During the war it'll do. Afterward, of course . . . What do you think the lords would say if they came back and saw the *umlaut?* Their eyes would pop.

Two customers leave the coffeehouse and say goodbye to each other. One says "adieu," the other, "addio."

FIRST: What's that ? Adieu ? Addio ? Frenchmen and Italians patronize your café ? You seem to have an international crowd . . . most suspicious!

OWNER: Now look, just because someone says "adieu" . . .

SECOND: But didn't you hear the other one say "addio" ? That's the language of the archenemy.

THIRD: Treacherous Italy!

FOURTH: The double-crosser at the river Po!

171

The owner has retreated, step by step, into the café.

FIRST: You British dago at the Po!

SECOND: Well, we taught him a lesson with them foreign words. Let's get some more.

THIRD: Hey, look, we're in luck today. Redcotz and Wapp. That's the same mixed brew as the coffeehouse owner's. Redcotz — everybody knows that's a Britisher. And Wapp, that's an Italian!

FIRST: Perfidious Albion and gangster Italy! Paper over the whole thing! We'll teach these drycleaners a thing or two about keeping clean, goddammit. That gets me! By this time tomorrow there isn't gonna be one un-German word in this whole neighborhood.

SECOND (*pastes over the sign.*)

FIRST: But now I've got to quit. I have a rendezvous with my fiancée. Ciao.

SECOND: Oh, bravo! Bon voyage.

THIRD: Cheerio!

Scene 8

In a grade school in Vienna.

TEACHER ZEHETBAUER: Now that higher ideals have burst into full-blown glory upon our horizon, attention to the tourist trade has taken a back seat. That's no cause for alarm, but it's our duty — after we have done our bit for the Fatherland — to continue resolutely and fearlessly along the tried and true road: The tender seeds of the tourist trade which we planted and which (with the help of our esteemed State Board of Education) have become firmly rooted in the fertile soil of your young hearts must not be crushed under the iron heels of our magnificent battalions, indispensable though they are in our heroic age. On the contrary, these seeds need to be nurtured lovingly, now and forever more. In these glorious times, each and every one of us must shoulder a man's burden, and that means you too. As young patriots it is your duty to approach your respected parents or guardians, and ask them to give you, as a birthday surprise, that splendid children's game, "We Play World War," or, with Christmas around the corner, that uplifting entertainment, "Death to the Russians." As a reward for good work and behavior, each and everyone of you should be permitted (with the ap-

172

proval, of course, of your respected parents or guardians) to drive a nail into the statue of the Iron Soldier, thus contributing a mite to this fund-raising endeavor. Every heller you pay to purchase a nail goes into the war chest.

THE CLASS: Oh, goody!

A boy raises his hand.

TEACHER: What do you want, Gasselseder?

GASSELSEDER: Sir, my father already allowed me to drive in a nail. May I drive in another one?

TEACHER: If your respected parents or guardians permit, the school administration will raise no objections to your patriotic zeal. (*Another boy raises his hand.*) What is it, Czeczowiczka?

CZECZOWICZKA: May I be excused, please?

TEACHER: This is no time for excuses. We all have to hold out.

CZECZOWICZKA: I can't, sir. I have to go.

TEACHER: Shame on you. Everyone has to remain at his post.

CZECZOWICZKA: I have an urgent need, sir.

TEACHER: Frivolous personal needs must be put aside in these times of emergency. You'd set a poor example for your classmates. The Fatherland is in need, too. The others hold out, and you must do likewise. Do your share. Help to sell war bonds, collect scrap metal, bring forth the gold that lies idly in your treasure chests. But back to the tourist trade. Promote the latter! I've already explained to you why we must not neglect it at this crucial moment. Although grim war clouds are whipping at the shores of our beloved Austria and our supreme commander is calling to arms thousands and tens of thousands of our sons and brethren, we can observe the first stirrings of an increased tourist trade. Therefore let us never lose sight of this lofty ideal. There is a beautiful story in your reader entitled "A River of Gold." We won't read it now, but let us raise our voices and sing the fine old tune by which we learned the vowels in an age when peace still reigned in our land. "A, a, a, the Winter Went Away." Now, as you know, it has been placed on a war footing, to promote the tourist trade. Let us all join in. (*Takes a violin and plays. The class sings.*)

A, a, a, the tourist brings the hay.
Times of hardship now have ended,
since the tourists have descended.
A, a, a, the tourist brings the hay.

E, e, e, we welcome you with glee.
All our cabs and girls are classy,
both are famous for their chassis.
E, e, e, we welcome you with glee.

I, i, i, we soak you low and high.
Loosen up your gold and riches,
we will take your shirt and britches.
I, i, i, we soak you low and high.

O, o, o, we love you for your dough.
We will sell you songs and schmaltz,
while you dance a Vienna waltz.
O, o, o, we love you for your dough.

U, u, u, and you and you and you.
Come and see the Danube blue
and let it cast its spell on you —
U, u, u — and you and you and you.

Scene 9

Street in Vienna. Two men of draft age meet.

FIRST MAN: Hi there, still in Vienna? Didn't the draft board get you?
SECOND MAN: I went over there and got things fixed up. But what are you
still doing in Vienna? Didn't the draft board get you?
FIRST: I went over there and got things fixed up.
SECOND: Of course.
FIRST: Of course.
SECOND: Wonder what happened to Ed Wagner. Did he get things fixed
up? He was called up in October, but I heard his old man bought him a
Daimler when his major promised to get him into the auto corps, and
then I heard he went to work in a munitions factory — office work, of
course — and then someone said he was classified as essential to the war
effort back in his own business, but I also heard that his uncle — the
sucker who paid for that military hospital on Fillgrader Street — told

him that if worst came to worst he'd get him into the Red Cross. I wonder where the poor devil ended up.

FIRST: I can tell you. His old man, the tightwad, changed his mind about the Daimler and got him a job with a Danish paper company instead. Ed got fed up with that and said he'd rather be in the service. He got assigned to the Blumau munitions factory, but that was a bore. So now he sits in the Chapeau Bar night after night, sometimes in uniform, sometimes in civvies. How he wangled it, I haven't the foggiest. I guess when all that pull didn't work, he just went over there and got things fixed up. Maybe he managed to get a medical exemption.

Well, so long, I have an appointment with a big dealer. I may get an order for a shipment, and boy what a shipment . . .

SECOND: You've always been a lucky dog. Did you hear that Kurt Seiffert was killed in action at Rawa Ruska ? So long now, I've got to run along too — a meeting at the War Welfare Office. Tomorrow they're having a tea and I promised to bring Leggy Peggy along. Be a sport and come too. And bring your doll. Bye now!

Both leave. Enter Old Man Biach and the Patriot.

BIACH: What do you say about the corruption in the French army ?
PATRIOT: Contracts for war materials were drawn up at exorbitant prices.
BIACH: They say some middlemen made enormous profits. Imagine, using middlemen!
PATRIOT: Where ?
BIACH: In France, of course.
PATRIOT: Disgusting.
BIACH: And it is being discussed openly in parliament!
PATRIOT: Couldn't happen here. Luckily we have . . .
BIACH: . . . no parliament, you mean ?
PATRIOT: A clear conscience, I meant to say.
BIACH: Well, and what about Russia ? They were forced to convene the duma, their so-called parliament, and the government had to listen to some very frank words.
PATRIOT: Wouldn't be possible here. Luckily we have . . .
BIACH: I know: A clear conscience.
PATRIOT: No parliament, I meant to say.
BIACH: And what do you say about the harvest ?
PATRIOT: A poor harvest in Italy. A catastrophic harvest in England. Crop failure threatened in Russia. Concern about the harvest in France. And what do you say about the currency ?

175

BIACH: Need I say anything ? The drop of the ruble speaks for itself.

PATRIOT: Heavens, if you compare that with our krone . . .

BIACH: Another currency that looks miserable is the lira — dropped thirty percent!

PATRIOT: And our krone, luckily, only twice that much.

BIACH: Apropos of Italy, did you read about their mess ? The papers in Rome are complaining about insufficient garbage collections. You can draw your own conclusions about conditions there.

PATRIOT: Compare that with our streets in Vienna! They are no dirtier in wartime than in peace. And have you ever seen our papers publish any complaints ? Well, occasionally an interesting feature story like "Garbage Men Fight the Horsefly."

BIACH: We've already done something about that — we've laid off some garbage men. Didn't you read it ?

PATRIOT: Did you hear the latest ? In France they throw people in jail because they're telling the truth. The other day a lady in Paris said Germany was prepared for war and France was not — and she was locked up. Just because she told them the truth to their faces!

BIACH: Yes, they can't take it, those French warmongers. Waging war — yes. Attacking a peace-loving neighbor like Germany, yes. That's the way they are.

PATRIOT: Golden words. Germany is waging a defensive war. No one here expected war. The defense industry was caught completely unprepared.

BIACH: Right. And when a simple woman in France speaks the truth . . .

PATRIOT: No, you are mistaken. She was sentenced because she said Germany was prepared for war.

BIACH: But the truth is that Germany was not prepared.

PATRIOT: But she said it was prepared.

BIACH: That's a lie.

PATRIOT: But she was sentenced because she told the truth.

BIACH: Then what did she say ?

PATRIOT: That Germany was prepared for war.

BIACH: How can she be sentenced for that in France ? For that she should have been sentenced in Germany.

PATRIOT: How come ? Now wait a minute — no — maybe — listen: the way I see it, she told the truth, but in France — the way the country is run — she was sentenced because she lied.

BIACH: No, no, you're all mixed up. What happened was that she lied, and she was sentenced because in France they cannot face the truth.

PATRIOT: Terrible, those conditions in France. What do you say about England ?

BIACH: Their potato prices skyrocketed.

PATRIOT: Yes, and they are still lower than ours were before the war. Imagine the conditions there.

BIACH: And what do you say about how they treat our civilians in Russian camps? Did you read how they suffer? And we pamper the Russian prisoners of war.

PATRIOT: Professor Brockhausen in his splendid article states that we never harass helpless prisoners, not even with words.

BIACH: And in the same issue of the *Neue Freie Presse* the mayor of Lemberg was unhappy because the Russian prisoners were cursed and jostled a little in the streets by a handful of Austrians. Such conduct, he said, was unworthy of a civilized nation.

PATRIOT: He admitted we are a civilized nation.

BIACH: Of course. All these issues show the tremendous difference between us and our enemies, the scum of mankind.

PATRIOT: Take, for instance, the civilized language we use for our enemies who are really the lowest goddam bastards on the face of the earth.

BIACH: And, unlike them, we are always humane. The *Presse* had a kind editorial even about the fishes in the Adriatic who now enjoy all those Italian corpses to feed on. That really is the height of humaneness, in these callous times, to think of the fishes in the Adriatic, when even people must go without food.

PATRIOT: We're not only humane. We are also way ahead in something still more precious: endurance! The enemy is discouraged. They would be glad if it were all over. But we . . .

BIACH: The papers are full of stories about defeatism in France.

PATRIOT: Listlessness in England.

BIACH: Despair in Russia! Cold feet in Italy!

PATRIOT: The mood of the allies is at low ebb.

BIACH (*visionary*): I can hear the crumbling of the walls!

PATRIOT: The heart of Poincaré is filled with fear.

BIACH: The tsar sleeps fitfully.

PATRIOT: Makes you feel good reading about it all. Doubts in London, Paris, Rome. Just look at the headlines — you don't need to read further to know what's up. You can see they are in trouble and we are on top. Our moods, thank God, are of a different sort.

BIACH: Yes, happiness reigns supreme. Confidence, joy, hope, and contentment everywhere. We're always full of cheer — why shouldn't we be?

PATRIOT: Take endurance, for example. We love to endure.

BIACH: Nobody in the world is better at it than we are.

PATRIOT: Particularly the Viennese. We bear all hardships as if they were bliss.

BIACH: Hardships ? What hardships ?

PATRIOT: I mean, *if* we had any hardships . . .

BIACH: Luckily, however, we haven't.

PATRIOT: Right. We haven't. But then, if we have no hardships, what are we enduring ?

BIACH: That's simple. We have no hardships, but we know how to endure them nevertheless — that's the trick. We have always been good at that.

PATRIOT: Correct. Take standing in line. It's fun. It's so popular. People practically stand in line for the privilege of standing in line.

BIACH: The only difference between now and the old days is that now there's a war on. If we didn't have a war, you'd think there was peace. But war is war, and we are forced to do a few things which in the old days we only wanted to do.

Scene 10

The apartment of the actress Elfriede Ritter, returned from Russia just before Russia's entry into the war. Her suitcases are partly unpacked. Reporters Cub, Feigl, and Halberstam are grabbing at her arms, crowding her.

REPORTERS (*all at once*): Do you still show welts from the Cossack whips ? Show us. We need details. How were the Muscovites ? What were your impressions ? You must have suffered frightfully, really you must have!

CUB: Tell us how they treated you like a prisoner.

FEIGL: Give us your impressions of your visit, for our late edition.

HALBERSTAM: Give us your thoughts on returning, for our morning edition.

ELFRIEDE RITTER (*smiling*): Thank you, gentlemen, for your warm interest. It's touching how my dear Viennese have kept a warm spot in their hearts for me. I really appreciate your coming here in person. I was quite willing to put off unpacking my bags, but for the life of me, gentlemen, much as I'd like to oblige, I can't think of anything else to say except that it was very, very interesting, that I experienced no inconvenience at all, that the return trip was tedious, but in no way troublesome, and (*roguishly*) I am deeeelighted to be again in my beloved Vienna.

HALBERSTAM: Interesting — a tedious journey, this much she admits.

FEIGL: "Troublesome," she said.

CUB: Hold it. I wrote the lead at the office. Now, to continue (*he writes*): "Relieved of the tortures of Russia's police-state atmosphere, after a tedious and troublesome journey, the star wept tears of sheer joy to be back in her beloved Vienna . . ."

RITTER (*wagging her forefinger*): I did not say that, dahling. On the contrary, I said that I have no complaints, none whatever.

CUB: Aha! (*Writing.*) "Our star looks back on her suffering with ironic composure."

RITTER: Well, I never . . . I must say . . . no, darling, I'm outraged.

CUB (*writing*): "However, when the visitor prods her memory, she is still outraged. In moving terms she describes how she was deprived of any chance to complain about her treatment."

RITTER: But Mr. Cub, what are you trying to do ? How can I say . . .

CUB (*writing*): "She cannot say . . ."

RITTER: Now really! I cannot possibly say . . .

HALBERSTAM: Aw, come on, you gave no idea *what* you can say! Look, dear lady, the public wants to read. Let me tell you, there's a *lot* you can say. In this country you can. Maybe not in Russia, but here — thank God — we have freedom of speech. Here you can say anything you like about conditions in Russia. Did any newspaper in Russia concern itself with you as we are doing ? Well, there you are.

FEIGL: Miss Ritter, be sensible. A little publicity won't hurt you, now that you are about to appear on the stage again in Vienna. See ?

RITTER: But, gentlemen, how can I . . . you're dragging things in . . . If you had seen . . . in the streets, in the public offices . . . If I had reason for the slightest complaint, say, about some harassment, do you think I would be silent ?

CUB (*writing*): "Shaking with agitation, Miss Ritter describes how the street mob dragged her about; how, upon the slightest complaint, she was harassed by public officials, and how she was forced to keep silent about all her experiences."

RITTER: You're joking! The police officers accepted me with open arms. They were most obliging. I was allowed to come and go where I pleased. I assure you if I had felt like a prisoner even for a moment . . .

CUB (*writing*): "Our star reports that one day she wished to go out, and police officers dragged her home by her arms so that she literally felt like a prisoner."

RITTER: This really makes me furious. I protest . . .

CUB (*writing*): "She gets furious when she remembers these experiences, her fruitless protests . . ."

RITTER: That's not true, gentlemen!

CUB (*looking up from his writing pad*): Not true? How can you say it's not true when I write down every word you say?

FEIGL: And when we want to publish it, you say it's not true.

HALBERSTAM: I have never seen anything like it.

FEIGL: It wouldn't be beyond you to write a correction to the paper.

CUB: You'd better make no trouble. It just might hurt you.

FEIGL: Don't do anything you may regret.

HALBERSTAM (*diabolically*): Isn't she soon due for the part of Gretchen?

CUB: If I tell the producer about this, the part will go to Susi Berger, you can bet on it.

FEIGL: Hasn't Fox always treated you with kid gloves in his reviews? But you don't know Fox! When he hears about this he'll tear you to pieces at your next premiere.

HALBERSTAM: Let me tell you, Wolf didn't like the way you played the lead in his play. He hates the Russians, and if he hears that you have no complaints about them, he'll chew you to bits in his next review.

CUB: I'll say! And Lyon? Better not tangle with Lyon. An actress cannot afford to antagonize the press.

FEIGL: On the other hand, it would do you a world of good with the public and the press if you let it be known that you were mistreated in Russia.

HALBERSTAM: Think it over. You came from Berlin, and Vienna rolled out the red carpet.

CUB: Returning from Russia with no tales of suffering — ridiculous! And a first-rate actress at that! Let me tell you, your career is at stake.

RITTER (*wringing her hands*): But . . . gentlemen . . . I thought . . . darling, please . . . I only wanted to tell the truth. Forgive me, please.

FEIGL (*furious*): The truth you call this? So it's *we* who are lying?

RITTER: No . . . that is to say . . . I thought it was the truth. But if you gentlemen believe . . . you are newsmen, after all, you know better. Please understand . . . I as a woman don't quite have the right perspective, you see? Please try to understand . . . This is a war, we are so easily intimidated . . . One is glad to return safely from a country with which we are now at war.

HALBERSTAM: See, your memory's coming back.

RITTER: But dahling, of course. You know, the first emotional wave of joy to be back again in your beloved Vienna . . . Everything I went through seemed so much rosier . . . only for a moment, of course . . . but then, one is once more overcome by anger and bitterness.

HALBERSTAM: There you are. We knew it all along.

CUB (*writing*): "Anger and bitterness overcome the actress even today, when she remembers the tortures she endured. Now, after the first joyful wave of her return to our metropolis has receded and given way to her terrible recollection . . ." (*He turns to her.*) Well, is it true *now*?

RITTER: Yes, gentlemen, it's the truth. You know, I was still so much under the influence of . . . One is so intimidated . . . so . . .

CUB: Wait. (*He writes.*) "She is still too intimidated to dare speak about it. Now, back in the land of the free, she sometimes still has the nightmare of being in Russia where she had to go through the humiliating experience of being deprived of her civil rights, of free expression of opinion, and of free speech." (*He turns to her.*) Well, it is true now ?

RITTER: Really, dahling, what a gift you have for interpreting the most secret emotions!

CUB: That's better.

HALBERSTAM: Finally, she admits that she suffered . . .

FEIGL: She endured . . .

CUB: What do you mean, "endured"! She lived through hell.

HALBERSTAM: We got our story. Let's go. We aren't here for the fun of it.

CUB: I'll write the last paragaph in the office. We won't worry about your sending in a correction, right ? That would be all we need.

RITTER: But dahling! Delighted you came. Come again soon . . . Adieu, adieu!

FEIGL: That's a sensible girl. So long, honey. (*To the others while leaving.*) Here she has survived a nightmare, and doesn't have the courage even to talk about it, poor kid!

Elfriede Ritter slumps into a chair.

Scene 11

Barracks in Vienna. A well-dressed gentleman, about forty, is waiting in a dirty room without chairs. A sergeant enters.

GENTLEMAN: Pardon me, sergeant, could you please tell me . . . I've been standing here for three hours, and there was no one here to talk to. I was classified for office work only, and I volunteered to start work before my orders came. I was told to stay right here but I'll have to . . .

181

SERGEANT: Shut up.

GENTLEMAN: As you say, but I'll have to let my family know . . . I'll have to get a few things . . . a toothbrush, a blanket . . .

SERGEANT: Shut up!

GENTLEMAN: As you say. But please consider . . . I did volunteer . . . I didn't know . . . I'll have to . . .

SERGEANT: You fat pig, one more word outa you, and I'll slap your trap but good.

The gentleman takes a ten-kronen bill from his vest pocket and offers it to the sergeant.

My dear man, I really can't let you go home, it's against orders. But if you want a blanket I'll see that you get one. (*He leaves the room.*)

A young lieutenant enters.

LIEUTENANT: Are you the one having trouble with the sergeant. Hi. Don't you recognize me ? Wogerer, Athletic Club.

GENTLEMAN: Oh, it's you!

LIEUTENANT: You got a desk-job classification ? Say, how can an intelligent man like you argue with a sergeant ?

GENTLEMAN: What can I do ? I've been standing here for three hours. I have to go home . . . My family has no idea . . . I volunteered . . .

LIEUTENANT: Oh, so you fell for it. Whoever talked you into that ? If you want to go home, you can of course go.

GENTLEMAN: How do I do that ?

LIEUTENANT: Oh, come on, you are a man of the world . . . I'll tell you what to do. You go to the captain . . .

GENTLEMAN: And he'll let me go home ?

LIEUTENANT: Not normally, of course. He's very strict. But you tell him, right to his face, straight, with no words minced, smart (*he salutes*): "Captain, reporting respectfully, I've got to find me a girl!" You'll see, the captain will say, I bet you: "So you're horny for a girl, eh ? Well then, take off, you old stud!" And then you can go.

Scene 12

Room of the Chief of the General Staff, Franz Conrad von Hötzendorf. He stands alone, in contemplation, rocking slightly from side to side.

CONRAD (*looking toward the sky*): If only Skolnik were here now!

MAJOR (*entering*): Your Ex'lency, reporting respectfully, Skolnik is here.

CONRAD: Skolnik ? What Skolnik ?

MAJOR: Skolnik, the court photographer from Vienna who took that beautiful shot of Your Ex'lency pondering the map of the Balkans during the Balkan War.

CONRAD: Oh yes, I seem to recall dimly.

MAJOR: No, Your Ex'lency, he used bright lights, all on you.

CONRAD: Yes, yes, I remember. It was glorious.

MAJOR: He claims that Your Ex'lency called for him again.

CONRAD: Well, I wouldn't say I called for him, but I did drop a hint because the man takes pretty good pictures. He wrote to me he is swamped with requests from the illustrated magazines. His picture of me was a great success, and so . . .

MAJOR: He is also requesting, as long as he is here, to be allowed to take a photograph of the generals.

CONRAD: No. Let them call their own photographers.

MAJOR: He says, since their faces aren't worth the waste of a photographic plate, he really just wants a chance to shoot all their medals.

CONRAD: Ah, that's different. All right, show him in, that fellow Skolnik. Let's see . . . shall I again be pondering the map of the Balkans . . . It was exquisite . . . But, maybe Italy this time for a change . . .

MAJOR: That's definitely more appropriate now.

Conrad spreads out a map and tries out different poses. When the photographer enters with the major, Conrad is absorbed in studying the map of the Italian front. The photographer bows deeply. The major takes a position next to the table. He and Conrad stare fixedly at the map.

CONRAD: What's the matter now ? Isn't it possible, even for a moment, to study a map in privacy ?

MAJOR (*winks at the photographer.*)

SKOLNIK: Just a quick shot, Your Excellency, if I may be so bold.

CONRAD: Here I am busy making world history, and you . . .

SKOLNIK: I've been asked to take a picture for the *Illustrated Journal*, and so . . .

CONRAD: Ah, something for posterity.

SKOLNIK: And also for *This Week*.

CONRAD: But I don't want to wind up on the same page with the generals. I've seen that before. I'd much rather . . .

SKOLNIK: No, Excellency, you may rest assured on that point. In view of Your Excellency's immortal name, Your Excellency's photograph will appear completely by itself. The others will be lumped together under the heading "Our Illustrious War Leaders." Individually, they'd rate picture postcards at best.

CONRAD: All right. And don't forget Höfer. He's smart. Draws a 20,000-kronen bonus for service at the front while he sits in Vienna reading his name in the papers.

SKOLNIK: Noted, Your Excellency. He'll be in the front row.

CONRAD: Front row ? Now let's not overdo things. By the way, where in the magazine will you squeeze me in ? I don't want to be conspicuous, my good man, and not with the others. The subtle touch, always the subtle touch.

SKOLNIK: A space has been specifically reserved for Your Excellency. The cover picture of *This Week*. A most interesting issue. It will contain some shots of models from Vienna, and one of Treumann, the idol of the Vienna stage, but I'm assured that His Majesty, the German Emperor, will also be in the issue — a boar-hunting shot never shown before. So you see that Your Excellency . . .

CONRAD: Well, all right, not bad, not bad . . . But, dear friend, just now I'm rather busy. Couldn't you possibly come a little later . . . I am, confidentially — and don't let this get around — I'm studying the map of the Balkans . . . Ah, what am I saying, I mean the map of Italy.

The photographer wants to step back, but the major winks at him to go ahead.

SKOLNIK: What luck! This is the moment of highest concentration, a moment I must catch. I can see the legend: "Colonel General Conrad von Hötzendorf and his Aide, Major Kundmann, Studying the Map of the Balkans." Ah — what am I saying ? — "of the Italian Front." Would this be all right, Your Excellency ?

CONRAD: All right, then . . . to please Kundmann. He can hardly wait to see his picture in the magazine. (*He keeps staring at the map. The major,*

who has not moved an inch, does the same. Both stroke their mustaches.)
Will it take long ?

SKOLNIK: Just one historical moment, if I may be so bold . . .

CONRAD: What do you want me to do, then ? Continue to study the map
of the . . . of Italy ?

SKOLNIK: Don't let me disturb you, Your Excellency, just continue . . .
just like this . . . entirely unposed . . . casual . . . No, that would look
just a teensy bit unnatural and people might get the idea the picture
was posed . . . Now, Major Kundmann, if you'd be so obliging as to
step back a trifle . . . Now your head . . . fine . . . no, Excellency, still
more casually . . . and boldly, please, a teeny weeny bit more boldly!
The gaze of the Commander-in-Chief, if you'd be so kind . . . It's supposed to be, after all . . . it's supposed to be a histeri- — a historical commemoration of these heroic times . . . So, there, that's just right . . .
Just a bit to the . . . yes, that's it! Would Your Excellency kindly look
grim, please ? There we are, thank you!

Scene 13

Optimist and Grumbler, talking.

OPTIMIST: You put on blinkers so you can't see how much noble spirit
and self-denial the war has brought into the open.

GRUMBLER: No, I merely refuse to overlook the amount of inhumanity
that was necessary to achieve that result. If arson is needed to find out
whether two decent tenants will carry ten invalid tenants out of a
burning house while eighty-eight crooked tenants use the occasion for
looting, there's still no reason to delay calling the fire department and
the police while praising the virtue of man. To prove the virtue of the
virtuous is not necessary; and to give evildoers the chance to become
more evil makes no sense. War, at best, is an object lesson, because it
points up contrasts. It may be useful by teaching us to avoid it in the
future.

OPTIMIST: But you cannot deny that it strengthens those who are forced
to face death; it lifts them to higher spiritual levels.

GRUMBLER: I don't envy Death for having to face so many poor devils
who were abruptly lifted to higher spiritual levels through conscription — if indeed they are lifted.

185

OPTIMIST: Good people become better, and bad ones good. War purifies.

GRUMBLER: It makes good people lose their faith, if not their lives, and makes bad people worse. The contrasts were great enough in peacetime.

OPTIMIST: But haven't you noticed how the war has raised the spirit on the home front?

GRUMBLER: It's raised as the street dust is raised by the brush of the street sweeper. It falls back onto the street again.

OPTIMIST: Nothing changed, then?

GRUMBLER: Oh yes. Dust changes to slime, because after the sweeper comes the sprinkler.

Act II

		Act/Scene of the German original

Scene 1

Vienna. Ringstrasse next to the Opera House. A moving mass of people, among them cripples, invalids, panhandlers, blind people, and figures bent over looking for cigarette butts.

FIRST NEWSBOY: Extra! Eyetalian disaaaster! Eyetalian army annihilated!

SECOND NEWSBOY: Extra! The Amurrican note by Vilson!

FIRST OFFICER: Hi, Povolny. Well, what do you say? I mean about politics. What about America?

SECOND OFFICER (*with cane*): They're bluffing.

THIRD OFFICER: Of course.

FOURTH OFFICER: No question. Say, that was one helluva big party last night . . . Did you see the unbelievable redhead on the cover of *Muskete?* A real classic.

FIRST OFFICER: Know what I think? It's American propaganda.

FOURTH OFFICER: Advertising. Business. They want to sell. The paper says so today.

THIRD OFFICER: If they go to war, it'll be against China.

SECOND OFFICER: No — against Japan.

THIRD OFFICER: Or Japan. It's the same thing. I always get those two mixed up.

SECOND OFFICER: They're bluffing, I tell you. What can they do against our U-boats?

FOURTH OFFICER: That's right, we have them everywhere.

SECOND OFFICER: Besides, even if the Americans do get over here — one Austrian regiment can take care of all their divisions. It will be child's play. (*Runs his forefinger across his throat.*) Kkkch — kaput.

THIRD OFFICER: High time it's peace again.

SECOND OFFICER: I beg your pardon?

THIRD OFFICER: So we could dine again at the Gartenbau.

SECOND OFFICER: Oh, that's what you mean.

FIRST OFFICER: About politics . . . Let's hear it from the political wizard! I keep reading in the papers about a blockade. Tell me, just what is a blockade?

SECOND OFFICER: It's this way: We — that is, the Austrians and the Germans — we form a bloc which they cannot beat, so they turn off the food supplies instead.

FIRST OFFICER: Oh, that's the way it is. Say, is it true that the Socialists are responsible for the Czechs stabbing us in the back ? Hey, look . . . isn't that the dame we met . . . ?

THIRD OFFICER: Right. It's the one from last night . . . She's a knockout. (*Runs after her.*)

THE OTHERS (*calling after him*): Let's meet at Hopfner's afterward!

THIRD NEWSBOY: Eeeresistible advaaance of our troops!

COUNTESS (*to her girl friend*): Look at that chestful of medals on that officer! I bet he fought gallantly! I adore men who fight gallantly! (*They leave.*)

Old tired men pass by singing a sentimental song about returning from the war.

BERLIN EXPORTER (*a thick, expensive cigar in his mouth, to his companion*): Our German boys get over the shock in a hurry. One of our most eminent professors has proved they're adjusting psychologically while still in transit. You Austrians are more scared on the home front than we Germans in combat. You are as blue as your Danube. All that commotion — you can hardly wait till peace breaks out! (*They leave.*)

OFFICER'S WIFE (*to her companion*): Look at them lining up for tomorrow! I don't care if the war lasts ten more years. My husband sends me everything from brigade headquarters. (*They leave.*)

FIRST PASSER-BY: If you don't follow regulations, you're fined. If you do follow regulations, you die.

SECOND PASSER-BY: What do you mean ?

FIRST PASSER-BY: Didn't you read about the professor who starved to death ?

SECOND PASSER-BY: How come ?

FIRST PASSER-BY: He didn't buy on the black market but tried to live on his rations.

SECOND PASSER-BY: Crazy fool! (*They leave.*)

FIRST PATRIOT: When the first attack comes, take my word . . . (*Runs his forefinger across his throat.*) Kkkch — kaput!

SECOND PATRIOT: And the Jews are next — the works! (*They leave.*)

A stout lady in Red Cross uniform, with a lorgnette, alights from an electric car.

CAPTAIN OF THE CAVALRY (*rushing to her and kissing her hand*). Baroness! How sensational! Not on vacation ? How fetching you look in your uniform!

BARONESS: So do you, in yours. How about breakfast at the Bristol? My husband is waiting.

CAPTAIN: The better half. Delighted. You're working for the Red Cross — sensational!

BARONESS: Works out fine. This way I can keep the car. My husband had trouble keeping it, so I decided to join the Red Cross. Between you and me, the work is just a formality . . . a status symbol. Actually, I nurse . . .

CAPTAIN: You really do?

BARONESS: I nurse a grudge because they would not let me have my car without this Red Cross bit. But the war will be over soon, so what do I have to lose? How smart you look in your uniform, much better than in civvies. I bet that's why you're wearing it. Right? Oh, you men!

CAPTAIN (*flattered*): You really think so?

BARONESS: And the Distinguished Service Cross! Wellwellwell!

CAPTAIN (*with false modesty*): Oh, it's nothing.

BARONESS: You might even get the notion to serve at the front. Did you ever?

CAPTAIN: I can't . . .

FLOWER GIRL (*passing by*): Yellow pansies!

CAPTAIN: . . . the Board of Directors won't let me. I insisted, but . . . (*Both leave.*)

FIRST MAN: Whatever happened to your artist friend? Did he land a soft job in the army?

SECOND MAN: Well, yes. First he designed crosses for cemeteries . . .

FIRST MAN: Great!

SECOND MAN: But then the gravy dried up and he was transferred to a marching battalion.

FIRST MAN: Oh, too bad!

SECOND MAN: But he got a break. His captain turned out to be a lover of art.

FIRST MAN: And?

SECOND MAN: So now he draws nudes for the captain.

FIRST MAN: Great!

A gentleman gets out of a horse-drawn carriage.

COACHMAN (*holding out his hand*): But sir, my fare comes to much more . . . (*Turning over his hand.*) Look at those scars . . .

Scene 2

A gun emplacement at the front.

ARTILLERY OFFICER: Look at that; here's our army chaplain visiting from his infantry post. Isn't that nice of him!

CHAPLAIN: God bless you, my good people. God bless our arms. Are you letting the enemy have it, with the cannons?

OFFICER: Right on the button, father.

CHAPLAIN: God willing, I'd like to try a shot.

OFFICER: Help yourself, father. I hope you hit a few Russkies.

The chaplain fires a shot.

CHAPLAIN: Boom!

Shouts of "Hurrah!"

OFFICER (*to his men*): There is a good and noble priest! And a native son of our beautiful Styria, too! I'll have to send in the story to our local paper in Graz. (*To the chaplain.*) This regiment of boys from Styria is proud of its field chaplain and brave fellow fighter who is setting a great example for us. (*Shouts of "Hurrah!" The chaplain leaves.*)

OFFICER: Now that our father has fired a shot, our arms have been blessed.

ALICE SCHALEK (*a woman war correspondent, at the head of a group of male correspondents*): Thank you, my brave countrymen! We have pushed ahead to this advanced position. I wish it were more advanced, but it's a good beginning.

CANNONIER (*spitting*): Morning.

SCHALEK: Lord, how fascinating. There he sits as though carved from wood. I think there's even a hint of a twinkle in his eye. The common man, in person. What are you thinking? What emotions are sweeping your soul? Why did I never before the war see these splendid figures I now meet every day? Some on the home front may call the war the abomination of the century — I did so myself when I still sat at home. But those in it are gripped by the fever of the adventure. Call it patriotism, you idealists; hatred of the enemy, you nationalists, call it sport, you modern men; adventure, you romantics; call it blissful strength, you students of mankind — *I* call it liberated humanity!

191

OFFICER: What do you call it ?

SCHALEK: Liberated humanity.

OFFICER: If only they would give us a furlough once in a while!

SCHALEK: Say, lieutenant, I'd like to take a potshot.

OFFICER: I wish I could let you, ma'am, but not right now — it might alert the enemy. We're having a lull in the fighting and we're glad . . .

SCHALEK: Aw, come on, don't be difficult. You let the chaplain, so why not me ? Why do you think I've come all the way out here ? You know my reports are always based on personal experience.

OFFICER: I know, but I can't take any responsibility . . .

SCHALEK: But I can! Let me at it. How do you shoot this thing ?

OFFICER: Like this.

Schalek fires a shot. The enemy shoots back.

OFFICER: Now you've done it.

SCHALEK: What do you want ? That's fascinating! I'm gripped by the fever of the adventure! Lieutenant, tell me, what are you thinking ? What emotions are sweeping your soul ?

Scene 3

Optimist and Grumbler, talking. A group of gray-bearded recruits walk by.

OPTIMIST: Look, they're marching to war.

GRUMBLER: They're not marching, they're being marched. In Germany they're even beyond that stage.

OPTIMIST: What do you mean ?

GRUMBLER: In Karlsruhe I saw a poster saying, "Free the Soldiers!" At the gate of army headquarters.

OPTIMIST: I don't believe it — that would be revolution! How can army headquarters . . . ?

GRUMBLER: They are looking for office help, and want civilians to volunteer so the soldiers doing office work can be sent to the front. Therefore: "Free the Soldiers!"

OPTIMIST: Your grumbling doesn't even stop at army headquarters.

GRUMBLER: I memorized verses from another poster at a police station. They go like this:

> Beat the rascals, beat the traitors,
> throw them in volcanic craters!
> Boil them in hot lava masses,
> kick the bastards in their asses!

> Kick their balls and kick their butts,
> kick them till they spill their guts!
> Rip all feelings from your heart,
> rip those criminals apart!

> Fill with dynamite their valleys,
> bomb their picnics, parties, rallies!
> Bash the skulls of everyone,
> and be proud to be a "Hun"!

OPTIMIST: This could have been written in other countries, too.

GRUMBLER: You may be right. In England they may write something like this after a few more years of compulsory military service. Every country will eventually come to understand that valleys were created to be filled with dynamite. But the line, "kick them till they spill their guts!" has real German flavor.

OPTIMIST: An outburst of brutality. Could've been written anywhere.

GRUMBLER: Not in England, yet.

OPTIMIST: Even in Germany it's an isolated instance.

GRUMBLER: Which, however, could happen only in Germany. And the fellow who concocted that piece of poetry sits in an office and jumps when a paper bag is popped.

OPTIMIST: So?

GRUMBLER: But at the front he becomes a passionate murderer who finishes off a dying man with his bayonet, brags about it at home, and jumps again when a paper bag is popped.

OPTIMIST: What does that prove? There are good and bad people in the world.

GRUMBLER: Including editorial writers and churchmen. A sermon for peace is not as effective as an editorial for war. But since all sermons are preached to support war . . .

OPTIMIST: I'll admit, that wasn't the method of salvation prophesied at Bethlehem.

GRUMBLER: Oh, but Bethlehem in the United States corrects the mistaken prophesies of nineteen hundred years ago.

OPTIMIST: In the United States?

GRUMBLER: Bethlehem Steel, the greatest arms manufacturers in the world. Every German church contributes its mite to that new spirit of Bethlehem.

OPTIMIST: A mere coincidence that Germany's enemies are supplied with arms by a company called Bethlehem.

GRUMBLER: Headed by Germans.

OPTIMIST: You must be joking. The American steel trust is headed by Carnegie.

GRUMBLER: No, by Charles M. Schwab.

OPTIMIST: What? German-Americans produce weapons for the enemy?

GRUMBLER: No, German nationals.

OPTIMIST: Who says so?

GRUMBLER: The *Wall Street Journal*. It says that twenty percent of the Bethlehem stock is held by Germans — not German-Americans, but German nationals. And why not? Business is business.

OPTIMIST: In politics, success is success. That's why I think that the sinking of the *Lusitania* will not fail to impress the world.

GRUMBLER: Yes, indeed. At least that part of the world where people are not yet numb to horror. The reaction in Berlin is characterized by an announcement in a cabaret showing a film about the catastrophe. It says: "The Sinking of the *Lusitania*. See It As It Happened! During This Number Smoking Is Permitted."

OPTIMIST: A lapse of taste. But to me the *Lusitania* is not a matter of sentiment.

GRUMBLER: No, it's a matter of crime.

OPTIMIST: The people had been warned.

GRUMBLER: What you call a warning was a threat to commit a crime — the mass murder was preceded by blackmail. A blackmailer cannot plead innocent for having announced his crime in advance. If I threaten to kill you unless you do what I have no right to ask you to do, I'm not a warner but a blackmailer. And afterwards I'm not an executioner, but a murderer. Smoking permitted. My country right or wrong; so what if a few children are drowned.

OPTIMIST: The U-boat had no choice but . . .

GRUMBLER: . . . to play the part of the iceberg that struck the *Titanic* a few years back. At that time it was the wrath of God about the

194

arrogance of this technical age that tried to teach man through horror what he wouldn't learn through reverence. But now the God of technology does the teaching — that's progress. As the smasher of the *Titanic*, the name of the Lord was still mentioned. This time the heroes of the U-boat remained anonymous. The story that the captain received an award is branded enemy propaganda.

OPTIMIST: Of course, the captain has no such claim to heroism as, say, William Tell.

GRUMBLER: Why not? His *deed* is being praised as heroism, instead of being kept secret like his name.

OPTIMIST: The deed may not be heroic but it served a purpose. The *Lusitania* carried arms that would have killed Germans.

GRUMBLER: And were manufactured by Germans.

Scene 4

Two retired privy councilors meet on a street.

FIRST PRIVY COUNCILOR: Can't wait to see if the *Journal* will publish my poem tomorrow. The *Journal* is my favorite paper, you know. Sent in the poem yesterday. Want to hear it? Here . . . (*Takes a sheet of paper from his pocket.*)

SECOND PRIVY COUNCILOR: You wrote another poem, eh? What about?

FIRST: You'll see what it's about. "Violent Night." Instead of "Silent Night," get it? (*He sings.*)

Silent night, holy night.
All is calm, all is bright . . .

SECOND: But . . . funny . . . that's my poem!

FIRST: What? Yours? It's a Christmas song. But listen, you'll hear the difference. I'll sing you my version. (*He sings.*)

Violent night, victory night,
don't be calm, plan to fight.
Round yon cannon, the gunner gets wild,
shoots a Frenchman with mother and child.
They sleep in heavenly peace,
they sleep in heavenly peace.

195

Isn't that funny how I made it fit? I just put in the cannon instead of the Virgin, and the Frenchman instead of the Holy Infant. If the *Journal* publishes it, I'll send it to the staff chaplain. I'm a great admirer of his.

SECOND: Now this is really funny. Because yesterday I wrote exactly the same poem. I meant to send it to *Muskete*, but . . .

FIRST: You say you wrote the same poem? Oh, come off it.

SECOND: But I changed more than you did. It's called "In England." (*He sings.*)

> Island night, English night.
> Do you have an appetite?

FIRST: But yours is different. It's more humorous.

SECOND (*sings*):

> Eat your words now, my treacherous child.
> You cooked your goose, but it's still running wild.
> No, you won't eat your geese,
> till you come begging for peace.

FIRST: It's funny. It's like telepathy.

SECOND: But now I've done this work for nothing. I'll see if yours is published. If the *Journal* prints yours, I can't send mine to *Muskete*. They might think I parodied you.

Scene 5

An office room at an army command post.

MEMBER OF THE GENERAL STAFF (*telephoning*): Hi there. Have you finished your report on Przemysl? Not yet? Not quite awake yet, eh? Come on, get it done, or you'll be late for our party tonight. What, you forget the directives again? Ah, you people . . . ! Now listen, here are the main points once more: First, the fortress wasn't worth the trouble — that's most important. What do you say? Impossible to make the public — what? Make the public forget that this fortress has always been the pride of . . . Oh, one can make the public forget

196

everything, my friend. Now listen: The fortress wasn't worth a hoot, the armaments were old junk ... What ? The most modern guns ? Junk, I'm telling you, understand ? All right, then. Secondly, now pay attention: Not taken by force of arms but by hunger! Get it ? At the same time, don't stress the angle of insufficient supplies too much — you know, play down the bungling, the mixups. Hunger, that's the main point. Pride in hunger, get it ? Not by hunger but by force of arms ... ah, what am I saying! Not by force of arms but by hunger! Yes, that's it ... What, won't work ? People will say that supplies were short ... What ? And will wonder how come ? Awright, let 'em have it their way and say: Impossible — can't pile up as much food as is needed because the enemy will get it when he takes the fortress ... What ? How could he, then, take the fortress through hunger ? No, in that case, of course, by force. Don't ask so many questions! Can't you get it through your head ? If he takes the fortress by force and we have a lot of supplies, then he will also take the supplies! That's why we mustn't have many supplies so he won't get them. So he takes the fortress by hunger and not by force. Oh, you'll know how to handle it. Got to run now, to the mess hall — have no intention to surrender through hunger. So long.

Scene 6

Restaurant. Grumbler at one table.

WAITER: Have you ordered yet ?
GRUMBLER: May I see the menu ?
WAITER (*hands him the menu.*)
GRUMBLER: What's ready to eat ?
WAITER: What it says on the menu.
GRUMBLER: It says here, "Down with Perfidious Albion." That's not my dish.
WAITER: Maybe some Fatherland mutton with Valhalla nectar ?
GRUMBLER: Fatherland mutton with Valhalla nectar ?
WAITER: It used to be English mutton with Worcestershire sauce, before the war.
GRUMBLER: Which they think they can win by renaming food. What is "Wicked rabbit" ?
WAITER: Used to be Welsh rabbit.

GRUMBLER: And what in the world are "Traitor's noodles"?

WAITER: Spaghetti.

GRUMBLER: Of course. Well, let's see. Bring me some Teutonic ersatz steak with warmonger fries, and apple pie à la Kaiser.

WAITER: Yessir. (*Exits.*)

MAJOR BATTLEDASH (*shouting and banging on the table*): Goddamit, what's the matter with the service here? Hey, you there, eyes right!

WAITER: Be with you in a moment, major.

OWNER: What can I do for you, major?

MAJOR: You can get me something to eat. Why is the service so lousy? Where are all your waiters?

OWNER: At the front, major.

MAJOR: At the front? Why are they all at the front?

OWNER: Because there's a war on, major.

MAJOR: You're down to four waiters. For such a large place! I've noticed it all year.

OWNER: Since the war started, major.

MAJOR: Preposterous! I want you to know the other officers are complaining, too. They won't patronize your place if things don't change.

OWNER: Yes, major, we all hope things will change and we'll have peace again.

MAJOR: Peace? I don't want to hear any of this whining about peace. I took part in the Emperor Maneuvers. What if our supreme commander could hear you? Endurance, my friend! Endurance is the call of the hour! (*Waiter passes by.*) Hey you, attention! Hup, two, three, four! Come here or I'll send you to the front! (*To the Owner.*) See what kind of service you have around here?

OWNER: What would you like to order, major?

MAJOR: A steak, rare, with . . .

OWNER: Sorry, but today is meatless Monday.

MAJOR: Meatless Monday? What kind of a trick is that?

OWNER: There's a war on, major.

MAJOR: Cut those excuses. What does the war have to do with your running out of meat? It's never happened before!

OWNER: But now there's a war on, major.

MAJOR (*jumping up in excitement*): Stop rubbing it in. War! War! That's all you know. The other officers will hear about this place. And you won't see any of them eating here again! (*Runs off.*)

Scene 7

Optimist and Grumbler, talking.

OPTIMIST: Well then, in your opinion, what is a hero's death?

GRUMBLER: An unfortunate accident.

OPTIMIST: If our Fatherland thought that way it would be in poor shape.

GRUMBLER: Our Fatherland does think that way.

OPTIMIST: It calls a hero's death a misfortune? An accident?

GRUMBLER: Just about. It calls it a cruel blow.

OPTIMIST: Who? Where? Every military obituary speaks of the privilege for the soldier to die for his country. In death notices, the plain citizen who ordinarily might have spoken of a cruel blow of fate, announces in simple words, proudly if you will, that his son has died a hero's death. See here, for instance, in the *Neue Freie Presse*.

GRUMBLER: I see it. But turn a few pages back. Here the chief of the General Staff, Conrad von Hötzendorf, thanks the mayor for his condolences "on the occasion of the cruel blow of fate" when Baron Conrad's son was killed in the war. He used the same words in the death notice. You're quite right that every little shopkeeper who loses his son accepts the official line and poses as a hero's father. But the chief of the General Staff drops the mask and expresses the plain old feeling — justified here as for no other death — that is contained in the conventional phrase, "cruel blow." A Bavarian princess congratulated her relative on the hero's death of his son: on such high levels of society there is a certain obligation to glorify the murder of one's child. But the chief of our General Staff not only accepts condolences, he also laments the cruel blow of fate. This man, who is more intimate with that fate than the soldiers who are killed by it and their fathers whose hearts are broken by it — this man speaks of its cruel blow. He speaks the truth, and the others are lying.

OPTIMIST: No, they're not lying. The people see the hero's death as something glorious, and the prospect to die on the field of honor is soul-stirring for the nation's sons.

GRUMBLER: And also for its mothers, I'm sorry to say. They have surrendered their power to save our era from this disgrace.

OPTIMIST: Apparently they have not yet advanced to your subversive thinking. And neither has the rest of our country. Our leaders must think as patriots. The case you mentioned was incidental. Baron Conrad simply wrote a conventional phrase. He was caught unawares . . .

GRUMBLER: Yes, with an emotion.

OPTIMIST: At any rate, the case proves nothing. But here I want to show you an item proving the miraculous unity that joins all classes in these times of common suffering. I'll read it to you so you'll get the impact of every word: "Official release from the Ministry of War. The wire services report: The Imperial Ministry of War has declared the emperor's birthday a special holiday for all workers in munitions factories. The Ministry takes this opportunity to pay tribute to the workers who, through their loyalty and their untiring efforts, have helped our glorious armed forces to gain sublime laurels by their death-defying heroism." Well? (*The Grumbler is silent.*) You don't seem to be able to find words. The Social Democratic press prints this item under the headline "The Workers' Achievement Is Recognized." And many of these workers will be unhappy to get only one day off, even if it is the emperor's birthday . . .

GRUMBLER: That's true.

OPTIMIST: . . . instead of getting the satisfaction of being released from factory work altogether . . .

GRUMBLER: True again.

OPTIMIST: . . . and having the opportunity actually to use at the front the ammunition which they so far have been allowed only to produce. These brave men must be heartbroken that they can join their compatriots only through the work of their hands and not also through death-defying bravery. The opportunity to serve at the front is the highest reward that can be given to any mortal.

GRUMBLER: Mortality seems to be the main prerequisite for being a soldier. You really believe that combat service is considered the highest reward — by the recipient?

OPTIMIST: Yes, I believe that.

GRUMBLER: Maybe so. But is combat service also bestowed as a reward?

OPTIMIST: Why, of course. You seem lost for words.

GRUMBLER: You're right. All I can offer you, in place of my own words, is the official text of an announcement. I'll read it to you so you'll get the impact of every word.

OPTIMIST: From a newspaper?

GRUMBLER: No, a newspaper would hardly be the place for such a thing. It would come out as a censored, white space. The announcement I want to read to you is posted in factories that, having been placed under government protection, have managed to suppress worker unrest.

OPTIMIST: But you've just heard how enthusiastically the workers support the war effort, and that they are restless only because they cannot participate more directly. Even the Ministry of War acknowledges their dedication.

GRUMBLER: You seem to want to supply the words I was not able to find. Let me read what the Ministry of War itself has to say: "June 14, 1915. It has come to the attention of the Ministry that the discipline and morale of workers in many factories operating under the War Production Law has been extremely unsatisfactory. Insubordination, arrogance, rebellion against management, passive resistance, wanton destruction of equipment, absenteeism, are among the offenses against which even criminal proceedings often prove ineffective . . ."

OPTIMIST: Clearly the men are impatient to get to the front. The glory is withheld from them . . .

GRUMBLER: No, it is offered to them. Let me continue: "The Ministry of War, therefore, is compelled to decree that such cases are to be prosecuted to the fullest extent of the law. Penalties to be inflicted are severe and can be made more so by special punitive measures. In addition, those convicted are not to be paid any wages during their prison terms, in order to make them an even more effective deterrent . . .

OPTIMIST: Well, yes, those are harsh penalties. And in addition such men forfeit all hope of being sent to the front.

GRUMBLER: Not quite. Quote: "After completion of their sentence, workers of draft age who were found to have been ringleaders are not to be returned to their places of work but are to be handed over to their local induction posts for reclassification and immediate combat service with the nearest march battalion." Unquote. (*The Optimist is speechless.*) Signed for the minister by General Schleyer with his own hand. *You* seem lost for words now. You see, the men who are pining for the blessings of combat service are being assigned to it as a punishment.

OPTIMIST: Even as a special punitive measure!

GRUMBLER: The Fatherland regards the opportunity to die for the Fatherland as the most severe punishment. The citizen regards it as the highest honor. He wants to die a hero's death. Instead he is called up and attached to the nearest march battalion. He wishes to volunteer and is being volunteered instead.

OPTIMIST: I can't believe it — a punishment!

GRUMBLER: There are degrees. First, corrective measures. Second, court penalties. Third, special punitive measures. And fourth, the most severe punishment: combat service. The incorrigibles are sent onto the field of honor. The ringleaders! Repeaters are sentenced to the hero's death. For the chief of the General Staff, the hero's death — if his son suffers it — is a cruel blow of fate. The Ministry of War calls it a punishment. Both are right. The first words of truth spoken in this war.

OPTIMIST: You make it difficult to be an optimist.

Scene 8

A hangar somewhere near the Adriatic Sea.

ALICE SCHALEK (*enters, looking around*): What fascinates me most in war is individual courage. Even before the war I often speculated about the essence of heroism — I often met men who lived dangerously: American cowboys, pioneers in the jungle, missionaries in desert countries. These men looked the part of heroes, every muscle taut as if forged of steel. How different are the heroes one meets in the Great War! These men are given to telling boyish jokes, quietly craving hot chocolate with whipped cream, and then nonchalantly describing experiences which must be classified among the most amazing stories of world history. And yet . . . (*A lieutenant has entered.*) I don't have much time, so be brief. You are a bombardier — what emotions does dropping bombs arouse in you ?

LIEUTENANT: Usually we circle over the enemy coast for half an hour, drop a few bombs on military targets, watch them explode, take a few pictures, and return to base.

SCHALEK: Have you faced death ?

LIEUTENANT: Yes.

SCHALEK: What were your emotions ?

LIEUTENANT: My emotions ?

SCHALEK (*aside*): He eyes me a bit dubiously, unconsciously wondering how much understanding he can expect for feelings still in ferment. (*Aloud.*) We noncombatants have such stereotyped concepts of courage and cowardice that the man at the front is afraid he won't be able to communicate to us his vast range of changing emotions. Have I guessed right ?

LIEUTENANT: You are a noncombatant ?

SCHALEK: Do not resent it. You are a combatant, and I'd like to find out how it feels. Most of all: how do you feel afterward ?

LIEUTENANT: Well, it is strange. I feel like a king who has suddenly become a beggar. You know, it feels almost like being a king, so high above the enemy city. There they are below — helpless. No one can run away, no one can save himself or hide. You have power over them all. It's majestic — all else becomes insignificant. Nero must have felt that way.

SCHALEK: I can identify with that feeling. Did you ever bomb Venice ? . . . What, you have scruples ? Well, I'll tell you something. Venice is a problem worth thinking about. We entered the war filled with romantic ideas . . .

LIEUTENANT: Who did ?

SCHALEK: We did. We intended to wage it with chivalry. Slowly and after painful lessons we had to change our attitudes. As recently as a year ago, who among us wouldn't have cringed at the thought of dropping bombs on Venice! And now ? Everything has changed. If Venice shoots at our soldiers, we have to shoot at Venice — calmly, openly, and without sentimentality.

LIEUTENANT: Don't worry. I've bombed Venice.

SCHALEK: Good for you.

LIEUTENANT: In peacetime I used to spend my vacations in Venice. I loved it. But when I bombed it from the air — no, I didn't feel a spark of false romanticism. We all flew home, happily. It was our day of honor — our day!

SCHALEK: That's what I wanted to hear! Now your buddies from the U-boats expect me. I trust they are as gallant as you! (*Exits.*)

Scene 9

In a U-boat that has just surfaced.

MATE: Here they come!

OFFICER: Quick! Down again! . . . No, it's too late.

Members of the press headquarters enter, led by Alice Schalek.

OFFICER: Gentlemen, yours are the first faces we see. It's a strange feeling to see daylight again.

REPORTERS: Well, tell us, how does it feel to be down there ?

OFFICER: Terrible. But up here . . .

REPORTERS: Give us details. Are these here the torpedo tubes ?

MATE: No, that's a sighting hood.

REPORTERS: Aren't these the diesel motors?

MATE: No, these are the water tanks.

OFFICER (*to Schalek*): Why so quiet?

SCHALEK: I feel as though I've lost my power of speech. May I touch on a delicate problem? Tell me, what did you feel when you drilled that colossus of a ship into its wet and silent grave with so many human beings aboard?

OFFICER: My first feeling was one of unmitigated joy.

SCHALEK: That's what I wanted to hear! I have now gained a conviction: The Adriatic Sea will remain ours!

Scene 10

A factory placed under war emergency administration.

MILITARY SUPERVISOR: Chains, whipping, arrest, and — well — reclassification. That's all we can do to make 'em work. Not much, but that's all we've got.

FACTORY OWNER (*a dog whip dangling from his arm*): I try kindness as long as possible. (*Points to the dog whip.*) But what can you do if those union swine keep stirring up trouble — negotiations about working conditions, complaints about food? How can we keep the plant going with all their legal claims, demands for better terms, insistence on workers' rights in wartime . . .

SUPERVISOR: Yes, I know. My remedy is to reclassify 'em — including, if possible, the union representatives. We've milked the War Production Law for what it's worth. We've done pretty well by it. Take the story of the blacksmiths and mechanics last August 14. In the morning they still earned six kronen for piece work; at noon we transferred 'em to military authority and told 'em they were soldiers now; and in the afternoon they did the same work at the same place for soldier's pay. Not one let out a peep.

OWNER: Good for you.

SUPERVISOR: They complained about rough treatment only once. I had 'em report to me and asked 'em who had given 'em ideas. This bastard answers: "We're organized workers and asked our unions for advice, and they sent us a couple of representatives." "All right," I say, "I'll send

204

for these gentlemen; they'll be at your side and work instead of making trouble." So the bastard says: "We are organized workers doing our duty for the Fatherland, but we also seek protection through our union . . ."

OWNER: The dog whip — that's the only answer. What did you . . . ?

SUPERVISOR: What did I do? "You're criminals," I told 'em, "it's high treason, and to learn you not to complain again, thirty days in the barracks. That's final! Curtains!"

OWNER: I'm amazed at your leniency. For high treason!

SUPERVISOR: Well, you know, one mustn't overdo it. The sad part of it is that the civilian courts support them bastards.

OWNER: I've heard of such a case. It happened to that man Lenz, in Traisen; he was paying the bastards twenty-five kronen a week. Two of them sued because they used to get forty-four. The local court decided against Lenz. When the two left the courthouse, in high spirits . . .

SUPERVISOR: I know the case. Two policemen picked 'em up and led 'em back to the factory. The military supervisor there, my buddy, stuck 'em with ten days in the clink, and then back to work. Those judges are nothing but a bunch of bureaucrats! Luckily Lenz is mayor, so he can throw people in the clink himself. That's what he did with some women workers. On Christmas Day he had 'em picked up at home by military patrols — to work, and then the clink.

OWNER: Once they complained about me, with their union, because of "ill-treatment" and not enough pay. I sent for one of their ringleaders and said: "Look here. You complained; you know what this dog whip is for?" And I shook it at him. So the bastard said: "We're not dogs." I pointed at my gun holster and told him: "For you, I also have a gun." He babbled something about "human dignity." But you know, the bastard really got the grievance committee to decide that his pay was not enough!

SUPERVISOR: Well, I'm sure the man was immediately . . .

OWNER: Of course he was called up. Your predecessor was very cooperative in this respect. Once I whipped a man when he complained about low pay, and your predecessor sent him to the clink for three weeks for it.

SUPERVISOR: You'll find me just as cooperative. Between you and me, the bastards are lucky they don't work in a mine.

OWNER: The military headquarters in Leitmeritz make it easy on the mine owners. The mine workers are told that since they took their oath on the statutes of war, complaining may be mutiny, in which case the ringleaders can be court-martialed and executed.

SUPERVISOR: In the Eibiswald coal mine they have to work Sundays. No inn stays open after 8 P.M. Out of every five days in jail, three are fastdays. They take arrested men directly from the mine to jail, a long walk. In Ostrau, everybody who gets arrested gets whipped, systematically. They've done this since the war began: on a bench at the police station, held by two soldiers. One bastard told his union representative about it and got whipped a second time. Those who complain get called up. That's the way!

OWNER (*sighing*): Yes, the mine owners, they got it made!

SUPERVISOR: Well, you other employers are not exactly unprotected either. The foremen see to that. They're pretty good at slapping. I myself order handcuffs for jail, six hours every day. And workers are led from the factory through the streets, between fixed bayonets — that sets an example! No washing up, and the head shaved as soon as they arrive in the clink, even if they draw only twenty-four hours. We take the cost of food off their wages, and of course no pay while they're in jail — then, to top it off (but only in severe cases), they're called up for military service. No, employers have nothing to complain about!

OWNER: You're quite right, I didn't mean it that way. And I don't bother the military authorities except in emergencies. I'd rather rely on self-help. I always say, as long as kindness will do . . . (*He points to the dog whip.*)

Scene 11

The grocery store of Vinzenz Chramosta.

CHRAMOSTA (*to a woman*): The pot cheese? Four kronen for four ounces. What, too much? Next week it'll cost you six, and if you don't like it, go someplace else and buy crap. It's cheaper. And now get the hell outa here . . . (*To a man.*) *What* do you want — sample it? Are you nuts, mister? There's a war on! If you'd rather eat crap, try it! (*To a woman.*) You there, quit pushing! Everybody gets his turn! What do you want? A pickle? They go by weight, and the smallest is two kronen! (*To a man.*) A sausage? Get lost, you idiot, how d'you expect us to get sausages these days? The ideas people get — it's unbelievable. (*To a woman.*) Whatya staring at? My scales are right but the paper weighs something too. There's a war on! If you don't like it, tough shit, but don't let me see your face here again, you fat goat, and that's final! (*To a man.*) No arguments back there — don't think I can't hear you. I won't sell you nothing today — customers like you give me a pain in the ass. Beat it! (*To a woman.*) The lettuce is twelve kronen. What? Marked? Of course it's marked eight, so what? It costs twelve. Those are my prices, and you can't talk me down one lousy heller! If you don't want it today come again tomorrow, then it'll be fourteen. And now clear out, get lost, scram. Understand? (*Grumbling among the customers.*) What do I hear? Wanna start something? One more gripe outa you, and I'll run you all in. I've had it! And now, git, alla you! You spoiled my day! I won't sell a thing to a bunch of freeloaders!

The customers leave, grumbling. A commissioner from the Price Administration enters.

COMMISSIONER: Inspection!

CHRAMOSTA (*surprised*): Inspection . . . ?

COMMISSIONER: Let me see the invoice for the lettuce.

CHRAMOSTA (*taking a long time finding it before handing it over*): Yes . . . But it doesn't mean much. I had to pay something under the counter to get it.

COMMISSIONER (*taking notes*): Purchase price, four fifty. What are you selling it for?

CHRAMOSTA: Eight. Can't you read? They don't give away food for free nowadays. And anyway it's up to us to set the prices! That's our job! If the customers don't mind, the government better keep its goddam nose out of it.

COMMISSIONER: Watch your language. I'm going to report you for a price violation.

CHRAMOSTA: What? You dirty dog, you want to fix me? I'll fix *you!* (*He throws a heavy bowl of soft cheese at the commissioner, without hitting him.*)

COMMISSIONER: You'll take the consequences for this!

CHRAMOSTA: What? I . . . ? Have I hit you? No. So there. I'm way ahead of you, mister! Who do you think you are? I'll show you who I am — you're not going to pin anything on me. I bought war bonds, see? And anyway, what do you want here? I'm a taxpayer, remember that! To hell with you! It burns me up to have some bum like you come in here and snoop around! You should be ashamed of yourself? Take your ass out of here right this moment, or I'll kick the stuffing outa you! (*He picks up two knives.*)

COMMISSIONER (*retreating toward the door*): I'm warning you!

CHRAMOSTA: *You* are warning *me*? You bureaucrat! You penniless scum! I'll fix you but good! (*He throws a basket of nuts after the commissioner.*)

Scene 12

Optimist and Grumbler, talking.

OPTIMIST: The development of weapons, including poison gas, tanks, U-boats, and the 120-mile cannon, has made it possible . . .

GRUMBLER: . . . to suggest that the army be dishonorably discharged from the Armed Forces for cowardice in the face of the enemy. If military honor still means anything this war ought to stop right now. It still needs to be discovered what the discoveries of chemists have to do with courage, and how we can gain battle fame by a "chlorious" attack without choking in shame on our own poison gas.

OPTIMIST: What's the difference which weapon does the killing? How far do you go along with the technical development of arms?

GRUMBLER: I could do without any of them, but if you forced me I'd say: to the bow and arrow. Of course, if men cannot live without killing each other it doesn't matter how they do it, and mass killing is the most practical. But the romanticism of war is undercut by the inventions of this technical age. Tanks and gas will get bigger and better and eventually give way to bacteria. Epidemics, which used to be the results of war, will become the weapons of war. But even then man will need to keep up the romantic image of himself as the heroic killer, so the general who is being kept in business by the bacteriologist will still be wearing his uniform, his hero costume, just like the general of today who is being supplied by the chemist. The Germans can claim the glory of inventing the new weapons, the others the shame of perfecting them. Or the other way round — it makes no difference.

OPTIMIST: But by their highly developed war techniques the Germans have proved . . .

GRUMBLER: . . . that their methods are even more efficient than those of Joshua. Modern techniques are better suited to destroying the enemy, which, after all, is the purpose of war. A breakthrough after gassing three Italian brigades surpasses even the military miracles of Jehovah!

OPTIMIST: You see similarities between the modern German and the ancient Hebrew forces?

GRUMBLER: Yes, even in their ideas of their gods. All nations on this crazy planet share the delusion that they are backed up by the same god; the Germans, however, like the ancient Hebrews, have in addition their special relationship to this god, to whom they offer their terrifying battle sacrifices. The Germans have appropriated exclusive rights to being the chosen people; they even consider the word "German" an adjective of praise with comparative and superlative forms. The ancient Hebrews at least paid lip service to the commandment "Thou shalt not kill," which caused them a grim but genuinely felt conflict. But the Germans today have simply twisted Kant's categorical imperative into a "Go and get them!" as their moral justification. They have made the Lord into their Supreme Commander-in-Chief and direct superior of Wilhelm II.

Scene 13

A Protestant church.

PASTOR BUZZARD: This war is a punishment inflicted by the Lord upon the nations for their sins, and we Germans, together with our allies, are the executors of divine judgment. Without a doubt, the Kingdom of God had been tremendously strengthened and deepened by this war. And let us acknowledge clearly and unequivocally that Jesus' commandment "Love thy enemies" applies only to relationships between individuals and not between nations. In the struggle of the nations there is no room for loving one's enemies. Here the individual soldier need have no scruples! In the heat of battle, Jesus' command of love is suspended! In combat, killing is no sin but a service to the Fatherland, a Christian duty — indeed, even a service to God. Yes, it is a service to God and a sacred duty to punish forcefully our foes, to destroy them if need be. Thus I repeat unto you: "Love thy enemies" no longer is binding. Away with all doubts of conscience! But, you may ask, why have so many thousands of soldiers been crippled? Why have so many hundreds been blinded? Because, I tell you, this is God's way of saving their souls! Look about you and pray, as you are witnessing the Lord's miracles: "Deliver us, O Lord, to paradise!"

209

Scene 14

Another Protestant church.

PASTOR CROW: Therefore — fortify your blood with steel! And to the fainthearted I say: Once a war has started, it is our right, and sometimes indeed our duty toward our Fatherland, to regard treaties as scraps of paper to be torn up and tossed into the fire if this will save the Fatherland. War is the last resort, God's ultimate means of bringing the nations to their senses, by force if they won't let themselves be guided in any other way, along the path that God has chosen for them. Wars are God's trials and His judgments in world history. And that's why it is also the will of God that in war the nations use all their strength and all the weapons He has given them to carry out the just punishment of their enemies! Therefore — fortify your blood with steel! German women too, the mothers of fallen heroes, reject sentimentality in war. Their beloved husbands and sons are fighting or have been killed, but they refuse to listen to wailing and moaning. God wants us to have an iron will. He urges us to the supreme exertion of our strength. Therefore, once again — fortify your blood with steel!

Scene 15

Another Protestant church.

PASTOR HAWK: Look about you: German genius has strung together brilliant achievements like the pearls of a glittering necklace. It has created the miracle of the U-boats. It has produced that fabulous gun that shoots missiles high into the atmosphere, carrying destruction to the enemy one hundred twenty kilometers away. But German genius not only provides us with weapons; it untiringly safeguards and fortifies our minds. For example, Schultze in Hamburg, on a grant from our Foreign Office, is doing basic research on the desecration of corpses and graves by the British and the French. Our Information Service will spread his findings all over the world, findings which are bound to win us the sympathies of the neutral nations, especially — we hope — those of our neighbors who still have doubts. Everywhere in our German lands spirits rise, ready to help our just cause, to arouse the sluggish, to convert the backsliders, and to win new friends. Our government in its wisdom has realized that Switzerland not only can serve as a transit area for our bombs but will gratefully learn methods of warfare from our pictures and words. Our films, showing our U-boats sinking untold tons of food to the bottom of the sea, cannot fail to have a devastating effect on neutral audiences. People faint; women especially are most likely to be impressed by the loss of priceless goods. Such films gradually make people all over the world realize the magnitude of the damage we are inflicting on our enemies. The German word is equally effective. Listen, for example, to the magnificent poem, a soldier's prayer, I found in a splendid publication that our Information Service is distributing in neutral countries to enlighten foreigners about the true German character and gradually overcome the hatred with which we have been persecuted:

Do you hear the soldiers praying?
We seek blessing from above;
from the gullets of our cannon
sound the pledges of our love.
Through the barrels of our cannon
we will shoot the Good Lord's Prayer;
we'll plant bayonets upon them,
stuck like crosses in the air.

Buddies, sprinkle dumdum bullets
like a holy-water rinse;
let our cannon smoke like censers.
Unexploded mines are sins,
let's repent then and do better,
true omission sins are they!
But when land mines start exploding,
then our sins are blown away.

Let us string our hand grenades like
rosaries around our chest;
when the beads go popping, watch them
crush the enemy's fighting zest.
Let us say our angry prayer,
yes, let's sing the "Wacht am Rhein."
Praying hands will turn to talons
wringing necks of godless swine.

For we are the Lord's own agents,
carrying out the will divine.

And thus look around you and pray, as you are witnessing the Lord's miracles, "Deliver us, O Lord, to paradise!"

Scene 16

A Catholic church.

SEXTON (*speaking to tourists*): Here you see an interesting devotional gift presented to our holy shrine by two soldiers who fought at Col di Lana: a rosary whose beads are shrapnel bullets. The chain is fashioned from barbed wire. The cross is cut from a burst Italian grenade and has three Italian rifle bullets as pendants. The figure of Christ has been shaped from shrapnel. The cross carries on its back the engraved inscription: "In gratitude. In memory of the war in Italy, Cima d'Oro, July 25, 1917," and the initials of the donor. For prolonged praying it requires a strong hand. Would one of you gentlemen care to lift it?
VISITOR (*trying*): Ugh! Damned heavy! (*A church bell is ringing.*)
SEXTON: Listen! It's ringing for the last time. Today it'll be taken down. We make rosaries from shrapnel, and cannons from church bells. We render unto God what is Caesar's, and unto Caesar what is God's. Everybody does his share.

Scene 17

Office room at an army command post.

MEMBER OF THE GENERAL STAFF (*telephoning*): Hi there. Have you finished your report on Przemysl? Not yet? Not quite awake, eh? Come on, get it done, or you'll be late for our party ... Oh yes, tonight we'll definitely have a party. What, you forgot your directives again? Now listen, here are the main points: When we lost Przemysl our troops were defeated by hunger — but now it's a different story: The enemy was defeated by our superior forces, and not by hunger — get it? Only by our strength. The Russians had enough supplies but couldn't withstand the assault of our brave troops . . . the force of our attack. Furthermore, the fortress was taken completely intact, in perfect condition . . . it has the most modern guns. What? We can't make people forget? Old junk? No, no, not anymore, of course. We can make them forget anything, my friend! So listen and don't get it all mixed up: Most modern fortress, Austria's pride, retaken in perfect condition. Not by force but by hunger . . . ah, what am I saying! Not by hunger but by force! You'll know how to handle it . . . as long as you make people believe it. You'll have no trouble this time . . . So long!

Scene 18

Room at the Ministry of War in Vienna. A captain sits at his desk. Before him stands a civilian in mourning.

CAPTAIN: Well, what else do you want? We can't keep complete records in such cases. How should *we* know whether a man is dead or wounded or taken prisoner? Go and ask the Italian minister of war, my friend! There — you see? What do you want us to do? Incredible, the things people expect of us!

CIVILIAN: Yes . . . but . . .

CAPTAIN: My good man, that's all I can tell you. It's almost three, and I think we're entitled to a little consideration; office hours are over. We're only human. Look, just between you and me: You haven't heard from your son in six weeks, so you can assume he's dead.

CIVILIAN: Yes . . . but . . .

CAPTAIN: There's no but. We'd be swamped if in every such case . . . This sort of thing happens thousands of times. There's a war on, my good man! A civilian is expected to do his part, too. Look at us standing at our post by sitting here. And besides — you must know it anyhow but I'll tell you again — just between you and me, and don't quote me: For a soldier there can be no higher ambition and greater award than to die for his country. Well, so long.

CIVILIAN (*bows and leaves.*)

Scene 19

A palatial villa, "Wahnschaffe," in a German spa; crenelations, turrets, ornaments; from the gabled roof flutter the two flags — black, white, red and black, red, gold; below them a bust of Wilhelm II. Above the entrance a sign: "With heart and hand for God, Kaiser, and Fatherland." Before the entrance two cannon models, one carrying the sign "Up and at 'em!", the other, "Hold out!"

"Councilor of Commerce" Ottomar Wilhelm Wahnschaffe steps from the villa and sings. Each stanza is followed by a musical passage sung by an invisible choir representing the laughter of the world.

Both day and night I slave away;
I need a longer working day
to help the boys to watch the Rhine
and speed up the assembly line.
Because I worked like hell before,
our loafing enemies went to war.
We'll beat the foe with ammunition,
we'll beat with goods the competition.
I'm a German!

Our honor no one must attack.
No, Belgium we will not give back.
On honor Germany insists;
in honor we are specialists.
And when the victory proves us right
the earth will be our satellite —
a market without parallel
for any junk we want to sell.
Made in Germany!

Of this I'm absolutely sure:
We Germans have much more *Kultur*.
Among the gifts with which we're blessed
Our German *Kultur* tops the rest.
And in a world of knaves and stinkers,
we are the poets and the thinkers.

They call us Huns and Krauts, and killers —
where are their Goethes and their Schillers?
German *Kultur!* (*Exits.*)

FRAU WAHNSCHAFFE: I am a German mother. I have two children. But, alas, neither is fit for military service; one, unfortunately, is a girl. So I have to make do with fantasies that my boy served at the front and, naturally, that he met a hero's death; otherwise I would die of shame — if he had returned, for example, without a scratch. This fantasy is my greatest comfort. My children are really disadvantaged in two ways: they were born too soon to die for the Kaiser and too late to be named for one of our heroes. Our boy might have been named Hindenburg, and our girl Zeppelina.

Scene 20

Optimist and Grumbler, talking.

OPTIMIST: Are you planning to visit Switzerland again?

GRUMBLER: I'd like to, although I would be sure to run into the same people there whom I'm trying to avoid here. Well, at least I could still keep an eye on the characters from the play I'm writing about this catastrophic war. In Berne you'd think you were in Vienna. Austria exports all her scoundrels, diplomats, black marketeers, and hack writers to Switzerland. They have no trouble leaving Austria because they beat the propaganda drums in Switzerland for our obnoxious government. For someone like me it's not easy to travel, and all the red tape is enough to keep me here.

OPTIMIST: Yes, our passport mess. One agency doesn't know what the other one requires. But, after all, war is . . .

GRUMBLER: . . . war, I know. But even more disgusting than to deal with this bureaucracy when it forbids something, is to deal with it when it grants something. You have to give a "valid reason" for wanting to leave this country.

OPTIMIST: Don't you have one?

GRUMBLER: A thousand. One of them would be the hope of getting a slice of buttered bread — no, I won't list that. I'd rather list the single sum total of all my reasons for wanting to leave: the fact that I live in

Austria. The government could save itself a lot of paper work if it required the person who wants to leave to state a valid reason why he wants to stay. Well, anyway — the requirement to give a valid reason for wanting to leave is in itself a valid reason for wanting to leave. It is a good reason not only for visiting abroad . . .

OPTIMIST: But also . . . ?

GRUMBLER: For emigrating.

OPTIMIST: You'll find a reason. Is there anything for which your sophisticated mind couldn't think up a reason?

GRUMBLER: Yes. For returning.

Act III

Scene 1

Vienna, Ringstrasse next to the Opera House. Evening, drizzly and cold. A mass of people mill around, staring silently ahead, moving through a lane formed by two lines of the wounded and the dead.

VOICE OF A NEWSBOY: The *Journal* . . . ! Late edition!

FIRST OFFICER: Hi, Povolny. Well, let's hear it from the political wizard. What do you say about Bulgaria?

SECOND OFFICER (*with cane*): I say: don't even bother to ignore it.

FOURTH OFFICER: Touché. Say, that was one helluva good party last night . . . Did you notice the unbelievable brunette on the cover of *Muskete*? A real classic.

VOICE OF A NEWSBOY: Peeeee feeelers by the Allies!

THIRD OFFICER: Nothing doing here tonight.

FIRST OFFICER: I met Slepička von Schlachtentreu in the Ministry of War this morning. He said we're approaching the giant with peace steps . . . ah, what am I saying? We are approaching peace with giant steps. Is that true? Isn't that optimistic?

SECOND OFFICER: It's pessimistic.

FIRST OFFICER: Pessimistic? He said Turkey has a soft underbelly, and Austria will get one, too. What does that mean?

SECOND OFFICER: He means the general situation.

FIRST OFFICER: I see.

THIRD OFFICER: I wonder where all the broads are tonight.

SECOND OFFICER: Skunkie will join us later.

FOURTH OFFICER: Know what they call him at the Ministry? Hero, they call him.

FIRST OFFICER: How so?

FOURTH OFFICER: Don't you get it? He was at the front. He says he preferred it there.

FIRST OFFICER: Then why do they keep him here? To each his own.

SKUNKIE (*entering*). Hi, everybody.

FIRST OFFICER: Hi, hero.

ALL: Hi, hero.

SKUNKIE: What's this hero stuff?

FOURTH OFFICER: How was the war? Let's hear all about it at Hopmer's.

FIRST OFFICER: Yes, tell us. You're a real killer.

SECOND OFFICER: Give it to us straight. How was it out there?

SKUNKIE (*smirking*): Killing.

FLOWER GIRL (*passing by*): Forget-me-nots!

FIRST OFFICER: Well, Skunkie old boy, what's the word?

SKUNKIE: Live and let live.

Two invalids in rags, their legs shot off, move into their path.

SECOND OFFICER: Let's go; nobody here but loiterers. (*The officers leave.*)

VOICE OF A NEWSBOY: Extra! Staggering losses of the Allies!

A WHISPERING VOICE: Come here, I'll tell you something.

Silence. Then the voice of a coachman.

COACHMAN: In wartime my fare goes up five hundred percent.

Scene 2

*A railroad station near Vienna. A sheepish crowd of five hundred
has been waiting for two hours at the closed ticket window.*

FIRST VIENNESE: It will be here in ten minutes.

SECOND VIENNESE (*to a ticket checker*): Can you tell me when it'll be here?

TICKET CHECKER: The timetable says 5:15 but it usually comes around
seven.

THIRD VIENNESE: But it's already a quarter of eight.

TICKET CHECKER: That's right. It's going to be two and a half hours late.
It says so on the board.

GRUMBLER: Is that reliable?

TICKET CHECKER (*annoyed*): How do I know? All they know is a bunch of
crap, and if they do know anything they won't tell the public.

GRUMBLER: But it says so on the board.

TICKET CHECKER: The board! The board! That doesn't mean a thing.
It always comes later.

GRUMBLER: Is that the rule?

TICKET CHECKER: Not exactly the rule, but it would be an exception if it
came as early as the board says it's late.

GRUMBLER: Then why do they bother writing the time on the board?

TICKET CHECKER: It's the regulation. They out there don't tell us, and we in here don't know.

FOURTH VIENNESE: I think I hear it coming.

TICKET CHECKER: See ? But it's a mere coincidence that it's as late as it says on the board.

GRUMBLER: How can things be so messed up ?

TICKET CHECKER: Look, mister, bellyaching to me does no good. Go ask someone else. Trains are late, that's the way it is. Nobody tells us nothing. There's a lot of traffic — there's a war on.

FIFTH VIENNESE: The train's coming.

SIXTH VIENNESE: The ticket agent is asleep!

CALLS: Come on! Open up! (*The Grumbler knocks his cane against the window.*) That's it!

The ticket window opens. The Austrian Face appears. It is extremely undernourished but filled with diabolic satisfaction. A thin forefinger wags from side to side, and appears to squash all hope.

THE AUSTRIAN FACE: No tickets sold today! No tickets sold today!

Grumbling, rising to a tumult. Groups are formed.

ONE WHO KNOWS: Come on, I'll show you a back door. You won't need any tickets there! (*All leave through the back door.*)

Scene 3

A meeting of physicians in Berlin.

PSYCHIATRIST: Gentlemen! Here you see the most remarkable case I've ever come across. It was lucky for me that this man was released to me from protective custody. He has committed so many crimes that no man could live long enough to serve time for them all. There was no other way but to send him to the psychiatrist. In his case we need not find out if the criminal is responsible for his actions; his actions prove his irresponsibility. This man has declared publicly that the food situation in Germany is precarious! (*Commotion.*) More than that —

this man has expressed doubt in Germany's final victory! (*Restless-ness.*) To top it off, this man has questioned the usefulness of an inten-sified U-boat war — in fact, he questions the U-boat altogether! He rejects that weapon not only as useless, but as immoral! (*Excited calls.*) Please, gentlemen, do not hold responsible either this unfortunate creature or me, who happens to be called upon to present you with this revolting case of insanity. Responsibility is lifted from him by his illness, and from me by science. (*Calls of "True, true!"*) Gentlemen, this man suffers from the fixed idea that Germany is being driven to her destruction by her "criminal ideology," as he chooses to call our noble idealism. He blames our government and not the British (*calls of "Phooey!"*) for the deaths of our children. (*Boos.*) He believes our children are dying because we don't have enough food; this alone proves his mental confusion. (*Calls of "True, true!"*) I have given you the background of this case, my esteemed colleagues of internal med-icine, so you can try to straighten out the patient with firsthand in-formation about health conditions in wartime Germany. From his reaction I hope to gain a more complete clinical picture, perhaps establish his criminal responsibility, and to come to a decision, one way or another. (*Calls of "Leave it to us!"*) Now I should like to ask my esteemed colleague, Dr. Boas, to probe the mind of our patient.

PROFESSOR BOAS: I have said it many times and I'll say it again: reduced food consumption has not lowered our health standard. (*Calls of "Hear, hear!"*) Cutting our protein rations in half has not reduced our vigor and working ability. The fact is: our weight has gone up and our health has improved.

THE INSANE: You probably buy on the black market! (*Excited calls.*)

PSYCHIATRIST: Please, gentlemen, do consider the mental condition of the patient.

PROFESSOR BOAS: In our research no harmful effects of the food situation on infant mortality have been found.

THE INSANE: *Must* be found, my dear sir! (*Calls of "Shut up!"*)

PROFESSOR BOAS: In the past, our affluence and our extravagant nutri-tional standards did much to sap our health. But under the pressure of certain privations, millions of people have found their way back to nature and the simple life. Let future generations not forget the lessons of today's war. (*Calls of "Bravo!"*)

THE INSANE: The man is right. The rich stuffed themselves too much before the war. And they still eat too much. But the other people — those who need not consult Boas about their obesity — will produce children born with rickets. Germany's next generation will be a generation of child invalids! Those dying during the war are better off than those born during the war and destined to walk on crutches! I predict that the perverse mentality that finds pride in endurance and in enemy losses, as well as in the hero's deaths of our own sons, will result in a crippled Germany! (*Boos.*) As for Boas's statistics, I dare him to deny that so far 800,000 civilians have starved to death this year alone. (*Calls of "Enough!" and "Some gall!"*)

PSYCHIATRIST: Gentlemen, please. Professor Zunz will now continue our probing of the patient's mind with information on the effects of wartime nutrition on our priceless national asset, German efficiency.

PROFESSOR ZUNZ: German efficiency has in no way been impaired by our wartime diet. Some undernourishment, however, may have resulted from some people's refusal to eat a sufficient amount of ersatz vegetables.

PSYCHIATRIST: Is it correct to say, then, that the population itself is to blame?

PROFESSOR ZUNZ: That is correct.

PSYCHIATRIST: Professor Rosenfeld will continue our probing.

PROFESSOR ROSENFELD: Research shows that wartime nutrition does not affect resistance to disease . . .

THE INSANE: It only affects the hypocrisy of doctors! (*Shouts of indignation.*)

VOICES: Throw him out! Call the police!

PRESIDENT OF THE MEDICAL BOARD OF GREATER BERLIN: I should like to take the opportunity of this outrage to raise my voice in an appeal to the medical profession. You are the father confessors of your patients. It is your patriotic duty to encourage endurance, oppose timidity, reject unfounded, malicious, or thoughtless rumors. We on the home front can, should, and will hold out! Colleagues! The simple life and the modest intake of protein and fats have profited many!

THE INSANE: The black marketeers and the doctors! (*Calls of "Disgrace!" and "Throw the bastard out!"*)

PRESIDENT: The doctors have proved without a doubt . . .

THE INSANE: . . . that Germany can be successfully brainwashed with lies! (*Boos.*)

PRESIDENT: . . . that today's youths are as healthy as before.

THE INSANE: Infant mortality has increased thirty-seven percent! (*Calls of "Shut up!" and "Traitor!"*)

PRESIDENT: Infant mortality has fallen off. A prominent health expert has stated that the health of our infants is at an all time high. (*Calls of "Hear, hear!"*) Children's hospitals are less crowded than before.

THE INSANE: Because the patients are dead. (*Noise.*)

223

VOICE: Let the bastard prove it!

THE INSANE: Doctors' reports from hospitals sound desperate. They describe hungry patients looking for food in garbage cans. A report from an old-age home simply states: "All inmates have died." But you, who are alive and gathered here, have been ordered what to say and will find the courage to tell the truth only after the unavoidable collapse of the German Reich and its lies. By then it will be too late, and no amount of confessing will spare you the contempt of the world. German science has become a whore and its practitioners are her pimps! General Headquarters has commandeered you into the service of the Big Lie. You have been ordered to deny infant mortality and to make black look white. But you are more responsible for the bloodshed than those who are drowning the world in red!

Noisy commotion. Some of the professors want to lay hands on the insane and are held back by others.

PSYCHIATRIST: Gentlemen, we have just witnessed a wild outburst of hatred by a man against his own fatherland. Such hate could not have grown on German soil. Clearly, the man is not insane but in the pay of the Allies! This is an acute case of British propaganda, and the Medical Society of Greater Berlin is duty-bound to stop it. The poison of pacifism has entered even healthy minds, and opposition to war, masquerading as idealism, encourages weaklings and draft dodgers. Criminal enemy propaganda threatens to paralyze our vigor when final victory is just around the corner. This mood of defeatism strengthens the backbone of our enemies and clips our wings in fighting this defensive war that was forced upon us by British jealousy . . . (*calls of "A nation of shop-keepers!"*), French revenge . . . (*calls of "And Russian greed!"*) and Russian greed. The case here is typical. We are dealing with a hardened criminal. These are not the words of a mentally sick person; these are the words of a traitor! And I can also tell you, gentlemen, that this man, through his revolting attacks on everything that is holy to us Germans, has attracted attention in the highest quarters, and that a personality whom we all revere, our Crown Prince (*the audience rises*), has declared that the bastard deserves to be slapped across his mouth. (*Calls of "Hurrah!"*) It is our task, gentlemen, to declare this case as lying outside our competence because it does not concern medical science, and to turn this man over to the police. (*He opens the door.*) Officer!

POLICEMAN (*enters*): Okay, in the name of Law and Order, come on, get going!

The policeman takes the insane away. The assembly rises and sings the "Wacht am Rhein."

Scene 4

Resort town of Semmering, near Vienna.

IMPERIAL COUNCILOR: What do you say about the news today ♪

BIACH: It cannot fail to depress the Allies.

IMPERIAL COUNCILOR: I don't know . . . I have a feeling . . . today's news . . . What do you say about the loss of Luzk ♪

BIACH: The Allies are hiding behind big words but are feeling their weaknesses.

IMPERIAL COUNCILOR: Well, but Luzk ♪

BIACH: The battle of the Upper Isonzo started this morning and we do not want to anticipate its course.

IMPERIAL COUNCILOR: Yes, but Luzk . . .

BIACH: In the words of the press headquarters, we sense the breath of history.

IMPERIAL COUNCILOR: Yes, of course. But Luzk . . .

BIACH (*enthusiastically*): Cleopatra's nose was one of her most beautiful features.

IMPERIAL COUNCILOR: Just a moment. What does that have to do with Luzk ♪

BIACH (*excitedly*): You don't know ♪ You don't know ♪ ♪ That's how "he" starts his editorial today . . .

IMPERIAL COUNCILOR: Oh yes, of course. But out of context it was unfamiliar at the moment. I know every one of his words by heart . . . But to tell the truth, I don't like the news about Luzk. Of course, it's a first-rate strategic withdrawal . . . yet . . .

BIACH: In Russia, they hear the crumbling of the walls!

Scene 5

A Court-martial Chamber.

CAPTAIN JUDGE DR. STANISLAUS VON ZAGORSKI (*pronouncing the verdict. One hears only the sentences and words that he particularly stresses*): ... taking into consideration that defendant Hryb is only twenty-six years old, cannot read or write, therefore lacks education; taking further into consideration that, in the judgment of the Court, defendant Hryb was guilty to a lesser extent than the other defendants, the Court has decided that in view of these extenuating circumstances the death penalty pronounced in accordance with section 444 of the Military Penal Code is to be carried out first on defendant Hryb.

... death sentence to be carried out second on defendant Struk because his crime, compared with that of the first defendant, is more severe ...

... because defendant Maeyjiczyn has been in contact with the Russians, he is to be third ...

... because of severe guilt ... death penalty ... fourth ... his dishonest defense ... fifth ... his complete submission to Russian influence ... sixth ... in consequence of his traitorous actions ... seventh.

... because Fedynscyn was convicted on two counts, he is to be eighth ...

... taking into consideration the enormity of his crime, Fedor Budz is to be ninth ...

... Petro Dzus is to be tenth ...

... the Court has decided that his crime was the most severe of all eleven men convicted; thus he is to be the last on whom the death penalty is to be carried out. Case concluded. (*The defendants are led away.*)

FIRST OFFICER: Nice going! One can tell you're a lawyer. Say, how many death sentences have you put away ?

ZAGORSKI: That was exactly the one hundredth. Or, counting them singly, number 100 and up to 110.

OFFICERS: That calls for a celebration! Why didn't you tell us ? Congratulations!

ZAGORSKI: Thank you, thank you. And, I'm proud to say, I've personally witnessed every execution I've ordered. Plus many pronounced by colleagues.

SECOND OFFICER: You drive yourself too hard. You are too conscientious.

226

ZAGORSKI: Yes, it's an exacting job.

FIRST OFFICER: Remember, he's a doctor of law; it's in his blood.

ZAGORSKI: Yeah, a death sentence must be well reasoned out — it's no fun.

SECOND OFFICER: Jeez, did we have trouble with the colonel who was here before you! He was dead set against court-martials, called them judicial claptrap. "Simply kill 'em off," he always said.

FIRST OFFICER: Same with Wild of the eleventh corps. He had twelve politically suspicious characters strung up between Christmas and New Year 1914, six on one day. He said he didn't fiddle around with court verdicts. He also used bayonets to finish them off.

SECOND OFFICER: Lüttgendorff didn't care for court-martials either. "Use the simplified method," he always said. Once he ordered a corporal to finish off three men with the bayonet because they were drunk. That was on the emperor's birthday, I remember it well. We also had whippings and house burnings, first-rate I tell you. He was tough on sabotage — in Syrmia we burned down every second house, as a warning. He marked the entire village for extermination. The pregnant women he marched off — whether he eventually bumped them off too, I don't know. But anyway, the ones who weren't bumped off right away had to stay with the corpses of their friends and relatives all night. The Hungarian gendarmes in charge always handled criminal cases by the simplified method and left the corpses on the spot — you know, the teachers and priests and local officials.

FIRST OFFICER: The internment camps were even more efficient.

SECOND OFFICER: That was later, when they carried out the final solution according to plan. The Hungarian camps were well equipped for it. Starvation, beatings, typhoid fever — it sure cut down them Serbians!

THIRD OFFICER: Yes, but to be honest, that's no longer a real judicial procedure.

SECOND OFFICER: Yeah, it's more administrative. And I can tell you, Lüttgendorff saw to it that every case was covered by an official form saying "Execution ordered." He just didn't go for real trials like we have here. Oooh, how he cursed at the judges! "Slowpoke!" he shouted at them. "Bonehead! Stickler!" He liked to string up people without fuss. Of course only under extenuating circumstances. Otherwise the bayonet.

FIRST OFFICER: Did you ever come across a Nazarene?

SECOND OFFICER: What's that? There are no such animals anymore.

FIRST OFFICER: Oh yes. Nazarenes are those finks who refuse to handle a gun because of their religion, or so they say. We had one once, a peasant — we used him as a driver. He behaved all right, had a good record, but he wouldn't handle a gun during drill. He made a helluva bad impression in court. I guess he knew we were going to sentence him to death, so he told us — without a trace of remorse, mind you — that he wouldn't carry a gun even if he got shot for it. Of course, clemency was out for such a stubborn ass, and the minister of war confirmed the verdict. But later the story got sticky because the colonel-judge reported to the Supreme Military Court that the verdict was based on a regrettable oversight. It turned out that the minister of war, in 1914, had decreed that Nazarenes were to be sent to the front as noncombatants and that their court-martial was to be held up until after the war. But we didn't hear about that decree until after the execution, in 1916, so there was nothing we could do about it. Except that the colonel-judge got three weeks military arrest.

SECOND OFFICER: All this wouldn't have happened under Lüttgendorff. With him, a Nazarene would have been . . . (*gesture of finger across the throat*) kkkch — kaput, my friend!

ZAGORSKI: Yes, but as men of law we don't have that much leeway. I go slow — and yet I've accomplished more than even Wild.

SECOND OFFICER: Yeah, you're doing fine.

ZAGORSKI: My most interesting case happened in 1914 when we still were full of enthusiasm. There were these three Ruthenian refugees, one of them a priest. Naturally I sentenced them to death and they were executed . . .

SECOND OFFICER: Did you arrange them nicely in order, too ?

ZAGORSKI: Don't be silly. They all three knew how to read and write, and besides, they all were equally guilty . . . or perhaps I should say, equally innocent.

FIRST OFFICER: Innocent ? How come ?

ZAGORSKI: That's the interesting point. Their case was later reopened by the military court and it turned out the three were innocent.

THE OFFICERS: Tough luck.

ZAGORSKI (*laughing*): Not really. The Ukranian national assembly complained about me to the supreme military commander. You can imagine what happened.

FIRST OFFICER: Of course. What rank did you have then ?

ZAGORSKI: First lieutenant.

FIRST OFFICER: And when did they make you captain ?

ZAGORSKI: When it turned out that the three Ruthenians had been innocent.

SECOND OFFICER: You think there's a direct connection ? That they wanted to make it up to you ?

ZAGORSKI: I wouldn't say that. They aren't that considerate at the High Command. But the complaint drew their attention to me. They saw how hard I was working. And then, you know what happens when a politically unreliable nation complains about us. A Ruthenian can't harm us by complaining, only by being alive.

THIRD OFFICER: Say, do you think the eleven we tried today might be innocent too? Actually, the only thing that was proved was . . .

ZAGORSKI: . . . that they were Ruthenians. And that should be enough. One o'clock! Let's go eat.

Scene 6

Schönbrunn. Emperor Franz Josef's study. The emperor sits at his desk, sleeping. On each side stands a chamberlain.

CHAMBERLAIN ON THE RIGHT: He's working again, untiringly.

CHAMBERLAIN ON THE LEFT: It's a quarter of nine. At 9:13 the audiences begin — it's a delicate situation.

CHAMBERLAIN ON THE RIGHT: Sssh — listen! His Majesty's saying something.

EMPEROR (*speaking in his sleep*): No, no, NO — I won't make peace with those Italian mobsters . . . I want to be left alone . . . They tricked me . . . How do you do . . . Go away . . . The second buttonhole is two millimeters high . . . Pleased to meet you . . . I couldn't care less . . . Everything happens to me . . . No, not yet, the audiences don't begin until 9:13 . . . Glad you could come . . . You're so right, I can't stand the Prussians either . . . It's a shame . . . They tricked me . . . There's nothing I can do . . . (*He wakes up.*) Huh? What is it? All right, I'll sign it. (*The chamberlain on the left hands him a pen; the emperor signs several documents.*) Say, who's coming today?

CHAMBERLAIN ON THE RIGHT: Herr Emmanuel von Singer will be here to be made a count.

EMPEROR: Ah yes, Manny. That's fine.

CHAMBERLAIN ON THE RIGHT: Then Herr Riedl is due to receive the Order of Franz Josef.

EMPEROR: Riedl, yes, yes. Pleased to see him again. How's he doing?

CHAMBERLAIN ON THE RIGHT: Not so well, Your Majesty. Was under the weather last week, they say. He may not be able to come today.

229

EMPEROR: That would be too bad — such a young man.

CHAMBERLAIN ON THE LEFT: Yes, Your Majesty, a good thirty years younger than Your Majesty, but as for his vigor — no comparison.

EMPEROR: True, true. Say, how is Beck?

CHAMBERLAIN ON THE RIGHT: Oh my, Your Majesty! (*He mimics a doddering old man.*)

EMPEROR: What? And he's only eighty-four, a mere child. The boy ought to be ashamed of himself. (*He laughs and has a coughing spell. The chamberlains hold him up.*) It's all right. (*The chamberlain on the left leaves the room.*) Where are you going?

CHAMBERLAIN ON THE RIGHT: To get your pills.

EMPEROR: I need no pills. No, no, NO — I won't take them.

CHAMBERLAIN ON THE LEFT (*returns with the pills and gives one to the emperor*): I just heard . . .

EMPEROR (*taking the pill*): They tricked me.

CHAMBERLAIN ON THE LEFT: I just heard that Herr Riedl is too sick to come today.

EMPEROR: Everything happens to me.

CHAMBERLAIN ON THE RIGHT (*to the chamberlain on the left*): Oh me, here comes the old song.

The emperor falls asleep. The two chamberlains tiptoe out.

EMPEROR (*singing in his sleep*):

When I was born to my mother
the world was a terrible mess.
I looked at all that bother
and really couldn't care less.
Wien was a dirndl-and-schnapps burg,
and schnapps was not *my* cup of tea.
Oh, why was I born a Hapsburg?
Everything happens to me.

They had a revolution
in 1848.
They said our constitution
was too little and too late.
So we shot every sympathizer
of rebellious anarchy.

At eighteen I was Kaiser —
everything happens to me.

For duty, not for pleasures —
my country right or wrong —
I've guarded Austria's treasures:
her women, wine, and song.
I dreamed of peace and quiet,
a happy monarchy.
Now we have war and riot —
everything happens to me.

I kept my image charming,
and the schoolbooks prove it, too.
They tricked me into arming —
there was nothing I could do.
And all the charm there was of me
has turned to tragedy.
Oh, nothing happens because of me —
but everything happens to me.

I gave my life to glory,
gave smiles to those who cheered,
to girls the Mayerling story,
to men a style of beard.
Will I become a bigger
concern to history ?
Or an operetta figure ?
Everything happens to me.

I've heard that ghastly saying:
old kaisers never die;
they spend their time decaying
and fade out by and by.
I hope it's all confusion,
some dreadful fantasy. (*Wakes up.*)
But no, it's no illusion —
it's really happening to me.

Scene 7

German headquarters.

WILHELM II (*to his staff*): Morning, gentlemen.

THE GENERALS: Morning, Your Majesty.

WILHELM II (*posing, eyes toward the sky*): Unquestionably, our Lord has His plans for our German people. He has chosen us Germans, who have preserved our idealism, as His instrument to usher in a glorious new age. He wants us to fight for justice, loyalty, and morality. We wish to live in friendship with our neighbors, but first they must acknowledge the German victory. The year 1917, with its great battles, has proved the Lord to be a staunch ally of the German nation. A divine judgment has struck our enemies! The smashing victory in the East fills my heart with deep gratitude. He has allowed us, once more, to experience one of those glorious moments when we, standing in awe, can admire His Majestic Self at work in history!

> *The Kaiser holds out his right hand. The generals and officers line up to kiss it. During the following he emits, when he is excited or amused, a noise like the barking of a wolf. In moments of excitement his face reddens, his expression resembles that of a boar, he puffs up his cheeks making the tips of his mustache stand on end.*

FIRST GENERAL: Your Majesty, you are no longer the instrument of God . . .

WILHELM II (*snorting and puffing*): Ha . . . !

FIRST GENERAL: . . . for God has become the instrument of Your Majesty!

WILHELM II (*beaming*): Fine, fine! Ha!

SECOND GENERAL: When we achieve our breakthrough, with the help of God and gas, we must credit it exclusively to the ingenious strategy of Your Majesty.

WILHELM II (*steps over to a large wall map*): Ha . . . From here to there it is fifteen kilometers. I'll throw in fifty divisions! Colossal, eh? (*He looks around. Murmurs of admiration.*)

THIRD GENERAL: Your Majesty, your strategy is one of the wonders of the world.

FOURTH GENERAL: Your Majesty is not only the greatest orator, painter, composer, huntsman, statesman, sculptor, admiral, poet, sportsman, Assyriologist, business expert, astronomer, and theatrical producer of all time but also . . . but also . . . (*he begins to stutter.*)

232

WILHELM II: Well?

FOURTH GENERAL: Your Majesty, I feel it beyond me to list all of the accomplishments in which Your Majesty excels.

WILHELM II (*nodding, satisfied*): Well, and what about the rest of you? (*They smile in embarrassment.*) What, you damned bastards, laughing at . . . ha! . . . your supreme commander? I'll . . . Seckendorff! (*He goes up to a staff officer and steps on his foot several times.*)

SECKENDORFF (*jumping in pain*): Your Majesty . . . Your Majesty . . .

WILHELM II: Ha! Click your heels! It's all right, Seckendorff, just teasing! Champagne!

AN OFFICER: Yes, sir. (*He leaves.*)

WILHELM II: Caviar! (*Another officer is about to leave.*) Ha . . . Halt! It's a disgrace for a German to live in luxury! Caviar! (*The officer leaves.*)

FOURTH GENERAL: Your Majesty . . .

WILHELM II: Yes? What is it?

FOURTH GENERAL: Your Majesty is also the greatest gourmet of all time.

WILHELM II (*beaming*): Fine, fine! (*Champagne and caviar on toast are served. He drinks.*) But this is French champagne. Phooey!

OFFICER (*pastes a German label on the bottle*): No, Your Majesty, it's German champagne.

WILHELM II: I can see it's excellent German champagne. Hanke, would you like some champagne too? Hurrah! (*He splashes at the general and roars with laughter.*)

GENERALS (*bowing deeply*): Much obliged, Your Majesty.

WILHELM II (*scraping caviar and butter off a piece of toast with his forefinger and smearing it into his mouth*): Ha . . . Hanke, would you also like some caviar? (*He throws the bare piece of toast to the generals and roars with laughter, slapping his thigh with his right hand.*)

GENERALS (*bowing deeply*): Much obliged, Your Majesty.

WILHELM II (*to an aide*): Ha . . . Duncker, tell me, how do you prefer your women? Fat or skinny? (*The aide smiles in embarrassment.*) He goes for fat ones. Likes to lie soft.

GENERALS: Hilarious, Your Majesty! (*The Kaiser laughs like a wolf.*)

WILHELM II: Ha . . . Krickwitz! (*He punches him in the belly.*) What does the rooster say?

KRICKWITZ (*crowing*): Cock-a-doodle-doo . . . Cock-a-doodle-doo . . .

FOURTH GENERAL (*to the general next to him*): His Majesty is divine.

WILHELM II: Ha . . . Flottwitz! Look — over there! (*Flottwitz turns. The Kaiser sneaks up to him and slaps his behind with great force. Flottwitz bends over in pain.*) Are you crazy? Why are you pissing on my boots? (*To the staff physician Martius.*) Ha . . . Martius, look over there!

233

(Martius turns around. The Kaiser sneaks up to him and grabs him between the legs. Martius staggers and steadies himself on a chair, white as chalk. The Kaiser breaks into roaring laughter, then turns away angrily as he notices the effect of his action on the others. With a red face and puffed-up cheeks, snorting and puffing.) You bastards are too goddam dull . . . Ha! No sense of humor!

GENERALS: Hilarious, Your Majesty! Hilarious!

Scene 8

Winter in the Carpathian Mountains. A man is tied to a tree.

COMPANY LEADER HILLER: How cold do you think it is ?

FIRST SOLDIER: About thirty below.

HILLER: Untie him. *(The soldiers untie the man, light-infantry grenadier Helmhake. He collapses. Hiller strikes him in the face several times with his fist.)* Now throw him into that ditch. *(They do it.)* Is it wet and stinking ?

FIRST SOLDIER: Yes, sir.

HILLER: Does he have a high fever ?

FIRST SOLDIER: Yes, sir.

HILLER: Double the guard . . . get going. The swine gets nothing to eat or drink. He's not to take a leak or crap day or night. *(Laughing.)* Won't need to, anyway. Same orders as yesterday. Anyone who doesn't like it I'll squash.

He leaves with his men. Two soldiers remain at the ditch. Whimpering can be heard.

SECOND SOLDIER: Don't you think it would be more Christian if . . . instead of this one . . . we got . . . *him?*

FIRST SOLDIER: Yeah.

SECOND SOLDIER: Two are dead already. He made Thomas undress in this weather, and Müller had to stand guard when he was sick. And to five others he . . . *(A groan is heard. It sounds like "Water!")* Hell, I can't stand this no longer . . . I'm gonna let him suck a snowball. *(He crawls into the ditch and comes back, tears in his eyes.)* Not yet twenty years old . . . he volunteered! *(Hiller returns with his men.)*

234

HILLER: I changed my mind. I want to see . . . Let the bastard come out. On the double!

SECOND SOLDIER: He . . . probably can't, lieutenant.

HILLER: What's the matter? Out with the filthy pig! (*Several soldiers pull Helmhake out and drag him along, lifeless, like a chunk of meat.*) God, what a sight! Ah, the swine's only playing dead. Kick his ass! (*He kicks him with his boot.*) Walk, swine! Hasn't the scum kicked the bucket yet?

SECOND SOLDIER (*bending down to the mistreated man, touching him, then lifting his hands up to Hiller as if in defense*): He has . . . just now.

Scene 9

In Hiller's dugout.

DR. MÜLLER: Frozen to death. Attempts at resuscitation in vain. The ticklish part is that he didn't receive food.

HILLER: We have to report it in a way so no one can get us.

DR. MÜLLER: No doubt the human resources are exhausted and sick. Nothing but canned soup, and some of it is dangerous to health. One symptom is a madness caused by exhaustion. It makes people dig in the snow and jump around like madmen.

HILLER: I admit — starving them, beating, and chaining no longer does the job of reviving their will to fight. So what can we do? As for Helmhake, I did all I could. Here is what I'm writing to his father:

Dear Herr Helmhake:

I am fulfilling herewith the sad duty of notifying you of the sudden demise of your son, light-infantry grenadier Carl Helmhake. The doctor diagnosed bloody dysentery. During his brief illness your son received the best possible physical and medical care. We have lost in the departed an able soldier and a good comrade whose passing we deeply regret. His remains rest at the cemetery in Dolzki.

Scene 10

Two generals, each in a car piled high with loot, arrive from different directions.

FIRST GENERAL: That's my last trip. That's all we can get.

SECOND GENERAL: That's all we can get.

FIRST GENERAL: Too bad. Such a rich country.

SECOND GENERAL: The Germans beat us to it again.

FIRST GENERAL: And we Austrians were late as usual.

SECOND GENERAL: Because of the Germans.

FIRST GENERAL: They're efficient, you have to admit it. They have special booty officers, everything is organized to a T. With collecting units. People like you and me have to pick up each little thing separately.

SECOND GENERAL: It's their organization. When they reached Udine, they immediately divided the city into North and South — Udine S and Udine N. In Udine S there was silk, so that belongs to the Germans.

FIRST GENERAL: In Udine N there was nothing. That belongs to us.

SECOND GENERAL: And we can't cross the line.

FIRST GENERAL: Sad.

SECOND GENERAL: Sad.

FIRST GENERAL: The German silk traders arrived there before our advance infantry units.

SECOND GENERAL: And the German booty officers are faster than our galloping diarrhea. You've got to hand it to them.

FIRST GENERAL: What did you liberate ? Some abandoned property ?

SECOND GENERAL: Not much. A few souvenirs from the front that weren't bolted down.

FIRST GENERAL: I liberated three carpets, thirty kilograms of rice, a little meat, two bags of coffee, three door panels, and four paintings of saints.

SECOND GENERAL: And I got a gramophone, twenty kilograms of macaroni, some copper, five kilograms of cheese, two dozen cans of sardines, and a few oil paintings. So long. (*He drives away.*)

FIRST GENERAL: So long. (*To a private.*) Hey, soldier, what are you doing — stealing an ear of corn from an enemy field ? I'll teach you! (*He gets out of the car and slaps the soldier's face.*)

236

Scene 11

Auditorium of Circus Busch. A mass meeting for "Peace on German Terms."

PASTOR BRÜSTLEIN (*with outstretched arm*): In the West, we'll never return the Flemish coast! (*Deafening applause.*) In the East, we'll firmly keep the notorious fortified line so that East Prussia is never again threatened! (*Warm applause.*) In the Baltic, we'll never surrender the Duchy of Courland and occupied Lithuania! (*Thundering applause.*) And linked with Courland are Livonia and Estonia. (*With outstretched arm.*) Their distress signal calls for our help. (*Shouts of "Hurrah, hurrah, hurrah!" The speaker steps down. The crowd sings "A Mighty Fortress Is Our God."*)

EDITOR-IN-CHIEF MASCHKE: My beloved compatriots! I shall be brief. I have only one demand, which is in everybody's heart: Down with the so-called world conscience! (*Calls of "Hurrah!"*) Down with the spirit of world brotherhood! Let our German conscience alone be our loadstar and guide! Its battle cry is: More power! More German power! Anyone writing or acting according to a world conscience or a feeling of responsibility toward mankind rather than the dictates of German power is a political dreamer, a confused visionary! (*Deafening applause.*)

A MALCONTENT: Let me remind this respected assembly of one fact: The Ministry of Finance is trying to boost our sagging morale by pointing to the brilliant victories of our army. But in the Bible we read: "For what shall it profit a man if he shall gain the whole world and lose his own soul?" Civilized man agrees with the wisdom of the Bible; no shining glory of our armies can hide the moral disintegration of our national fiber through fraud, theft, and deceit. Great national institutions such as the Post Office have become lairs of thieves, entire segments of the population vanish in the quagmire of immorality . . . And all this because of our greed for material profit . . . (*Shouts of "Throw the traitor out!" The speaker is thrown out.*)

PROFESSOR PUPPE: My dear audience! I shall not lose many words because the guidelines for a German peace lie so clearly before our eyes that we can touch them with our hands. (*Indicates the touching by gestures.*) Appeasement of France is impossible! (*Shouts of "Impossible!"*) We must render France so helpless that never again will she be able to attack us! (*Deafening applause.*) To this end we must push forward our western border. The iron-ore mines of Northern France must be ours! (*Warm applause.*) The former state of Belgium must remain ours — militarily, politically, and economically! In addition, we need a large colonial empire in Africa! (*Thundering applause.*) To protect this empire, we need naval bases. England must be driven from the Mediterranean, from Gibraltar, Malta, Cyprus, Egypt, and from her latest conquests! (*Shouts of "God strike down perfidious Albion!"*) And, of course, reparations must be paid! (*Tumultuous applause.*) Our enemies must be forced to hand over a substantial part of their merchant fleet and to supply us with gold, food, and raw materials. (*Shouts of "Hurrah!"*) Furthermore . . .

Scene 12

A street in the Austrian summer resort of Ischl.

BIACH (*arriving out of breath*): Guess what! According to "his" editorial, the pact between Austria and Germany has been strengthened and deepened!

SUBSCRIBER: What else is new?

BIACH: Imagine — strengthened and deepened!

PATRIOT: So what? Take hold of yourself!

BIACH: It's terrible.

SUBSCRIBER: What's bothering you?

BIACH: Listen. Are you aware of the difference between the version released in Vienna and the one released in Berlin? (*Desperate.*) A close examination of the text, "he" says, shows a startling difference.

PATRIOT: How so?

BIACH: Both announcements are identical.

SUBSCRIBER: Well, then what do you want?

BIACH: With one single exception. (*He reads breathlessly.*) "Vienna and Berlin announce . . . Vienna and Berlin state . . . Vienna and Berlin report . . ." Here is complete agreement . . . a great cause for satisfaction. Nothing is more important than the rock of unity . . . Nothing strengthens the sense of security . . . like . . .

PATRIOT: So what's the trouble?

SUBSCRIBER: There is no difference. You're worrying about nothing.

BIACH (*with growing agitation*): But the announcement released in Vienna says, "the illustrious monarchs stand firmly behind their decisions of last May which have *deepened* the pact." The announcement released in Berlin says that the meeting "established the *identical and most faithful interpretation* of the pact." When these two statements are compared, one can detect no contradiction but simply the fact that the announcements refer to two different matters.

SUBSCRIBER: Then what do you want ?

BIACH: But as "his" editorial points out, the German public is informed about something which is not mentioned in the Austrian announcement and vice versa. One announcement says nothing about standing firm behind decisions that have *deepened* the pact of last May, and the other announcement remains silent about the *interpretation* of the *present* pact. The difference in the versions cannot be without significance.

SUBSCRIBER: Well, it's obvious, the deepening can be interpreted, but the interpretation cannot be deepened. I don't know why you are so upset.

BIACH (*begins to stamp his foot*): The German chancellor wants the *present* pact even if it *cannot be deepened*. Austria agrees. Cooperation is the cry of the hour. (*His strength begins to fail.*) What is needed above all is mutual assistance at the front against the enemy. That's how the Allies operate. But it's what *we* should do. (*Exhausted, he begins to stagger. The subscriber and the patriot support him.*)

PATRIOT: But that's what we are doing . . . Get hold of yourself, everything will be all right . . . Let's wait and see . . .

BIACH: There is a difference. Maybe you think there is no difference but I tell you there is a difference. (*He cries.*)

PATRIOT: Sure, sure, there is a difference. Just calm down, for heaven's sake . . . Everybody can see there is a difference.

SUBSCRIBER: Why do you get him more excited ? There is *no* difference.

PATRIOT: There is no difference ?

BIACH (*groaning*): There . . . is . . . no . . . difference ?

SUBSCRIBER: Haven't you heard ? Listen. Latest report from Berlin: "Contrary to certain interpretations in the Austrian press, informed quarters here emphasize that up to this moment no official statement about details of the discussions at the Supreme Headquarters has been released. Any talk about a difference between the German and the Austrian official reports is unfounded."

Biach collapses.

SUBSCRIBER: Oh my God, maybe all is not as well with him as it should be . . .

GUESTS (*gathering*): What happened ? Biach is under the weather. .

PATRIOT: It's nothing. He got excited.

BIACH (*groaning*): All . . . for nothing. There . . . is . . . no . . . difference! All . . . this . . . work . . .

SUBSCRIBER: My God, I never thought he'd take it so hard . . . Terrible!

PATRIOT: It really upsets him!

SUBSCRIBER: Well, you know, it's no trifling matter.

GUESTS (*forming groups*): I don't like the look of him . . . Someone ought to call a doctor . . . Someone ought to tell his wife . . . Yesterday he still was . . . I remember him when . . .

PATRIOT: You know what I think? (*Looking around cautiously.*) "He" has him on his conscience. "He" and his editorials!

SUBSCRIBER: Don't talk rubbish. Listen, he's saying something.

BIACH (*groaning*): Strengthened . . . and . . . deepened . . .

SUBSCRIBER: Listen . . .

BIACH (*happily*): Cleopatra's nose . . . was . . . one of her most beautiful features . . .

SUBSCRIBER: He's having hallucinations.

BIACH (*raising himself up*): I hear . . . the . . . crumbling . . . of the walls . . .

PATRIOT: He prophesies!

BIACH (*collapses*): This . . . is . . . the end . . . of . . . the . . . editorial!

SUBSCRIBER (*sobbing*): Biach!

Biach dies. Subscriber and Patriot remain, shaken. Silent groups of guests.

PATRIOT: What a pity!

SUBSCRIBER: It's all over for him now.

Scene 13

Office room at an army command post.

MEMBER OF THE GENERAL STAFF (*on the telephone*): Hi there . . . No, it's me, Kabatsch . . . Peham is on furlough. Now listen . . . Of course, there are lots of dead . . . Thanks, I'm fine. Now about those fantastic numbers of prisoners the Russians claim . . . Well, you'll have to write something like this: "How do the Russians know the numbers so exactly? Nobody can count noses!" What? Okay, I guess that's not very convincing. I tell you what. Why don't you say, as long as their claim stayed within reason — say, ten thousand prisoners a day — we let it go by, but now that it's jumped over a hundred thousand we have no choice but to challenge their figures. How? Well, just say that no one can count so many prisoners. What? How can we ourselves count them? Well, we are we; but the enemy, that's different. What? What will they say? That the enemy takes so many prisoners that he can't count them so fast, and that it's easier for us to count our losses? Now wait a minute, hold everything! We did count the prisoners they took, but after careful consideration arrived at a much lower figure. Get it? The main thing is that you keep repeating over and over again: "Their numbers are pure fantasy." Keep saying that, it's very important. Oh, you'll know how to handle it . . . If you say it's official, that's already half the truth — and, well, the other half you add yourself. You're smart, you'll handle it. So long now.

Scene 14

Battlefield near Saarburg.

CAPTAIN KILLEM: Our boys keep hesitating. And they know the orders from General Gloribee, to use rifle butts and guns to finish off prisoners, wounded or not, and to shoot the wounded in the field just as the lying atrocity propaganda of the enemy claims.

COLONEL SLAUGHTER: Gloribee faithfully follows the directives of our supreme commander: "Pardon will not be given, prisoners will not be taken." Besides, His Majesty has ordered the sinking of hospital ships, and we on land must do at least as well!

CAPTAIN KILLEM: I saw to it that the order about the handling of prisoners was passed on by word of mouth. But the bastards still hesitate.

COLONEL SLAUGHTER: We'll see about that. Here's an opportunity. (*He kicks a seemingly dead French noncommissioned officer.*) There, he still opens his eyes. (*He waves at two soldiers to come; they hesitate.*) Don't you know your orders? (*The soldiers shoot.*) There's another one crouching . . . (*He waves to a soldier to come.*) Listen, Killy, you take charge here, I've got to put my own house in order. (*He leaves. The wounded French soldier falls to his knees before Killem and holds up his hands, pleading for his life.*)

CAPTAIN KILLEM (*to the soldier, who hesitates*): "Prisoners will not be taken!"

SOLDIER: A moment ago I dressed his wounds and fed him . . .

CAPTAIN KILLEM: He'll pay you back by gouging out your eyes and cutting your throat. (*Furiously, when the soldier still hesitates.*) They snipe at us from the back and from above. "Shoot 'em from the trees like sparrows," the general said. "Shoot everything in sight," the general said. Do I have to order you, you bastard ? We killed twenty this morning, and you bastard are still hanging back ? And you call yourself a German ? I'll hold you responsible for this! Do I have to do everything for you shitheads ? There — that's how it's done! (*He shoots the kneeling man.*)

Scene 15

Near Verdun. German prisoners are lined up, and French noncommissioned officers drive them on by beating them with their fists, striking them with horsewhips, and knocking them with rifle butts. Some wounded men fall to the ground, exhausted. After the column of prisoners has passed, General Gloirefaisant appears. He waves, and the captured officers are paraded past him. A French officer whips one of them across the thighs.

GENERAL GLOIREFAISANT (*to Captain de Massacre*): Too many prisoners! My soldiers are too lazy to use their bayonets. You must be prepared to run into a German who will plead with you. "Have pity," he will say, "I have ten kids!" Kill him, or he'll have ten more. The only reliable men come from our colonies. Their knapsacks are full of trophies, all those cut-off ears and heads which the atrocity reports of the Boches lie so much about. We Frenchman from France must do at least as well as our auxiliary troops from the colonies! (*He leaves.*)

CAPTAIN DE MASSACRE: One can never do right by him.

COLONEL MEURTRIER: How come you have so few prisoners ? Twenty ? I thought you had a whole company.

CAPTAIN DE MASSACRE: I did. We finished most of them off down there, in the trench. I ordered my men to use their bayonets on 180 of them. When the boys stalled I told them the alternatives, and they went to work.

242

COLONEL MEURTRIER (*indignantly*): A hundred and eighty ? That's too many. Even the general would say so. Keep the matter quiet, or your name may be stricken from the list of the Legion of Honor.

CAPTAIN DE MASSACRE (*self-confident*): On the contrary. I have reason to believe that in a few days I'll wear the cross of the Legion of Honor. And then they'll put me in charge of the regiment from Corsica. My accomplishments here open up a glorious career!

Scene 16

The subscriber and the patriot, talking.

SUBSCRIBER: What do you say about the rumors ?

PATRIOT: I'm concerned.

SUBSCRIBER: Rumors are rampant in Vienna about rumors being rampant throughout Austria. They've passed from mouth to mouth, but no one knows . . .

PATRIOT: No one knows anything for certain, but there must be something to it if even the government announces that rumors are rampant.

SUBSCRIBER: The government explicitly cautions against believing or spreading the rumors, and asks everybody to do his utmost to suppress them. I do what I can: wherever I go I say, "Who believes in rumors ?"

PATRIOT: The Hungarian government too says that in Budapest rumors are rampant about rumors being rampant throughout Hungary. And it, too, cautions.

SUBSCRIBER: In other words, it seems that rumors are rampant throughout the empire.

PATRIOT: I'm afraid so. I wouldn't say anything if those rumors about rumors were presented as rumors, but both the Austrian and Hungarian governments present them as facts.

SUBSCRIBER: Then there must be something to them. But why pay attention to rumors ?

PATRIOT: That's exactly what I say. When I meet a friend I ask him if he's heard the rumors. If he hasn't I tell him not to believe them but to do all he can to counter them. That's the least we can do — the first duty of a loyal citizen.

SUBSCRIBER: There must be something to them, though, or why would those three delegates go and see the prime minister and draw his attention to the rumors in circulation?

PATRIOT: Right. But the prime minister told them that he was well aware of the rumors in question — and in circulation.

SUBSCRIBER: You know what I think? Just between you and me: The rumors must have something to do with our most illustrious imperial . . . (*He claps his hand over his mouth.*)

PATRIOT: You don't say! But I know even more: Those rumormongers are trying to undermine the people's faith in the aforementioned illustrious . . .

SUBSCRIBER: You know, they say the rumors start spreading from different places at the same time, which shows . . .

PATRIOT: . . . an organized conspiracy.

SUBSCRIBER: Say no more. But don't forget, these are mere rumors . . . Who can check rumors starting in different places at the same time?

PATRIOT: Don't say that. The government can check everything. You know what they say? They say that the spreading of rumors is fresh proof that the enemy is trying to create confusion. But his efforts are in vain.

SUBSCRIBER: Absolutely. Rumor has it that the rumors are part of enemy propaganda, and that the Allies are trying to shake the foundations of our monarchy by undermining our loyalty to the most illustrious . . . (*He claps his hand over his mouth.*)

PATRIOT: You don't say! But I'll tell you something: they will not get anywhere!

SUBSCRIBER: You know what?

PATRIOT: What?

SUBSCRIBER: I'd sure like to know how much truth there is in those rumors.

PATRIOT: That I can tell you: none whatsoever! And the best proof of it is that no one even knows what the rumors are all about. You know what?

SUBSCRIBER: What?

PATRIOT: I'd like to know what those rumors are all about.

SUBSCRIBER: Well, what *can* they be all about? What can there be in rumors that are spreading from mouth to mouth without anybody knowing what they are about?

PATRIOT: Yes, one has nothing to go by but rumors!

Scene 17

Optimist and Grumbler, talking.

OPTIMIST: What do you say about the rumors ?

GRUMBLER: I haven't heard them but I believe them.

OPTIMIST: Everybody knows that they're lies invented by the Allies . . .

GRUMBLER: But not nearly so dangerous as our truths.

OPTIMIST: The only thing that could feed these rumors is . . .

GRUMBLER: . . . that we can't feed the people.

Scene 18

Vienna grade school. Several benches are empty. The surviving children are undernourished. They wear cheap wartime cloth-substitute suits.

TEACHER ZEHETBAUER: Beware of rumors and do your utmost to fight them. Our scheming enemies hope to confuse you but they will not succeed. Close your ears to stories that we might give up because of famine. It's an enemy trick — for who is responsible for the famine if not our enemies ? And now they are trying to undermine our foundations and to poison our well springs . . . (*A boy raises his hand.*) What is it, Gasselseder ?

GASSELSEDER: Can't we drink any more water, sir ?

TEACHER: Sit down, stupid. I didn't mean this figuratively but literally. The enemy can't defeat us on the battlefield, so he is trying to demoralize us on the home front. Therefore, beware of rumors! Remain steadfast. Take the Iron Soldier as your model. There he stands, built for eternity, so long as the Habsburgs' double eagle soars above our heads. Go look at him, visit the Iron Soldier (with, of course, the permission of your respected parents or guardians) and drive a nail into it if you can still find a bare spot. And pay no attention to the whispers that the days of the Iron Soldier are numbered and that he'll be replaced by a sausage peddler. We haven't sunk that low yet, thank heaven. The battle seesaws back and forth, and yet . . . (*A boy raises his hand.*) What do you want, Trembler ?

245

TREMBLER: I want peace, sir.

TEACHER: Sit down, you good-for-nothing. You'll end up on the gallows, once you start out in life. For shame! Hey, you there in the third row. Merton! What are you whispering?

MERTON: My dad says he doesn't understand why everybody is for peace. He's doing fine now and is in no hurry for peace to break out.

TEACHER: Yes, Merton, your father bravely carries on, setting a good example. But you were talking without permission, and that shows how much the enemy has undermined our discipline. I won't say that you have sold out to enemy propaganda, which has its tentacles everywhere, but I cannot help being concerned about such conduct now that we see the light at the end of the tunnel. I repeat: be steadfast! Do you realize what would happen if you, too, started wavering? Foreigners would invade us; and woe unto all of us then! Unto our sisters and brides! Our parents! Our guardians! (*A boy raises his hand.*) What is it, Sokol?

SOKOL: My pop says it's high time the foreigners came again.

THE CLASS: Yes, promote the tourist trade!

TEACHER: No, that's not what the slogan means! The tourist trade is a tender seedling that needs proper care. But do you want to be overrun by a bunch of macaroni eaters?

THE CLASS: Why not? Then we'd get something to eat.

TEACHER: For shame, you good-for-nothings! What must our illustrious emperor, God bless his imperial soul, think of you, looking down at you from his picture on the wall? He surely never expected a moral collapse when he was forced to take up his sword against superior forces and to defend himself in a wantonly trumped-up war! Woe unto us if the enemies invaded our land! They would stay at our finest hotels, and you would be miserable. Our women, those guardians of hearth and home, would have made all their sacrifices in vain. Have you forgotten the lesson for the day? Let's hear it.

THE CLASS: The grim storm clouds of war are sweeping across our land and our illustrious supreme commander is calling to arms thousands and tens of thousands of our brethren and sons. Yet, we observe the first stirrings of an increased tourist trade. May we never lose sight of that high ideal. Let us intone together the old song we first learned to sing in times of peace: "Promote Our Tourist Trade." (*They sing.*)

A, a, a, the tourist brings the hay.
Times of hardship now have ended,
since the tourists have descended.
A, a, a, the tourist brings the hay.

246

Scene 19

In the village of Postabitz.

A WOMAN (*sitting at a table, writing*):

Derely beloved husband:

I beg to inform you that Im in trouble. I could not help it,
dere husband. I am sure you forgive me for what I have to inform
you. I am expecting a happy event by someone else. I know you
are kind-hearted and will forgive me. He talked me into it and
said you wont come back from the war, and I had a week moment.
You know how week a woman is, what can you do but forgive, it
already heppened. I was sure something heppened to you, too,
because you have not wrote in three months. I got all scarred
when I got your letter and you was still alife. I wish you
well but forgive me, dere Franz, perhaps the child will die and
then everything will be all right. I dont care no more for this
fellow because I know that you are still alife. Here everything
is very expensive, it's a good thing you are not here. In the
army you dont have to pay for your food. The mony you sent me
is very useful. Love from your unforgetable wife.

Anna.

Scene 20

*A parade ground near the front after the winter offensive. The
remnants of a regiment, soldiers emaciated to skeletons. In their
tattered uniforms, worn out shoes and dirty underwear they look
like a bunch of sick and ragged beggars. They get up tiredly and
practice rifle drill and saluting.*

FIRST WAR CORRESPONDENT: Watch their eyes light up when they hear
that the supreme commander, on his visit to his gallant troops at the
front, has consented to inspect the victorious regiment.

SECOND WAR CORRESPONDENT: He'll be here any minute. I think they sense it.

FIRST SOLDIER (*to second*): *Now* he's coming, the jerk!

SECOND SOLDIER: He never shows his face where the action is!

FIRST WAR CORRESPONDENT: The Kaiser enjoys the blind confidence of his soldiers.

SECOND WAR CORRESPONDENT: They're happy when he so much as smiles in their direction.

A CAPTAIN: Get going, goddammit. His Majesty will be here any minute! Furlough, sure — that's all you think about. When you were sent back here, you thought you'd get some leave? Fat chance! His Majesty's coming to inspect his glorious regiment, and no man's going to be missing, you assholes!

FIRST WAR CORRESPONDENT: Look! That's interesting! They're getting new uniforms. They're being freshly equipped from head to toe.

SECOND WAR CORRESPONDENT: What happens to their old rags?

FIRST WAR CORRESPONDENT: They'll get them back after the Kaiser has left.

SECOND WAR CORRESPONDENT: These companies are down to fifteen to sixty men. Will they fill up their ranks?

FIRST WAR CORRESPONDENT: *Will* they? That's what they're doing now. You think they'd show the Kaiser losses of twenty-five hundred men?

SECOND WAR CORRESPONDENT: How will they fill the ranks?

FIRST WAR CORRESPONDENT: Oh, with butchers and bakers, orderlies, cooks, mule drivers, stablemen, sick people, and whoever is around. They already have rifles and are drilling. I wish he'd show up; it's damned cold.

SECOND WAR CORRESPONDENT: What are they doing with their faces?

FIRST WAR CORRESPONDENT: Rubbing snow on them, you dope, so they'll look healthy.

SECOND WAR CORRESPONDENT: Great idea! They look better already. Now they're passing out something.

FIRST WAR CORRESPONDENT: Postcards with the Kaiser's picture. To pay for them their bread rations will be cut in half.

SECOND WAR CORRESPONDENT: And no small number of these stout hearts will be happy with that exchange! Listen! The cars!

The cars arrive. Fat officers get out, among them a less heavy figure wrapped in thick fur and with large ear pieces. Little more than two bulging lips can be seen.

FIRST WAR CORRESPONDENT: Imagine, you are actually witnessing the supreme commander inspecting his troops at the front, right after a victorious battle . . . striking up conversations with the lowliest of his men.

SECOND WAR CORRESPONDENT: His manner is captivating. Their hearts beat faster . . .

FIRST WAR CORRESPONDENT: He quickens their pulse.

SECOND WAR CORRESPONDENT: I wish I could hear what he's saying. What is he saying?

FIRST WAR CORRESPONDENT: Nothing. But he's smiling.

One now hears, as the Kaiser walks from man to man, from company to company, at regular intervals of five seconds, either "Ah, very nice!" or "Ah, very good!" or "Ah, very fine!" or "Ah, carry on!" This takes two hours. Then the officers say goodbye. The cars leave.

COLONEL (*to the major*): The following order is to be made public. His Majesty expressed special praise for the regiment. Both the spirit and the appearance of the troops are excellent. The courage, mirrored in the eyes of each man, is unequaled. His Majesty was particularly pleased that the losses of the regiment were so light. His Majesty concluded with the words: "Isn't it true, colonel, the regiment will, as always in the past, be among the most loyal troops of Kaiser and Fatherland, and in its battles ahead, which will be hard but victorious, it will bravely discharge its duty and add laurel after laurel to its flag?" To which I replied, "Yes, Your Majesty, this I promise."

CAPTAIN (*to the soldiers*): What you have experienced today, you will be able to tell your children and your children's children. If you want to. But for the time being, our motto is: Forward to new victories! And now, get going, and take off those new uniforms!

FIRST WAR CORRESPONDENT: Tell me frankly, do you think it was worth it? It's not much fun at twenty-eight below.

SECOND WAR CORRESPONDENT: You're telling me. I've been sick of this assignment for a long time . . . I'm a theater critic. I'm going to talk to the division leader again about a theater at the front. He was interested in the idea.

FIRST WAR CORRESPONDENT: Theater at the front? They're already taking off their make-up!

Scene 21

A side street. In the doorway of a house, a soldier with two decorations on his chest. His cap hangs low over his forehead. Next to him walks his little daughter who has been leading him and who now bends down to pick up a cigarette butt, which she then puts in his pocket. In the courtyard of the house an invalid plays his hurdy-gurdy.

SOLDIER: That should be enough. (*He pulls out a wooden pipe, and the girl stuffs the tobacco from the butts into it.*)

A LIEUTENANT (*who has passed, turns around, gruffly*): Can't you see?

SOLDIER: No.

LIEUTENANT: What? Oh . . . I see.

He leaves. The soldier, led by the child, goes off in the opposite direction. The hurdy-gurdy plays the "Long Live Habsburg" march.

Scene 22

German tourists in a Swiss mountain train. Two giant blobs of human fat occupy one entire bench of the compartment. One is wearing winter sports pants and knee socks. The other, with a quadruple chin, wears an overcoat. Both have alpenstocks. The wife of the first sits on the opposite bench, wearing a pin that reads "Down with Perfidious Albion!" Through the window a brilliant snow-covered landscape can be seen, with a deep blue sky.

GOG: I'm in the market for beautiful paintings. They don't have to be Rembrandts or Böcklins . . .

MAGOG: I have oodles.

GOG: A beautiful painting is something beautiful. Right, Gretchen? Gimme a smacker. (*He kisses her.*)

MAGOG (*after a moment*): A man who doesn't get rich in this war doesn't deserve to live in these times.

GOG: True.

MAGOG: I'm concentrating on miniatures, preferably sixteenth century. Tapestries, snuffboxes, armorials — gimcracks like that are a lot of fun, too. The idea is to snap up culture, and the older the better.

GOG: And what about books? That kid of yours is one of the finest rare-book hounds in the Reich . . .

MAGOG: Yeah, we buy up everything that's available in numbered editions on handmade paper. There's not much left.

GOG (looking at his newspaper): Look at this German wire report: "Sixty thousand kilograms of bombs dropped in twenty-four hours! Dunkirk in flames! Our bomber squadrons performing extraordinary feats. Their effects on Fortress London positively confirmed!"

MAGOG: The West is in the bag.

GOG: What a ball it must be for our bomber pilots! You get a taste of it in the book by our Richthofen. The way he smashed those Russki train stations! Pure joy! Magnificent, how he worked his way up from rookie to ace flier! What a thrill to have the world beneath you while you flatten everything — like a king, loaded with bombs! Like a god!

MAGOG: Our U-boats aren't exactly made of cardboard, either.

GOG: Right. (Looking at his newspaper.) Look here, another German wire report: "Tremendous successes! Our U-boats sink sixteen ships in two days!"

MAGOG: Our boys in blue are winning, hands down.

GOG: Mark my words, the big cannon alone will show those essobees. That bull's-eye on the church the other day, smack into their festivities — man, that must've put the fear of God into them!

MAGOG: Another two months, and England will be brought to her knees. Maybe three. Leave it to us. They know they've lost the war — you can tell it from the humanitarian kick they've started.

GOG: A bunch of baloney. What do you think of their manifesto against gas war?

MAGOG: Shows our gases are effective.

GOG: Right. We Germans cheerfully support international law but we refuse to be suckers.

MAGOG: We face the future with calm hearts and a clean conscience.

GOG: We know their line. The old chestnut about negotiations. Reuter accuses us of "evading an honest agreement on the principles of an emerging legal order." Have you ever heard such hogwash?

MAGOG: Legal order? We've got gas!

GRETCHEN (looking out the window): Dearie, look at that beautiful . . .

GOG: Yes, honey. As long as the destructive will of our enemies remains unbroken . . .

MAGOG: Allied propaganda is trying to trick us into a negotiated peace!

GOG: And we know *that* tune! We'll insist on a German peace, and a German peace is no soft peace — understand that, Lloyd George, sweetheart ♪

MAGOG: We'll wipe them out all right, don't you worry. They're a bunch of crooks, I tellya. Trying to make us believe the Americans wouldn't have stepped in if we hadn't stepped up the U-boat war. The U-boat war cannot be stepped up enough! That arch-hypocrite Wilson is a slippery old shyster, isn't he ♪

GOG: He's at the top of my shit list. He's bluffing — trying to pull the wool over our eyes. The situation is simple: by a stroke of genius we freed a tremendous number of our troops at Brest-Litovsk. And once the Russians are out of the way, everything else will be easy. *Then* it'll get sticky for the brothers. *Then* Uncle Samuel is welcome to come across the Big Pond!

MAGOG (*looking out of the window*): For heaven's sake, still not on top ♪ Engine out of steam ♪

GOG: Inefficient bunch, the Swiss. The whole country needs to be reorganized. The other day, I heard someone speak French on a streetcar in Zurich. I told him off — it's a breach of neutrality. Wish you'd been there. I shut up his big mouth, but good. And in a pastry shop in Berne, Gretchen made the salesgirl say cream instead of *crème*. Right, Gretchen ♪ Gimme a smacker. (*He kisses her.*)

GRETCHEN: Yes, baby.

MAGOG: Too few tourists go to that trouble, unfortunately. Our embassy ought to get tougher. We don't do enough to win the sympathy of the neutrals.

GOG: Our information service is slipping. Here and there we scare them with a bomb but they still don't understand us.

MAGOG: That will have serious consequences. True, after the war they'll fear us because we're the victors, but we've got to make them love us — no matter how.

GOG: Oh, things won't change much. Here at home, yes; but . . .

MAGOG: What changes do you expect in Germany, after the war ♪

GOG: Simple. Before the war we worked from eight to seven. After the war we'll work from seven to eight.

MAGOG: Right. This damned war was forced on us by British avarice . . .

GOG: . . . French thirst for revenge . . .

MAGOG: . . . and Russian hate. Nevertheless, we do have to take the foreigners into account. Even after we've conquered them, we'll have to make them admire and love us. That's important. Reducing the hate is a job for our propaganda. Even if we bleed them half to death, these customers must never be allowed to forget that we are the nation of Goethe.

From the next compartment comes the sound of a French song.

GOG: The nerve! In a neutral country! Come on, let's show them! (*He sings "Deutschland, Deutschland über alles." Gretchen and Magog join in. The song next door breaks off.*)
MAGOG: Okay — that's better! (*They get off the train.*)
GOG (*outside*): Well, what do you say to this sunshine and this sky?
MAGOG: Good show. And the snow is worth every pfennig!
GOG: And that glacier's not made of cardboard, either.
MAGOG: And the air!
GOG: Nosiree, we don't need any gas mask here. Ahhh! Fountain of youth! Here Germany has her place in the sun! Well, Gretchen, aren't you glad hubby doesn't need to defend the ole Fatherland?
GRETCHEN: Yes, Siegfriedchen.

As the group moves on, it seems for one moment as if their giant silhouette of black blots out the world of brilliant white and blue.

Scene 23

Vienna. Terminal of the Northern Railroad. The platform bathed in pale morning light. Nurses, officials, dignitaries. A train with invalids has just arrived from the front. Bodies, writhing in convulsions, are taken off the train on stretchers. The stretchers are lined up.

A VOICE: Be sure that no relatives get in here.

The front row of the crowd is taken up by members of the "Laurels for Our Heroes Club" and by officials in tails. A military band takes its place.

A SECOND VOICE: The train was two hours late. We've been waiting here for two hours but the people who are supposed to be here aren't here yet.

A THIRD VOICE: Ah, what the hell — the wounded took eight days getting here. What difference do two hours make?

Ten reporters, in frock coats, appear and line up in such a way that they can observe the doorway but block the view for the public. From the time of their appearance the stretchers cease to be visible. While each of the ten pulls out a notebook, two officials approach the group, and each introduces the other.

ZAWADIL: Spielvogel.

SPIELVOGEL: Zawadil.

BOTH (*simultaneously*): A dismal morning. We've been here since 6 A.M. to make the arrangements.

ANGELO EISNER VON EISENHOF (*steps over to the reporters and speaks gravely to one of them. They begin to write. He points at various people who then stretch their necks and try to make themselves noticed. Eisner signals to each person that he has been noticed by the reporters and that they are taking note of his presence. Meanwhile Privy Councilor Schwarz-Gelber and his wife have managed to contact the reporters directly and tap one of them on the shoulder.*)

SCHWARZ-GELBER AND HIS WIFE: No power on earth could keep us from being here in person.

BUREAU CHIEF WILHELM EXNER: I am here as a pioneer in the field of artificial limbs.

DOBNER VON DOBENAU: As lord high steward I really am entitled to stand among the most prominent.

STUKART, CHIEF OF THE SECURITY BUREAU: My presence is a matter of course.

PRESIDENT LANDESBERGER OF THE ANGLO BANK: They call me a business tycoon . . .

A VOICE: Come over here, from where you can see them better, the returning warriors.

ANOTHER VOICE: I hear it took them eight weeks to cross Siberia.

A MOTHER: Don't get too close. You never know what sicknesses they might be spreading. Look at that one over there. He's in convulsions.

HER DAUGHTER: No wonder — shot in the stomach.

DR. CHARAS: The First Aid Service, of which I am president, has come out in force for this occasion, but has not yet had many opportunities to assist.

Commotion among the people. One of the wounded has died.

A VOICE: Look at the expression on his face. How happy he is now that he has reached his destination.

ANOTHER VOICE: He lives in our memory.

While the officials distribute war medals among the invalids, the band strikes up the Radetzky March.

A REPORTER (*to another*): Write down how they are listening!

Scene 24

The Grumbler at his desk, reading.

GRUMBLER: "The desire to determine the exact amount of time it takes to convert a tree in the forest into a newspaper prompted the owner of a paper mill to conduct an interesting experiment. At 7:35 A.M. he had three trees felled in a nearby forest and, after the bark was removed, had them shipped to his pulp mill. The trunks were converted into pulp so quickly that the first roll of newsprint left the machine at 9:39 A.M. The roll was taken by truck to the printing press of a daily paper, four kilometers away, and at 11 A.M. the newspaper was sold in the streets. Thus it had required only three hours and twenty-five minutes before the public could read the latest news on material made from trees in which the birds had sung that very morning."

From outside, very distantly, shouts of "Extraaa!"

The answer has come. It is the echo of my own bloodstained madness, the only sound reverberating from the smashed creation — the cry of ten million dying human beings accusing me of still being alive, of having had the vision to see the world in such a way that it became as I saw it. If this destruction is heaven's idea of justice, it was unjust of heaven not to destroy me first! Did I deserve to see come true my deadly fear of still being alive? I am the custodian of documents for a future that will not comprehend them, an era so far removed from today that it will say I was a liar. But no, there will be no future to say that. I have written a tragedy whose doomed hero is mankind. And, alas, because this drama has no hero other than mankind, it has no audience.

May I speak to you from this lecture hall of Europe? You will be forced to go on dying for something you call honor, and you don't know what it is. What did you die for? Had your minds grasped the contradictions, your bodies would have been saved. Contempt for death? Nonsense. Why should you have contempt for something you don't know? It's true you may have contempt for the life you have never known, the life you only just tested for the first time when some accidental shrapnel nearly killed you or when the beast in command, his mouth foaming, formerly a man like yourself, pounced on you — and you became aware that you stood on the threshold. And then the beast in command dared to say of you that you held death in contempt? And you did not use the occasion to shout at your commander that he was not the commander of God, that he had no business ordering Him to uncreate creation? No, you let him bully you, along with God, across that threshold where the secret begins that no traitor can sell to any earthly government! The secret after which every country sends its heroes but none sends its spies! Had you only known, at the instant of your sacrifice, about the war profits piling up in spite of — no, *because* of your sacrifice, and feeding on it! For never before, not until this war of machines, had there ever been such ungodly war profits; and you — both victors and victims — lost the war which your murderers won. Your cowardly, technically efficient murderers who killed and lived far from the scene of their crimes.

And that's why you lay for four years in mud and filth, that's why you had to wait so long for letters from home, that's why they delayed the books that were sent to comfort you. They wanted to keep you alive awhile because they had not yet stolen enough on the stock market, or published enough lies in their newspapers, or beaten enough men into submission, or strangled enough people in their red tape. They were not quite finished dancing at that tragic carnival in which dying men became newspaper copy for lady reporters, in which butchers received honorary degrees in philosophy. You on the front, and we at home, are expected to keep staring into the graves that the higher-ups have ordered us to dig for ourselves — as they ordered the old men in Serbia for no other reason than that they were Serbians and still alive, and therefore suspect.

Oh, if we, the survivors of this nightmare — drained of tears, impoverished, and aged — could by some magic of ultimate justice receive the power to make the ringleaders of this world-wide atrocity answer individually for their crimes, if we could lock them into their churches and, as they did to the old men in Serbia, force every tenth man to draw his death sentence from a hat! But then not to kill them — merely to slap their faces! And to ask them: So, you irresponsible fools, you were unable to see that among the millions of unspeakable consequences of a declaration of war would be children without milk, horses without oats, and people gone blind, even far behind the front, from methyl alcohol, if it suited the plans of the war profiteers? Did you ever fathom the agony of one empty hour suffered by a man held prisoner for years? The torment of one sigh welled up from a love torn apart, defiled, and murdered? Could you ever for one moment imagine the hells of one tortured minute suffered by a mother waiting day and night to hear the news of her son's "hero's death"? Help me, you victims of murderers! Help me so that I don't have to live among people who, out of ambition or to save their skins, gave the orders that made hearts stop and mothers' hair turn white! As surely as God lives, only a miracle can answer me.

Come back to life, and ask them what they did to you. Ask them what they did while you were struggling under their orders — before you died under their orders. Ask them what they did while you spent your winters on the eastern front. What they did that night when the officers' phone call to your forward position received no answer. Everything was quiet on the front. You had followed orders, as they later learned, standing fast, man to man, rifles ready to shoot. You were not among those who surrendered, deserted, or had to be warmed up — because they were freezing — with the machine-gun fire of their commanders. You held your positions and did not retreat into the murderous clutches of your Fatherland. Before you the enemy, behind you the Fatherland, and above you the eternal stars. Wake up from your cold graves! Step out, and demand that they give you back your lives! Where are you — you who died in hospital? My last letter was returned to me, stamped: "Shipped out. Address unknown." Step out, and tell them where you are and what it's like, and tell them that you will never again let them use you as they have. And you there, you with the face to which you were condemned in your last moment when the beast in command rushed into your trench — step out! Not that you had to die — no, but that you had to live through that nightmare   makes all our future sleep and all our dying in bed a sin. I long for vengeance — not for your death, but for the agony of what you had to live through.

I have exposed the heroics of your murderers for the empty shadows they are; I have stripped them of their flesh. But I have given body to their stupidities, their malice, their worthlessness, and have brought all these to life here on the stage. Time washes away the essence of events and would grant amnesty even to the most heinous crime ever committed under the stars; but I have preserved this essence. My ear has recorded the sounds of the deed, my eye the gestures of the talks, and my voice, by merely quoting, has preserved the base chord of this era forever.

This is world war. This is my manifesto to mankind.